ARCHIVE of the CONNECTED UNIVERSE

Volume One

Mike Ricksecker

Other Books by Mike Ricksecker:

Portals to the Stars: Inside Stargates, Atlantis, and Secrets of Ancient Egypt

Travels Through Time: Inside the Fourth Dimension, Time Travel, and Stacked Time Theory

Alaska's Mysterious Triangle

A Walk In The Shadows: A Complete Guide To Shadow People

Campfire Tales: Midwest

Ghostorian Case Files: Volume 1

Ghosts and Legends of Oklahoma

Ghosts of Maryland

System of the Dead

Deadly Heirs

Encounters With The Paranormal: Vol. 1-4

Join us at the Connected Universe Portal: connecteduniverseportal.com

Watch Mike on Gaia TV at: gaia.com/portal/mike

Follow the YouTube channel with 700+ videos at:
https://youtube.com/@mricksecker

Tune into the *Connecting the Universe* podcast on your favorite podcast platform, including Apple Podcasts, iHeart Radio, Spotify, & more!

© 2025 by Mike Ricksecker
All rights reserved. No part of this book may be reproduced, stored in a retrieval system or transmitted in any form or by any means without the prior written permission of the publishers, except by a reviewer who may quote brief passages in a review to be printed in a newspaper, magazine or journal.

First Edition:
First printing

Primary Front Cover Art by: Carlos Marquez with modifications by Katherine Swinn and Mike Ricksecker
Front Cover Book and Podium Art by: Nélia Cruz
Back Cover Art by: Nakorn

Author Photography by: Chris Loomis

All other photos within by Mike Ricksecker or Public Domain unless otherwise indicated.

PUBLISHED BY CONNECTED UNIVERSE PRESS
A Division of HAUNTED ROAD MEDIA, LLC
www.hauntedroadmedia.com

Cleveland, Ohio
United States of America

To Kate:
Together Together … as we begin our journey into the Connected Universe … and beyond.

Welcome to the world of illusion ... illusion of the world of welcome

ACKNOWLEDGMENTS

How do you properly acknowledge all of those who have been on this collective journey over the many years? And I mean *many* years. While this work is, primary, a compilation of articles I've written since 2021, there is plenty of research and material from years which long preceded that, and at points, I get into the very beginnings of my writing career which go all the way back to my days in elementary school. So, thank you Miss Steele and Mrs. Ahearn for your encouragement to write during those formative years. The biggest encouragement thanks I should give during those years, of course, is to my mother (and Dad, too), who always encouraged me to be creative during that era of my life and even let me bang away on her Smith Corona typewriter my father gifted her sometime during the early 1980s.

I must, once again, sincerely thank my good friend, Mohamed Ibrahim, the Egyptologist who is our tour guide for the Stargates of Ancient Egypt tour. As you'll see when you get to the Egyptian material in this work, there are several discoveries we've made together, but I would not have had the experience and knowledge to notice it and connect the pieces together without his tutelage. I must also thank his wife, Noha, who formally owns Saba Tours and the rest of the staff for always organizing such incredible tours for our guests. Similarly, I must also thank all of those guests who have joined us over the years and made those discoveries with us. From this past tour featured in the middle of this book, that would include Kate, Lisa, Wendy, Pam, Stefanie, Ellie, and Albert – I think we accessed a whole new dimension in 2024, especially with that "murder pudding." I must also thank Mohamed's team – Usama and Ahmed, especially – for making the entire Egypt experience thoroughly enjoyable.

Of course, I have to recognize all those "time travelers" who have been members of the Connected Universe Portal, those longtime supporters of the work and research I've been conducting, and the display of faith you've shown in me over all of this time. The work featured here is from the Connected Universe blog which would not exist at all without all of you. You've been absolutely incredible!

Most of all, I must thank my amazing partner in this life, Kate Swinn, who I met during our last adventures in Egypt. She's been immensely supportive and has also contributed to the greater work, as you'll encounter within the articles. Our connection on so many levels, including the ancient world, spirituality, writing, helping people through our work, and so much more has been an absolute wonder, and you'll see the fruits of that connection in upcoming works. I can't wait to see what she and I discover next!

Table of Contents

Introduction	13

Part 1: The Original Dozen

Our Place in the Universe	23
Types of Paradoxes	29
Exploring Ancient Mysteries of Egypt	37
Are Shadow Entities Extraterrestrials?	45
Inside Alaska's Mysterious Triangle	53
Seeing Shadows: A Peripheral View	61
Our Parallel Universe Running in Reverse Time	65
A Serpent Down the Rabbit Hole	71
Exploring Ancient Ireland	77
Real Time Travel: What Does it Look Like?	89
Stargates of Ancient Egypt	97
Mysterious Triangles of the World	105

Part 2: Finding the Way

An Odyssey of Exploration	121
Where to Start the New Book?	125
The Juggle is Real!	129
UFO Hotspots and Earth Energy	133
Shadows, Ireland, and Wine	145
Mammoths and Creating New Life Forms	149
The Mandela Effect and Paradoxes	155
Discovering Lost Locations with Ancient Documents	163

Time Travel: Consciousness or Physics?	167
Revisiting the Alaska Triangle	173
Anticipating the Solar Eclipse	179
Silver Circle in the Sky … and Heart	183
The Call Back to Egypt	191

Part 3: Stargates of Ancient Egypt

Getting the Hard Part Out of the Way	205
Like Visiting Old Friends	209
Discovering More Ancient Secrets	215
Pyramids, Tombs, and the Music of the Ancients	219
Epic Site and a Haunting Stare	225
Discoveries and New Theories in Egypt	231
Best Day of the Stargates Tour?	239
The Lord of the Pleiades	245
Super Hot Stargates and Tombs	249
Exploring the Origins of Atlantis and Murder Pudding	257
Did We Find the Ark of the Covenant?	263
How to Make the Great Pyramid Even More Mysterious	271
Egyptian Goodbye, But Not Goodbye	279
Evidence in Egypt of a Parallel Universe?	283

Part 4: Stargates and Portals

Are Portals Hiding in the Wilderness?	295
Embracing Stargate and Portal Synchronicities	301
What is a Real Stargate?	305
Last March of the Ents:	313
Not Your Grandfather's UFOs – Or Are They?	317
Portals and Star People of the Southwest	321
On the Trail of Atlantis in Egypt	327

Part 5: Earth Energy, Atlantis, and Antarctica

Unlocking Mysteries at Drombeg Stone Circle	335
Ancient Hermetic Secrets at Charleville Castle	339
I Could Have Used a Stargate	343
The Age of Atlantis	351
Atlanteans in Antarctica?	357
Secret Stargates in Antarctica?	361
Everything is Connected	369
Nikola Tesla's Earth Energy Quest	373

Part 6: The Writing Path

The Big Cover Reveal	383
Journey of a Lifetime	387
Stargates and Time Travel	401
Mysterious	405
Writing Portals to the Stars	409
Proving the Legends True	415
It's Unbelievable	419
What Lies Beyond the Holidays?	423
Adventures in Audiobooks	427

Part 7: Portals and Dimensions

What Lies Beneath	437
What Are the New Jersey Drones?	443
Droning on in New Jersey	447
Plasmoids, Portals, or Extraterrestrials?	453

Final Thoughts	459

Index   461

About The Author   473

Introduction

In a half century of lifetime, I have written millions upon millions of words. My current published works, such as *Travels Through Time*, *Portals to the Stars*, and others only reflect a fraction of that, and there is much of great import which has been included in blog articles and other media along the way which, after long periods of compounding said articles and media, have been lost in the cumbersome back end of the web sites where that information is housed. Unless someone is truly intent on drilling down into the deep recesses of my ongoing work, or unless I feel the need to bring it forth in one of my full-length books, this information largely becomes forgotten. That is quite unfortunate since one of the goals of my work has always been to try to make sure this information doesn't get lost to time, that this knowledge gets passed down to the next generation, and hopefully, curious souls from that generation pick up the mantel, carry that knowledge forward, and make new discoveries for themselves.

To be honest, the original goal of this archive was to create an audio version of those blog articles. As technology continues to progress and transform the way we ingest information, I find it quite amazing that, in many ways, we have come full circle to embrace a technology from our past: radio. Podcasts and audiobooks, our modern form of radio programs and newscasts, are now a staple of most people's lives, whether that's in the car on their way to work or in their ear buds as they're out for a jog around the neighborhood. There are many people who still enjoy sitting under a tree or the lamplight with a good book, but in our fast-paced society, overall readership has been on the decline. However, overall listenership is on the way up. Thus, it didn't make a whole lot of sense that I was keeping a written blog other than the fact that – hey, I'm a writer, and that's what I do. It's also nice to have a handy written reference to all this fascinating information we've been discussing.

As I write this introduction you're now reading, I am also recording the audio version it, but it makes no sense to the man of the written word to just simply have an audiobook. So, yes, I'm publishing a written version of it as well since there are those who, again, enjoy reading the old-fashioned way, but I won't mask that the primary goal was an audio format of the Archive. Welcome to the roaring 2020s.

The Connected Universe, specifically, has been my platform for some years now and is represented in the Connected Universe Portal (connecteduniverseportal.com), a treasure trove of videos and information I keep in what I call The Secret Library, and the *Connecting the Universe* livestream and podcast shows. Perhaps, one day I'll undertake the monumental task of transcribing those into a volume of this Archive as well. Within all of that, as well as within what you'll find here, is the common theme that *everything is connected*. **Everything**.

Some have scoffed at that notion, that everything being connected is some sort of mystical concept of the metaphysical community, and yes, there is certainly legitimacy to the human race being connected to each other on a spiritual and energetic level. Anyone who has seen my presentations on this subject knows I love saying things like ... we are connected right now through this book just like we are also connected to this planet, this planet to the Sun and the rest of the solar system, the solar system to the galaxy, the galaxy to the universe, the universe to ... ah, what's beyond that? However, we are also all connected on a very real and physical level. Just one look at images of the universe from such devices as the Chandra X-Ray telescope, and one can see with his or her own eyes that all the galaxies across the cosmos are connected to each other by gaseous filaments, making the universe look like one giant spider web.

This Archive, in many ways, is like that giant spider web. The concepts, ideas, and knowledge contained within may seem vastly different at times, but I assure you, it is absolutely all connected. I'm going to do my best for you to organize it in some sort of meaningful fashion, but you have to understand, first, how it was written.

The first section of a dozen articles was pulled from the Connected Universe Portal website where I periodically wrote a blog during the first couple years of the site's existence. I later began a more robust blog on the Substack platform which specializes in this kind of media, and that makes up the rest of the Archive in this volume. Technically, yes, anyone could go to **connecteduniverse.substack.com** and read almost everything that is here, but there are some differences between what is here and what is there.

Here, I'm going to provide some additional detail and insight with periodic small introductions in areas in which a little more clarity may be called for, and where opinions and information have changed, I will definitely let you know. There on the blog, you get all the included links to videos and supplementary articles, plus you can comment on the articles or message me directly with your thoughts and opinions on the subject matter. There are pros and cons to each, and if you're a reader, I do encourage you to find me out on the blog. This particular volume of the Archive ends on January 6, 2025, so there you would get all the latest information.

Now, you may be wondering, if there's a Volume 1, does that mean there's going to be a Volume 2? Of course! Some may point to my book *Ghostorian Case Files: Volume 1* and argue that there's never been a Volume 2, but I assure you that, at some point, there will be a follow up. I just never expected it would be more than ten years later. Hey, at least that's not as bad George R.R. Martin's long-awaited *Winds of Winter*. One of these days, right?

It's certainly my intention that Volume 2 will pick up right where Volume 1 left off and continue the journey through the Connected Universe, weaving our way through the web of mystery that has become our reality. You'll find throughout this work that there were weeks or months in which I was following a certain theme or following a certain line of research. Of course, right in the middle is the series of blog articles that were written daily while on the 2024 Stargates of Ancient Egypt Tour. Given the timing of this work, Volume 2 will cover the 2025 tour more toward its ending.

It's my hope you find nuggets of information in here useful, either for your own research or purely for your own curiosity. The universe is shrouded in mystery, and whenever we think we've answered one question it begs us to ask ten or twenty new questions. I don't expect we'll ever have it all figured out, but I believe it's enough to try to explore and understand as much as possible during our lifetimes and, again, pass it on to the next generation. We, today, just like those who came before us, are a steppingstone for the future.

To live in a world without becoming aware of the meaning of the world is like wandering about in a great library without touching the books.

Manly P. Hall

Part 1

The Original Dozen

Notes on Part 1

I believe it's important to note for Part 1 that while I am calling these articles the "original dozen," it's really the original dozen as it pertains to the Connected Universe Portal platform which I created in 2021. There are many other written articles and works that predate this era, especially on the old version of the **mikericksecker.com** website, which will be published elsewhere.

Also, the mention of the *Beyond the Shadows* broadcasts should not be confused with my film *The Shadow Dimension: Beyond the Shadows*. The *Beyond the Shadows* livestream show and podcast was a title I used for a couple years for what is now *Connecting the Universe*. The original title for this production was *Inside the Upside Down*, and sometimes the internet links still reflect the old titles, but they're all one in the same. Times and areas of focus change, and the titles reflected those changes. Connecting the Universe has been the title for several years now, and will be the title for the foreseeable future.

Our Place in the Universe

March 4, 2021

Article Notes: Orbital Assembly Corporation renamed their company to Above: Space Developments Corporation in 2022. They develop modular solutions for on-orbit platforms and continues to explore gravity solutions in space. More information about Above: Space can be found at: https://www.abovespace.com

Science fiction is becoming reality. When I scrolled through my social media feed this past Tuesday morning, I was instantly intrigued by a headline concerning the assembly of a space station and hotel with artificial gravity which will begin construction in 2025. To me, it was too good to be true. I clicked into the headline and began reading about the fascinating privately funded venture by Orbital Assembly Corporation to begin building this marvel and have it open for business by 2027. Amazing.

The entire concept is a huge step forward in taking our civilization out into space on a regular basis, creating new jobs above the Earth, and tapping into a whole new universe of

Voyager Space Station gravity ring concept by Above: Space.

opportunities (pun intended). The technology being developed for what has been called Voyager Station is literally straight out of our science fiction – a "Gravity Ring" which will rotate and create a type of artificial gravity in space, the first of its kind ever developed. The station will be able to accommodate 400 guests, including support for scientists to conduct experiments in Earth's orbit. The future is finally here!

Whenever I repost these types of articles and exclaim my joy at our progress reaching out into **the** world beyond our own, I'm always greeted with a handful of dissenters who state we should be more concerned with our troubles here on Earth. After all, there's still hunger and poverty, natural disasters – heck, we're still in the middle of a pandemic. I understand that, and no one is saying that what's happening on Earth isn't important, but we also need to think about the long-term future. Somewhere, there's a happy balance between taking care of our own on the surface and progressing our civilization out into space, which is absolutely necessary.

During several of my *Beyond The Shadows* broadcasts – and this article is based off a recent episode now archived in the Connected Universe Portal – I've talked about the inevitable extinction-level

Planet Earth's destiny with a red giant Sun in about 5 billion years.

event of the Earth, whether that's in the near future or whether it's a billion years from now when the sun starts entering its red giant phase and evaporates all the water off the planet. At the height of the sun becoming a red giant, it will engulf the entire planet as it expands to about the size of the orbit of Mars. It's a sad fact, but the destruction of our planet will happen at some point, and if we are to survive as a species, we need to figure out how to sustain our life out in space. The steps we're taking now are just the baby steps we need to take to eventually move our civilization elsewhere when the time comes. We may have even done this before. Perhaps we are survivors from another planet – but that's another discussion.

This destruction may have actually happened to a variation of our planet before. While the Earth was created from our sun as part of its ecliptic field of debris, the sun is barely hot enough to fuse hydrogen to helium. Because of this, many scientists believe that our solar system originally had a different "mother" star that exploded billions of years ago in a supernova and created our system today. It's fun to say we're all made of stardust, but supernovae, while beautiful in their brilliance, can unexpectedly wreak havoc upon our planet.

Russian scientist and cosmist Konstantin Tsiolkovsky.

When stars out in the universe explode into a supernova, they can be so powerful and bright that we can see them during the daytime here on Earth and can outshine the Moon at night. A supernova only 10 light years away could destroy all life on Earth, and some scientists believe a supernova about 120 lightyears away caused a minor extinction of sea animals on our planet two million years ago. The problem is, we can't predict the exact moment a supernova is going to happen, and the stars we see in the night sky right now are in the past as it takes years for the light to travel to us. A supernova could have already happened out there, and we won't know until decades from now. So, what do we do?

We need the flexibility to get off the planet.

Some of the media Orbital Assembly Corporation has posted regarding their space technology includes the following quote from Konstantin Tsiolkovsky: "The Earth is the cradle of humanity, but mankind cannot stay in the cradle forever." I agree; we need to grow up.

Who was Konstantin Tsiolkovsky, and why would he make such a statement? Tsiolkovsky was an early Twentieth Century Russian scientist and cosmist. As a scientist, he was a pioneer in rocketry and developed several equations that were used to launch the Sputnik satellite into space, including the equation for the mass of a rocket in 1897 and the horizontal speed for minimum orbit around the Earth in 1903. Yes, Tsiolkovsky was developing rocketry before we had successfully accomplished flight in airplanes.

He was fueled by the philosophy of cosmism -- the idea that we came from the stars and we need to return to the stars. He believed humans would eventually colonize the Milky Way and he was a proponent of panpsychism.

Panpsychism is one of the world's oldest philosophical theories, going as far back as Plato, and is described as a theory that, "the mind is a fundamental feature of the world which exists throughout the universe."

Plato probably stated it more clearly: "This world is indeed a living being endowed with a soul and intelligence ... a single visible living entity containing all other living entities, which by their nature are all related."

In this statement, we can see the idea of the connected universe. Given the description, one may also be able to find the idea behind the planet Pandora in the movie *Avatar*. It was a world completely connected, in which one directly affected the whole.

We can expand this out from just the planet to the entire universe. We, as a species, have always looked up to the stars as if that's where we belong ... and in many cases, have belonged before. When we look at ancient Egypt, they believed there are seven different parts of the soul, and at death, the spiritual aspects of the soul ascend to the stars and begins a journey to the constellation of Orion. This is a journey home.

There's also a prevailing idea in some circles that the human race may have originally come from Mars. There's plenty of evidence to show us there was once water on Mars, a necessary building block of life. Did civilization on Mars make it off the planet in time to get to Earth before it could no longer sustain life? Are our current journeys to Mars really a return home? If we've been planet hopping, how many planets have humans inhabited thus far?

Our place in the universe is not just relegated to Earth. Humans have always been explorers, and as we continue to grow and develop new technology, perhaps even meshing that technology with metaphysics, we're going to discover that it is really quite natural for us to move about the stars. We need to protect our physical bodies as our planetary situation evolves, preserve humanity as we forge forward, but we may discover that our consciousness plays a bigger part in how we travel through the cosmos and discover new worlds, including ones we can inhabit in the future. We'll absolutely need to discover those worlds to continue on.

Types of Paradoxes

April 19, 2021

Article Notes: This material on paradoxes was originally put together for a video called "Types of Paradoxes That Will Blow Your Mind" as part of a YouTube series, Haunted Road Media Learning Shorts, I produced for my YouTube channel. Back then it was the Haunted Road Media channel; today it's the Mike Ricksecker channel. (You can reach this either one of two ways: youtube.com/HauntedRoadMedia or youtube.com/@mricksecker). These learning shorts grew out of my weekly Friday Night Ghost Frights series, and while they were still released on Friday nights, I was no longer just telling stories about ghosts and hauntings. Later, this material became the backbone for my "Paradoxes" chapter in my book Travels Through Time.

Socrates: "I know one thing, that I know nothing."

Paradoxes are all around us, and they permeate throughout our popular culture. One of my favorites to throw at people is, "True or false? I'm lying." Trying to wrap your head around how those states of being can't exist properly with that simple question and answer combination makes it a paradox.

Let's take a look at some of these paradoxes and how we're familiar with them.

Bootstrap Paradox

The bootstrap paradox is a favorite in film and books. In a bootstrap paradox, self-existing objects or pieces of information in a causal loop have no origin. For example, a person travels back in time to give themselves an object to perform some act which they retain until that moment in the future when they travel back in time to give it to themselves again. The object is in a loop and has no origin.

I first saw this play out in film when I was a kid and fell in love with the movie *Somewhere in Time* starring Christopher Reeve and Jane Seymour. Reeve's character, Richard, receives a pocket watch from an old woman named Elise. When he travels back in time, Richard hands the pocket watch to a young Elise before he disappears, and Elise hangs onto it until she becomes an old woman and gives it to Richard. Thus, the watch has no place of origin.

The time-traveling Netflix series *Dark*, my absolute favorite series as of this writing, is loaded with bootstrap paradoxes. The book *A Journey Through Time* by H.G. Tannhaus is handled by multiple characters throughout the series and eventually ends up in the author's hands, at which point, he actually writes the book for the first time. However, he couldn't have written the book to begin with without having seen the book first.

Similarly, in that series, Michael's letter that he writes before he hangs himself is given to him by his time-traveling son, Jonas, before he even writes it. Jonas keeps the letter for himself (which he gives to another version of himself later), but Michael wouldn't have known what to write in the letter if Jonas hadn't shown him to begin with. Again, the information in the letter has no origin.

The bootstrap paradox also plays out in *Harry Potter and the Prisoner of Azkaban* when Harry is being attacked by the dementors and a patronus saves him. At first, he believes this is his father's doing, but when he and Hermione jump back in time and witness the event, Harry generates the patronus to save his other self, saying that he realized he could perform the spell because he had already done it when he had been saved. Again, this is another causal loop with no origin.

The use of "bootstrap" in this context refers to the expression "pulling yourself up by your bootstraps" and to Robert A. Heinlein's time travel story "By His Bootstraps".

Grandfather Paradox

The grandfather paradox name comes from the paradox's common description: a person travels back in time and kills his or her own grandfather before the conception of his or her father or mother, which prevents the time traveler's existence to begin with.

The most obvious depiction of this is Marty McFly's interference with his parents' past in *Back To The Future*. Although he doesn't kill his parents, he nearly prevents them from getting together and begins erasing his own existence from time. Marty's brother and sister begin disappearing from a photo he carries, and he almost disappears himself before his parents finally have their big kiss. Even if that kiss didn't happen and Marty did get erased from time, his existence before his erasure, even though he would have never been born, still would have had a profound effect on his parents' lives.

The most mind-bending grandfather paradox in pop culture has to be that of the film *Predestination*, based on the short story "All You Zombies" by Robert A. Heinlein. I encourage you to watch this

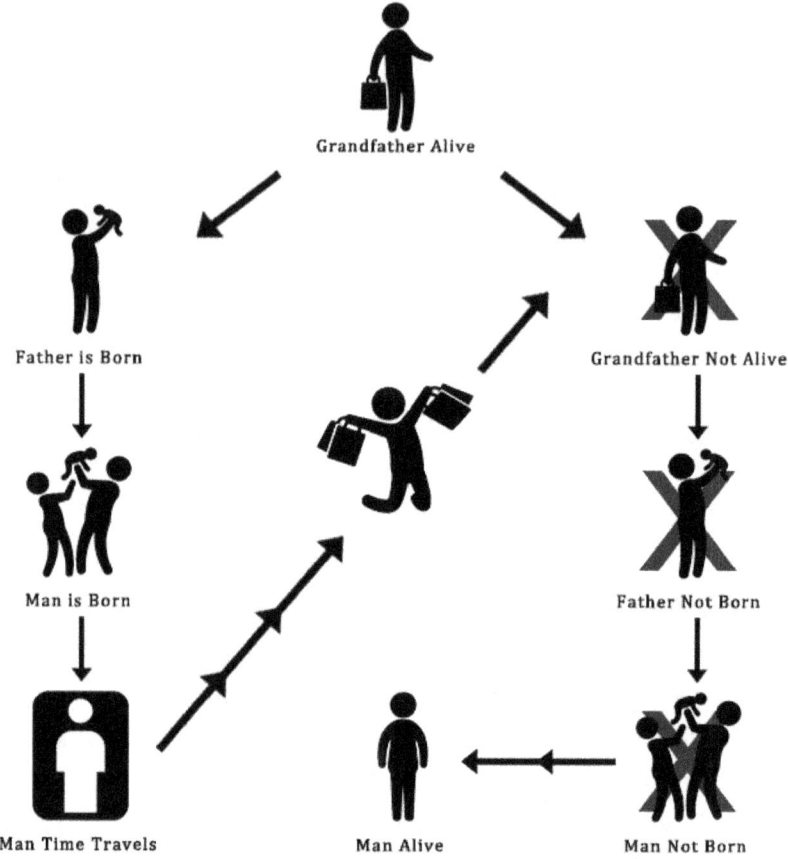

movie, so if you don't want a massive spoiler, please skip this part. This story involves an intersex time traveling agent who begins life as a baby girl, Jane, and through the course of events has a sex change operation when the birth of her own daughter results in massive complications. This baby is kidnapped from the hospital (and whisked away to the past) and Jane becomes John. At a bar one night, John meets an agent masquerading as a bartender who offers the invitation to become an agent and defeat the dastardly "Fizzle Bomber" terrorist, but only after completion of an initial mission into the past. During this mission, John meets college-aged Jane and they fall in love, conceiving … baby Jane. By the time the story is finished being told, you've come to realize that Jane, John, the bartender time agent, and the Fizzle Bomber are all different versions of the same person at different points in time all interacting with each other and affecting each other's lives.

Some also refer to these type of events as predestination paradoxes, and one can also contend that John and Jane are their own bootstrap paradox, their own physical body having no actual origin.

Some look at the concept of the grandfather paradox and believe that these alterations of the past actually generate parallel universes. The idea here is that when the time traveler kills his or her grandfather the traveler is killing a parallel universe version of the grandfather and the traveler's universe of origin is actually unaltered.

This may be what we see in the film *Looper* when Old Joe from the future has traveled back to kill "the Rainmaker" who is only a child at the time. When Young Joe kills himself to prevent this from happening, he states that he saw a world in which an angry child grows up to become someone destructive, but that world is destroyed when Young Joe destroys himself and Old Joe disappears.

Catch 22

A "Catch-22" is a situation in which someone is in need of something that can only be had by not being in need of it. This concept is based off the 1961 novel *Catch-22* by Joseph Heller in which a soldier who wants to be declared insane to avoid combat is deemed not insane for that very reason and will therefore not be declared insane.

We use this term in our everyday lives because we actually see this sort of thing play out, usually, when we're dealing with some sort of authority like health insurance, banks, the telephone company, etc. They want us to jump through some sort of hoop that we can't because of some sort of prerequisite that requires we've already jumped through that hoop.

The character Brantley Foster complains about this sort of problem in *The Secret Of My Success* while he's job hunting and no one will hire him because he doesn't have experience. He remarks, "How can I get any experience until I get a job that gives me that experience?"

J.K. Rowling finds a way to skirt around this paradox in *Harry Potter and the Sorcerer's Stone* when Professor Quirrell is trying to get the stone out of the Mirror of Erised ("desire" spelled backwards). He desires the stone, and the mirror shows him holding it, but the mirror won't release it because of a prerequisite Quirrell can't achieve. It releases the stone for Harry, however, because although Harry wants the stone, he doesn't actually want to use it. It's not precisely a Catch-22, but it's pretty darned close.

Fermi Paradox

On a recent broadcast of *Beyond The Shadows*, I was asked about the Fermi Paradox which I'll dive into a little bit here. The Fermi paradox is the apparent contradiction in the perceived lack of evidence of extraterrestrial life and the high estimates that extraterrestrial life throughout the universe actually exists.

I say "perceived lack of evidence" since there are plenty of people in the ufology community that have made a case for ET visitations on Earth, but for this paradox I'll digress we'll default to the traditional narrative that we haven't yet discovered extraterrestrials. In other words, how can we assume there are many untold number of species of extraterrestrial life out in the universe when we have yet discovered one? Simply stated, math. And perception. To me, this is rather easy to resolve.

When it comes to our place in the universe, humanity seems to be extremely self-centered and regards all other possible forms of life in the cosmos as extraterrestrial while blatantly disregarding one simple fact. To the rest of the universe, we are the extraterrestrials. The notion that there are Earthlings and everything else is an ET is preposterous, but that tends to be the narrow-sighted viewpoint many in the field take. Thus, given the universe as a whole, there is absolutely one planet upon which we know life exists: us. Score one for the Milky Way galaxy.

There are billions of stars with their own solar systems in our galaxy and there are billions of galaxies in the known universe, including recent reports from the James Webb telescope which indicate there are more than the number of expected galaxies in the distant parts of the cosmos. With all those nearly infinite possibilities, there should be some sort of life out there, and it's not just wishful thinking. It's a matter of perspective.

NASA estimates there are 100 – 400 million stars in our galaxy, which is about average for a galaxy per current estimates, and we know there is one planet there with intelligent life. We truly don't know how many stars are in our known universe since we are still discovering more galaxies today, but our current numbers have dozens of zeros at approximately 1,022 – 1,024 – that's a lot of stars! If we take what we know about our galaxy, that there is one planet with life per every (and I'll be generous to the Fermi Paradox) 400 million stars and divide 1,024 by that, we find that there may be approximately 2.515 (2,500,000,000,000,000 or two quadrillion, five hundred trillion) planets with life in the **universe**.

So ... I don't really think this is that much of a paradox. It's just perspective.

Optical Illusions

Speaking of perspective, here a couple of quick optical illusion paradoxes for you.

The Penrose Stairs is a favorite, the impossible staircase that goes round and round, never going up and never going down,

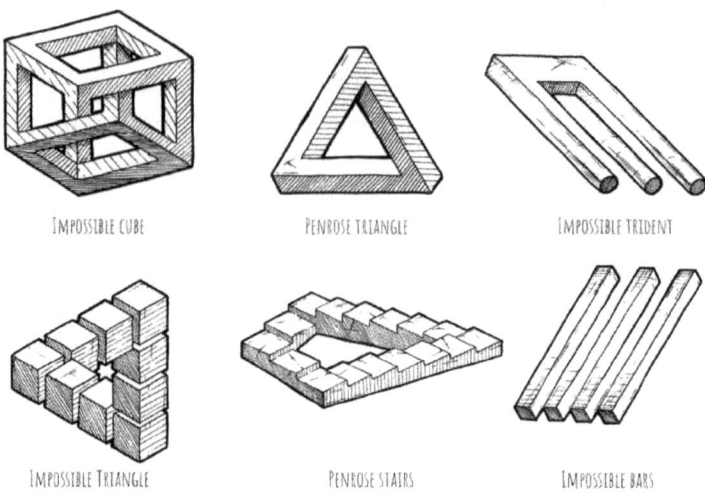

IMPOSSIBLE CUBE | PENROSE TRIANGLE | IMPOSSIBLE TRIDENT
IMPOSSIBLE TRIANGLE | PENROSE STAIRS | IMPOSSIBLE BARS

although those illustrated walking on it clearly appear to be going up or down.

This paradox was used in the Christopher Nolan film *Inception* as a method to keep the designed mazes smaller in size but larger in scope (and a cool way to beat a bad guy).

The impossible trident or blivet has many names, including The Devil's Tuning Fork, but it's an impossible object with three cylindrical prongs at one end which then mysteriously fade away and transform into two rectangles at the other end. A satirical article in *The Worm Runner's Digest* in 1968 by Roger Hayward, titled "Blivets: Research and Development" included a number of other variations and interesting drawings of this optical illusion, including the *Undecidable Monument*.

These are just a handful of paradoxes, and there are hundreds more, including Schrodinger's Cat, the tea leaf paradox, the Ship of Theseus, and on and on.

Exploring Ancient Mysteries of Egypt

July 7, 2021

Article Notes: This was written just after returning from my first tour in Egypt with Mohamed Ibrahim, but I was there as a guest on the tour and not as a co-host. It was on this tour, The Return of the Kheper Cycle, in which Mohamed and I first discussed co-hosting the current Stargates of Ancient Egypt tour which is held annually. Also of note, while Mohamed is known as the Guide of Egypt, the tour company he runs with his wife, Noha, is officially titled Saba Tours and is how you'll find the tours they have to offer.

Egypt is absolutely a mystical and magical place, rife with ancient secrets, enigmatic mysteries, and friendly people who welcome visitors with open arms. With many countries around the world still barring foreigners from touching their soil as continued fallout from the COVID-19 pandemic, Egypt is wide open and completely safe. I highly recommend you go, and here's why — my experience there was absolutely life changing. I will never look at the universe the same way again.

Where to start? I have an entire 14-day travel blog posted to the Member Site of the Connected Universe Portal, but let me give you some highlights. First of all, I was on the Return of the Kheper Cycle tour hosted by Mohamed Ibrahim of Guide of Egypt tours and Jonny Enoch who many will recognize as my co-star from *The Alaska Triangle* and several shows on the Gaia network. Mohamed's team is an absolute class act. From the moment you step off the plane in Cairo you are greeted with a friendly smile by his right-hand man, Usama, and Usama literally walks you through everything. This is huge for someone traveling internationally for the first time or has never been to Cairo. After Usama takes care of you at the airport, he places you with a driver who diligently takes you to the hotel where more of Mohamed's team checks you in. It was the smoothest experience I've ever had checking into anything before.

Our first several nights were spent at the Steigenberger Pyramids Hotel which sits right across from the Giza Pyramids. All I had to do was open the curtains and there the pyramids loomed outside my window. I spent quite a bit of the hotel time out on the balcony writing with the pyramids as my backdrop.

We wasted no time in diving straight into the action. On the very first morning, the very first thing we found ourselves doing was climbing down into the "Bent" Pyramid. Note for next time … hit the Stair Master before leaving for Egypt. I do quite a bit of walking throughout the day, but I wasn't really prepared for the descent, then climb up a series of stairs and passages (then do it all in reverse once we'd looked around). I was winded, but it was a fantastic way to start the entire tour, really just a prelude of what was to come in the following days.

Saqqara was even more impressive the second day as we ventured into the Step Pyramid and then the Serapeum after lunch. But that magical third day … this is what the Return of the Kheper Cycle was all about: the beginning of the new sun cycle starting on the summer solstice. And where were we on the summer solstice?

First day in Egypt in 2021 at the Bent Pyramid.

We were inside the Great Pyramid of Giza for two whole hours, just our group. Talk about amazing! We were able to climb down into the subterranean chamber, which is normally off limits, accessed the Queen's Chamber, up into Grand Gallery, and of course the King's Chamber. The entire complex is fascinating with plenty of secrets to unravel, and it's within the King's Chamber that I noticed something rather peculiar. You can watch myriad videos, look at photos, read books … but until you're actually viewing these places yourself it's just not the same. This box that mainstream academia likes to call a sarcophagus did not close like other sarcophagi. It had some sort of lid, for sure, but its lid was different than anything else we've seen.

The coffer in the King's Chamber ... a container but not a sarcophagus.

We continued around the Giza Plateau following the pyramid and later visited the Sphinx. All the while, Mohamed was pointing out discrepancies in the technology that would have been used to actually create these structures and what the mainstream has passed off as a story. My dad's occupation was as a machinist, a tool and die maker, by trade, and he maintains a rather significant shop in his basement where he has turned his attention to woodcraft. By proxy, I can certainly see where there must have been some kind of skilled machining in the ancient world. We'll get deeper into that another time.

The following day was a bit more relaxed as we hit the Civilization Museum to see the royal mummies as well as a Coptic church carved into a cave, and then we flew down to Aswan where a seven-day Nile Cruise awaited us. It was a fantastic strategy. Use the boat as a home base for a week while we visited all the temples up and down the Nile River.

The day we flew in we started with the temple at Philae which had been moved when they built the Aswan high dam. The following day we visited Elephantine Island which was an unexpected surprise for me. I hadn't recalled it on the original itinerary, but it was some place I'd always wanted to visit with its legends as a possible holding place for the Ark of the Covenant (some think it's still there). This was the first time I'd crossed paths with The Ark (and I was wearing a hat everyone told me looked like Indiana Jones). There are also stories there about stargates (we encountered these several times) and Egyptian depictions of Mayan headdresses. We concluded the day at Kom-Ombo temple and the crocodile mummy museum.

From there, much is a majestic blur. Esna, Luxor, and Karnak temples all in one day, Abydos and Dendera, Edfu ... These are all covered in detail in the travel blogs, but a few highlights ...

If you can successfully sneak doing it, go around the backside of the broken obelisk and Karnak, put your ear to it, and slap it. You'll hear the resonance resound from within. If you can get access to the Sekhmet statue do that as well. The eyes are amazing and appear to glow, gazing into your soul. Of course, Abydos has the controversial glyphs that appear to be vehicles from today's day and age, and it additionally has the Osirion out back with the "Flower of Life" inscription. Dendera ... the home of the Egyptian "lightbulb." It's not a straight up, physical lightbulb, but it does signify energy and is amazing when you get a peek at it. There are three of these "bulbs," by the way. The sheer height of the structure is what amazed me, with all the fantastic Hathor sculptures adorning the columns, unfortunately defaced in antiquity (the next time you want to deface a modern statue look at how frustrated we are that the ancients defaced theirs!). We also got access to a newly-opened crypt, first group inside to an area that had been off-limits for 20 years. And with the fresh chisel marks in the walls with large chunks of friezes missing, we can plainly see what they were doing for 20

Exploring a crypt in Dendera and feeling a bit like Indiana Jones.

years. And then Edfu… so much to see there, but things really got interesting when Mohamed and Jonny were having a nice back and forth dialog about the Atlantis origin story on the walls. That conversation in its entirety is a special feature in the Member Site.

After a slower day visiting the Nubian Museum (which contained important early history artifacts) and actually visiting a Nubian village for tea, we flew back up to Cairo … but not without a six-hour delay at the airport. I'll give Egypt Air props, however, since they gave us free food and drink while we waited.

Our final day together was spent back in Cairo visiting the fantastic Egyptian Museum in Cairo and then spending some time shopping in the Cairo markets. Like the other museums, the Cairo Museum has some important pieces with secrets hiding in plain sight like the Schist Disk, the sarcophagus with the failed cut on the backside, the giant coffin, and more. With its plethora of sarcophagi, it's where I performed a massive search for any box similar to the one in the King's Chamber of the Great Pyramid ... and found none.

These are just some of the highlights of an amazing two-week excursion to Egypt! For full details, check out the Travel Blog and the Special Features section of the Connected Universe Portal Member Site!

Are Shadow Entities Extraterrestrials?

August 15, 2021

Article Notes: My work on shadow people is what first landed me on Ancient Aliens *in the Season 18 episode "The Shadow People." There, I discussed the Albert K. Bender story (amongst other topics), and I also described this story in Darcy Weir's documentary* Who Saw The Men In Black. *I highly recommend watching both. I also recommend watching my docuseries* The Shadow Dimension *which, for some reason, I fail to mention in this article even though it had just been released that summer. Also to note is, since this article, I've gone deeper into the hypothesis about the shadow entity at Johnny V's being a type of time slip rather than just an ordinary interdimensional being.*

Supernatural shadow entities are extremely mysterious, and there have been a plethora of theories over the years as to who and what exactly they are. I've had many experiences with shadow phenomena, and I've written an entire book on the subject, *A Walk in the Shadows: A Complete Guide to Shadow People*. I also conduct lectures and have given many interviews on these shadow entities, and one of the more interesting questions I receive is, "Are some shadow people actually aliens?"

This is actually a very good question since there are likely a large variety of different types of extraterrestrials throughout our universe, and we still have many different ideas and theories as to how they interact with us in our own world.

One such theory about aliens and shadow people is that the shadow we see may actually be an attempt at some sort of cloaking device.

Here's a scenario to deliberate: An alien race is searching for a new home because its planet is dying, and they have detected Earth as a hospitable planet; however, they have also detected there are intelligent beings who have already populated the planet. They decide they wish to observe the human race to determine if we are beings in which they could cohabitate, so they deploy a few of their kind on reconnaissance missions to Earth. For their own protection, they utilize a cloaking technology they've developed for their space suits and send out their emissaries. At times, these emissaries stand in the corner of people's bedrooms or in their closets or outside a window and simply observe our nature. Unfortunately, this alien race is not familiar with our physicality and how our eyes receive and translate light, so instead of humans not seeing these aliens at all, we see a dark form standing and staring at us. The cloaking device works enough in that we don't see any discernible features of the alien wearing the suit or even any features of the suit itself; we only see a dark bipedal form that really could be anything, but it frightens most people.

That's one possible explanation, but true extraterrestrial beings may actually access our planet through other means than just a physical spacecraft. They may actually be accessing our planet from another dimension.

I'm of the belief that a "true" shadow person is an

On the right: the door at Johnny V's through which the shadow ran.

interdimensional being, an entity that lives on another plane of existence, but sometimes interacts with ours. Let me give you an example of when I believe I've witnessed this.

At a restaurant no longer in operation called Johnny V's in Muskogee, Oklahoma, we were just finishing up a paranormal investigation, and I decided I was going to take one last photo sweep of the restaurant. Some of the others from the team were upstairs in the bar area while others were out in the dining room when I waltzed through the main doors of the kitchen with my camera. That's when I saw it.

It was tall, narrow, translucent, and wispy. And it was so damn fast. I couldn't really say it had any significant discernible shape since it couldn't have been any more than six or eight inches wide, perhaps as tall as an average man, but it zipped out of there so quickly it was extremely hard to tell. From straight in front of me as I entered the room it immediately darted to the right side of the room, and I heard it blow right through the thin, flimsy metal doors in the wall that led to the back part of the dining room. The imperative word is *heard*. The doors didn't actually move at all. What had I just seen?

I called out to the others, "Did you guys hear that?"

"Yeah!"

I questioned them on the incident, even going so far as to ask them if they had thrown something at the door in case they were trying to give me a quick jump scare. They hadn't. They were too involved in their conversations, although I checked the floor outside the door just to make sure. There was nothing.

So, what happened here?

What I believe is some sort of entity was in that kitchen when I walked in and was resonating as just a vague bit of shadow. When I walked in and it saw me, I scared *it*, and it took off running through the door. On the shadow's plane of existence that flimsy metal door blew wide open as it ran away from me, yet I couldn't see that happen because the door remained stationary on *my* plane of existence. Yet sound is on a different wavelength and has its own frequency, so perhaps, that sound of the door being slammed into and its vibration resonated across both dimensions. While I couldn't see what actually happened on the shadow's plane of existence, I could certainly hear it.

In 1952, Albert K. Bender established the International Flying Saucer Bureau during what was known as the great UFO "Flap" that year. He published a quarterly journal for this organization called *Space Review* which reported UFO and extraterrestrial encounters witnessed across the country. Just a year after he started the IFSB, Bender was visited by what many have deemed as "the Men in Black" who threatened his organization and journal and insisted he no longer talk about these kinds of phenomena. He shared his experience with these men with Gray Barker who reported the encounter in his 1956 book *They Knew Too Much About Flying*

Shadow people, extraterrestrials, or the Men in Black?

Saucers, and Bender stepped back from his UFO research just a year after he'd begun.

In 1962, however, Bender reemerged with his own book *Flying Saucers and the Three Men* in which he retold the story of his encounter with these strange men. Late one night working in his office, Bender started to feel ill. He decided to lay down, and when he did so he saw three shadowy figures with shining eyes wearing fedoras materialize through the wall. Using a form of thought transference, these beings communicated that they wanted Bender to stop his UFO research immediately. Accompanied with an aroma of sulphur, these entities frightened Bender so much that he was unable to eat for three days.

Bender's conclusion was that these three hat-wearing figures were extraterrestrials trying to silence his work in the study of ufology. In his account, these beings represented an extraterrestrial race who came to Earth to harvest resources from the water in Antarctica, and they needed to be left alone until their mission was complete. While Bender painted these entities as extraterrestrials, others believed they were the "Men in Black," and yet other elements of the story sound eerily similar to accounts of hat-wearing shadow entities.

These three beings *seemingly* morphed from out of nowhere. They had a shadowy nature about themselves. They were wearing fedora-style hats. They had glowing eyes like some shadow entities do. When in groups, shadow entities are quite often reported in threes. They spoke telepathically.

I believe what Albert Bender experienced was what those who have encountered the hat-wearing shadow entities report experiencing. While these encounters could certainly be extraterrestrial in nature, they definitely have the aura of the supernatural attached and certainly seemed to be linked to each other in some fashion. I believe there are other men in black encounters which are a controlling, shadowy part of our government flexing its muscle, real human beings with some secret agenda. Having spent a brief amount of time at NSA (the National Security Agency), I've seen some of it. But what Albert K. Bender and so many others have experienced for centuries is something not of this plane of existence or world.

Another interesting example comes from a woman who approached me at a conference I was speaking at and related to me the following story:

She awoke in bed in the middle of the night startled by a flash of light from a room out in the hall. She wasn't sure what this flash was, but a shadow man rushed into her room and jumped on top of her. It pinned her down and she heard laughter. After a brief moment, it jumped off her and ran back into the other room after which she saw another flash of light.

The next day, she entered that room and flipped on the light switch. Two flashes of light burst forth in the room and the smell of burnt electronics filled the air. Most of the electronics in the room had completely fried, and she called the fire department.

Were those flashes of light possibly the shadow person entering our plane of existence and then later exiting? Was this an intentional

A shadow person may be an extraterrestrial ... or something else.

crossing of one dimension to another that required such a transfer of energy that it created a burst of light?

Now, when it comes to extraterrestrials, if an alien race has mastered the astral plane and can project themselves to our planet using the power of their minds or the power of another dimension, then it is quite possible for some of these shadow people to actually be extraterrestrial beings. Perhaps, with the way they are transmitting themselves into our dimension from their own, we are only able to see a certain wavelength of that transmission, and all we're able to see of their bodies is this shadow.

As I always say with paranormal and supernatural phenomena, it's all theory, and I'm not saying it's aliens ... but it may very well be that some of these shadow people *actually are* extraterrestrials.

Inside Alaska's Mysterious Triangle

December 19, 2021

Article Notes: This article served as a preview for my latest book at that time Alaska's Mysterious Triangle. *It's a brief chapter-by-chapter summary with some included quotes from the book. Unfortunately, we only got two seasons of The Alaska Triangle television show as the COVID-19 pandemic made production much more difficult to accomplish.*

Alaska's Mysterious Triangle is the latest tome by Mike Ricksecker exploring the strange mysteries of this universe, this time in the region of the world known as the Alaska Triangle, an area stretching from Juneau to Anchorage to Utqiagvik (formerly Barrow). The Alaska Triangle, much like its counterpart, the Bermuda Triangle, is one of the most enigmatic places on Earth. Since 1988, over 16,000 people have mysteriously gone missing across its landscape, and over the years this region has played host to some of the strangest phenomena ever recorded. What causes this unexplained activity and what ancient mysteries may be hidden in

Filming for The Alaska Triangle *television show in May 2019.*

the Last Frontier? You can find a copy of the book here: https://www.amazon.com/dp/1735668990

Let's take a glimpse, chapter by chapter with accompanying excerpts, of the areas this book explores ...

Introduction

Not only did I film with and have been featured on (as of this date) four episodes of *The Alaska Triangle* television show on the Travel Channel, but I also once lived in Alaska during the early to mid 1990s when I was stationed at Elmendorf Air Force Base as part of the USAF. Here, I recount some of those first impressions of The Last Frontier, arriving in Anchorage just after a volcanic eruption, and preview what's to come in the pages ahead.

Chapter 1: Cold Lessons in Triangles, Vortices, and Portals

What exactly are these triangle areas of the world? How are they powered? What's the difference between a vortex and a portal? How

Archive of the Connected Universe: Volume 1

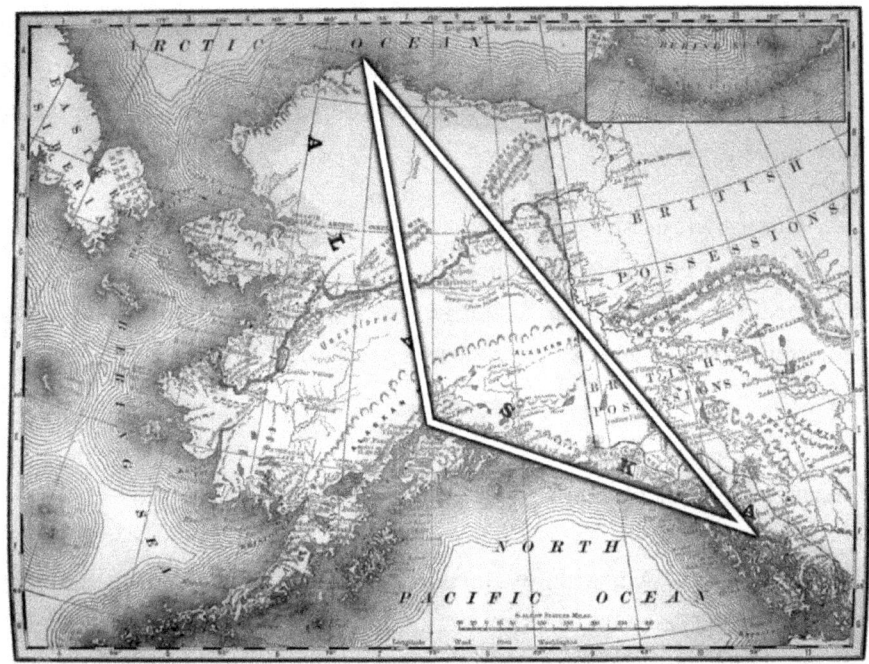

The triangle area is roughly the size of California.

are telluric currents and ley lines related?

This initial chapter sets up the whole rest of the book, defining precisely what we're talking about in these mysterious triangle areas all over the world and the phenomena that occurs within. How do elements like Earth energy, seismic activity, and the solar wind affect specific areas on the globe?

"There are a significant number of different types of anomalies occurring in the region due to the geological structure of the Alaskan ground and the stone within it down to significant depths. These anomalies are also exacerbated by the Earth's magnetic influence, field, and currents upon these types of rocks and minerals within the area known as the Alaska Triangle."

Chapter 2: Missing Airplanes

Thousands of people have gone missing in Alaska over the past several decades, but some of the most tragic have involved airplanes disappearing without a trace, including some extremely high-profile cases. Why have these planes never been found and where could they have gone?

"Although an extensive search was conducted twice over throughout the Portage Pass, no wreckage or evidence of the airplane's presence or of its passengers was ever discovered. Some say the Cessna must have made it through or it would have otherwise been located. But if it did make it through then where did it go? Decades later, it's still a mystery."

Chapter 3: Lost at Sea

Tales from Alaska's waterways are quite harrowing, ranging from missing vessels, to shipwrecks, to ghost ships. This is probably where Alaska seems most like the Bermuda Triangle.

"Winds off the Pacific blast islands and seaboard towns, and gusts have been known to roll and capsize poorly loaded ships. Fog can hang so thick and low that shoals and reefs go unseen until a vessel runs aground, arctic winds will coat ships in ice in a matter of minutes, and storms will kick up so quickly and heavily dumping enormous amounts of snow onto ship decks. All of that is before we even consider the strange electromagnetic properties of the region that may affect instrumentation and account for many of these tragedies."

Chapter 4: Walking In Shadows

Are there reports of shadow entities in Alaska? Following my work on shadow phenomena in my book *A Walk In The Shadows: A Complete Guide to Shadow People*, I also cover this type of supernatural activity in the great white north.

"Perhaps those shadows flitting about were actually images of those personnel who had previously worked in that basement decades beforehand, shadows of real human beings living and working in another point in time. Or, perhaps, they were images of those who would come after us, some future unbeknownst to us. Could they have even been ourselves?"

Chapter 5: Somewhere in Time

Time is simply a human construct used to describe our reality – it doesn't really exist. Yet, we seem to be trapped in what we've dubbed a "river of time," unable to move through it, backward or forward, at will. But what if we could? Have there been accounts of time travel in Alaska?

"Imagine that every moment that ever has occurred, is occurring, and will occur in a specific location are all stacked together in one extremely tall pile of photographs – a living picture captured every second, if you will. All these captured photos are still living and on-going within that tall stack without knowledge that the others in the stack are also living and on-going. The time slips we previously talked about would be when two of these moments in the stack of photos resonate at the same frequency and overlap for a moment. Time travel would be the ability to go to a location and move up and down this stack of moments at will."

Chapter 6: Extraterrestrials

Many of the conversations throughout *Alaska's Mysterious Triangle* could easily have an extraterrestrial influence to it. Were extraterrestrials or UFOs responsible for the missing Douglas Skymaster, any of the tragedies at sea, the shadow phenomena, or many of the other strange things that happen in Alaska? There have certainly been a plethora of sightings in the Triangle, including UFOs out of the water, many times occurring around the same time as other bizarre events.

"This is just one of many early reports for which we're left with no explanation and

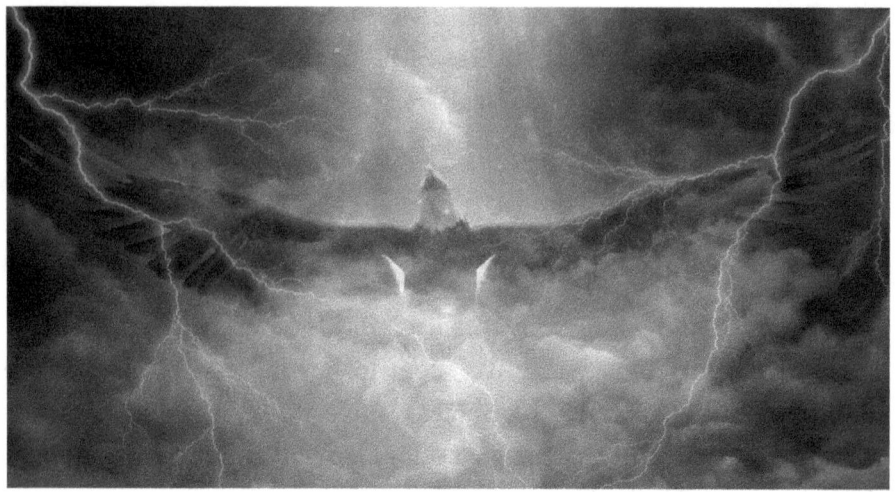

What are the true origins of the thunderbird legends?

the recent UAP report won't even touch. Why is it that our society has the propensity to withhold information, or spread disinformation, that hurts or prevents our own progress?"

Chapter 7: Cryptid Encounters

Alaska is rife with strange creatures from newly discovered animal species to Big Foot to ancient sea monsters. The native Inuit and Tlingit have their own legends of strange beasts as well, and the land has stories of once being inhabited by giants. What about science's new idea to resurrect the wooly mammoth? We explore many of these stories within this chapter.

"One can't help but to make connections from the Denisovans to accounts of giants in Alaska. In 1937, Alaskan Inuit native Michael Francis Kazingnuk began writing out by hand what would become a 500-page tome on the history and traditions of his people. Amongst the plethora of stories Kazingnuk compiled were ones of giants, some with connections back to Siberia across the sea."

Chapter 8: Specters of the North

Of course, Alaska is quite haunted as well, rife with ghost stories and legends of spectral beings at historic locations. Does the power of the Alaska Triangle increase the paranormal activity in this part of the world?

"The prevailing hypothesis is that energy can only be transformed, so when we lose the physical body at death, the energy within us continues on, and depending on your belief system, can go on to do a variety of different things either here on Earth, on some other world, or within some other dimension. So, what happens with that energy in a much more volatile and energetic place like Alaska?"

Chapter 9: Government Conspiracies and Cover-Ups

Alaska is a massive state, enormous in size and far removed from the rest of the United States. The vast wilderness and treacherous terrain make the Alaska Triangle area a much easier region in the world to lock away secrets.

"What concerned most people with this statement is the idea that HAARP was used to 'excite the electrons' and directly affect conditions in the Earth's atmosphere. This has led to a bevy of accusations of weather events HAARP is said to have been a direct cause of, including the 2011 earthquake and tsunami in Japan, the 2013 tornado in Moore, Oklahoma, a 2006 landslide in the Philippines, and the aforementioned earthquake in Haiti, among many others."

Chapter 10: Other Connections

I love this chapter. This is where I got to really explore some more esoteric topics outside the confines of Alaska as we discover the Triangle, like the everywhere else in the universe, is connected to many other areas on the planet. How might Alaska be connected to Antarctica? Egypt? Did the lost civilization of Atlantis also colonize Alaska? How did massive pole shifts affect the world when Alaska and the North Pole actually became the South Pole?

"In another ironic connection, there's a photo of a dark-colored unnamed mountain in Antarctica's Ellsworth mountain range that looks so much like a pyramid that several websites have used the photo in their articles about Alaska's Dark Pyramid (even though the Dark Pyramid is supposed to be underground). Many also believe the Antarctic mountain itself is an ancient pyramid. The photo serves almost like a visual double entendre, teasing us about two highly controversial structures in both Alaska and Antarctica shrouded in mystery and suspicion."

Seeing Shadows: A Peripheral View

February 26, 2022

Why do we see shadow entities in our peripheral vision and then they suddenly vanish? I just recently recorded the second edition of the audiobook version of *A Walk In The Shadows: A Complete Guide To Shadow People*, and there are some new additions! Just over a year ago, I released the print version of the second edition, which included over 40 pages of new content, so the audiobook companion has been a long time in coming. The additional content to the new audiobook version (due out in March) isn't nearly as substantial, but it does provide some additional interesting concepts and anecdotal stories concerning shadow entities.

The following is an excerpt from Chapter 17, "Interdimensional Shadows," which got the biggest additions, and briefly covers observing shadow beings in one's peripheral vision. Enjoy the early preview!

"[An] enormously valuable contribution to the cause of human enlightenment." -Andrea Perron

A Peripheral View

One other aspect to consider while examining the possible interdimensional implications of shadow people – the way our eyes work. Many times, when people witness shadow entities, they see them out of the corner of their eyes, they get a glimpse of something shadowy moving about in their periphery, and when they turn to look, it's suddenly gone. Why does this seem to happen so often?

Our eyes are made up of rods and cones, the rods being low-light receptors and the cones being like the HD camera of the eye and allowing full-color, high resolution eyesight. While cones reside near the center of your retina and help you see color and fine detail, rods mostly sit away from the retina, and although you see less detail with rods, the human eye is designed as such that the faintest objects in our range of vision can be seen 16 – 20 degrees off-center. Stargazers will use a technique called averted vision, a technique in which one looks off to one side to expose the most sensitive part of the eye in order to see fainter objects in the night sky.

Seeing shadows out of the corner of the eye is such a commonly reported phenomenon that in Episode 2 of *The Shadow Dimension* docuseries, I had three different people discuss this point: Esoteric

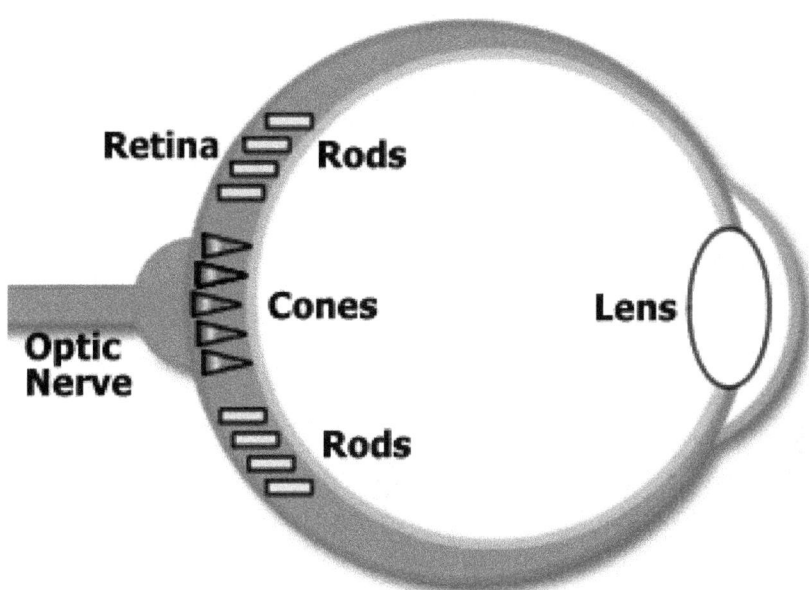

Researcher Jonny Enoch, Psychic Explorer Mark Anthony, and Medium and Researcher Mary Marshall. Together, they painted a fantastic picture of how this works with averted vision, and in one particular quote from Mark we come to understand what we're seeing in these moments in which we glimpse the shadows in our periphery.

"In our peripheral vision, we see slightly into the infrared range. It's like when you want to observe a comet, and if you try to look at it directly you don't see it so well. You see a comet better when you're viewing it out of your peripheral vision. Spirits, and particularly shadow people and other interdimensional beings, they're vibrating at a frequency which may be subtle. So, if you try to look at them directly you don't see it, but that's why you'll catch a glimpse of them out of your peripheral vision, because that part of your eye is more sensitive to low light. So, these entities are around us a lot, and it's learning, first off, like you, to be receptive to them, and then secondly, when you do encounter them, to learn how to observe them. Because people say, 'I thought I saw something out of the corner of my eye, and I looked at it and it vanished.' It didn't vanish."

The idea that the presence of the shadow entity may actually still be there with us when we turn to look at it may not be comforting to some, but the concept makes sense considering we know there is a world around us we cannot usually see with our range of vision. This world is composed of both physical and interdimensional elements, as well as many elements we still don't quite understand, yet it's all quite very natural.

In addition to the new audiobook, this new material will also find its way into the print version of *A Walk In The Shadows*, although there won't be any new edition number. This will simply be added to the existing paperback edition within the next month (you can call it Edition 2.5 if you like).

Our Parallel Universe Running in Reverse Time

April 4, 2022

Article Notes: Most of this blog article found its way into the first chapter of Travels Through Time, *"Cycles of Time." It still blows my mind that much of the traditional media swept this research under the rug. Yet, since that time, neutrino research has increased with the Sanford Research Facility (SURF) being built within old gold mines in South Dakota and Fermilab in Chicago beaming neutrinos at it 800 miles through the ground. Known as the Deep Underground Neutrino Experiment (DUNE) this will measure the oscillation of neutrinos to better understand the mysteries of matter and anti-matter ... in other words, duality.*

There's a parallel universe running in reverse time! *Seriously?*

In early 2020, as we were just learning about a virus called COVID-19, other media headlines were buzzing about groundbreaking experiments in Antarctica and reprinting information from an article *New Scientist* had published titled "We May Have Spotted a Parallel Universe Going Backwards in Time" which declared,

"Explaining the signal requires the existence of a topsy-turvy universe created in the same big bang as our own and existing in parallel with it. In this mirror world, positive is negative, left is right, and time runs backwards." The news sounded like something out of *Through The Looking-Glass* or the "Mirror Universe" episodes of *Star Trek*. What was this sorcery, and how could it possibly be real? Could the implications mean our ancient gods of lore may have actually been visitors from this twin universe?

The scientific studies *New Scientist* cited for this article were taken from the ANITA project in Antarctica. The ANITA (Antarctic Impulsive Transient Antenna) is a stratospheric balloon-based experiment which points a radio antenna back at Earth to try to detect radio waves that are emitted by high-energy neutrinos if they happen to strike an atom in the ice. Back in 2016, ANITA detected evidence of these high-energy neutrinos that were supposed to be arriving from space actually coming up out of the Earth's surface without a source. When these findings were published a few years later, *New Scientist* may have taken a bit of an initial leap in proposing a parallel mirror world running in reverse time. Or, perhaps, they knew what was coming down the road since, ultimately, the idea is not without merit and has recently been re-proposed by other sources.

At the time the article was published in 2020, traditional media and academia were quick to dismiss the claims, such as a *Forbes* article which stated, "It's all *way* overblown and misrepresents what the research in question is about." Since this interpretation of the data was being reprinted in tabloid-esque media outlets like the *New York Post*, *Daily Star*, and *Express*, traditionalists wanted to sweep it under the rug. That same Forbes article went on to state, "To be clear, there is zero evidence of what the *Daily Star* says is 'a parallel universe, right next to ours, where all the rules of physics seem to be operating in reverse.'" Perhaps, they shouldn't have been so

ANITA Project prior to launch. Drummermean photo, Wikimedia Commons.

quick to be dismissive. Two years later, it appears we may have the evidence they didn't believe existed.

In March 2022, popular media sources such as *Live Science* and *Space.com* started printing familiar headlines: "Our Universe May

Have a Twin That Runs Backward in Time." It was déjà vu of the 2020 articles, but this time they cited a new peer-reviewed paper published in the journal *Annals of Physics* which expanded on the neutrino research and supported a universal symmetry. Titled "The Big Bang, CPT, and Neutrino Dark Matter," this paper states, "We investigate the idea that the universe before the Big Bang is the CPT reflection of the universe after the bang, both classically and quantum mechanically ... The universe before the bang and the universe after the bang may be viewed as a universe/anti-universe pair, emerging directly into the hot, radiation-dominated era we observe in our past."

Within nature, physicists have defined a set of symmetries, three of the most important of which (CPT) are referenced in this paper:

(C)harge: If you flip the charges of all the particles involved in an interaction to their opposite charge, you'll get the same interaction.
(P)arity: If you look at the mirror image of an interaction, you get the same result.
(T)ime: If you run an interaction backward in time, it looks the same.

The idea here is that in order to preserve the CPT symmetry throughout the cosmos, there must be a mirror-image cosmos that balances out our own. This cosmos would have all opposite charges than we have, be flipped in the mirror, and run backward in time.

If this concept of symmetry and balance sounds familiar, it ought to. One needs to look no further than the yin yang symbol and the belief that there can be no positive without negative, no light without shadow, and there's a delicate balance of two sides throughout the universe. There **is** also an interconnectedness represented in the symbol in the way the curves flow together and how there is a little of each in the other. If our universe and this mirror universe came

from the same Big Bang then that means we originate from the same source material and were connected at birth, so we forever have a relationship with it. We see similar symbolism of duality and balance in the Andean Yanantin, the Norse rune Dagaz, the Celtic double spiral, and many more. It seems science may finally be catching up to what the ancients were telling us long ago

Furthermore, if our universe is operating from a beginning to an end then the other universe would be operating from end to beginning, meeting with us again and starting the cycle over. Again, we see this type of symbolism play out in the ancient world with the ouroboros, the symbol of constant recycle and renewal. The oldest allegorical symbol in alchemy with roots in ancient Egypt, the ouroboros represents mystical time flowing back into itself for eternity.

Taking this type of universal symmetry a step further, if this mirror universe is running in reverse time from us then its most sophisticated civilizations would have been thriving at a time when ours were at their most primitive. They may have started off as space-faring races across the cosmos and are now a society that has been slowly devolving for millennia. Is it possible in a time long ago they had the ingenuity and technology to traverse the universes and visit our world, possibly appearing as gods to our most ancient cultures? Have these beings tried to impart knowledge upon us because they've already seen what happens to humanity? In *our* future, will we be doing the same for them when they reach a more primitive state as their time continues to run backwards?

It's a lot to consider from experiments in one of the most remote areas of our planet on subatomic particles we can't see with our own eyes. But if it's true that this mirror universe is out there, then we may be getting reintroduced to something our ancient ancestors had been telling us about long, long ago.

For more information, including the role of dark matter in this mirror universe, watch our *Connecting The Universe* interactive class "Anti-Universe and Mirror Worlds" within the Connected Universe Portal member area.

The ouroboros by Theodoros Pelecanos in 1478.

A Serpent Down the Rabbit Hole

May 9, 2022

Article Notes: Like the previous article, most of this has also found its way into the first chapter of Travels Through Time. *I love diving down these rabbit holes.*

Alchemy. The word is derived from AL-KHEMET which originated in Egypt meaning "from the black land." The oldest known allegorical symbol in alchemy, the ouroboros, also has its origins in Egypt, depicted on King Tutankhamun's burial shrine (circa 1323 B.C.). At least that's the earliest we have found to date. And this symbol, while with us for thousands of years, seems to have found renewed interest in today's modern world. Apropos.

The ouroboros caught my eye some years back, or I should say ears, when viewing the film *Predestination*, starring Ethan Hawke and Sarah Snook. While I won't spoil any of the twisted paradoxes within this savvy film based on the 1958 short story "All You Zombies" by Robert Heinlein, there were several references to "the snake eating its own tail" that scratched at the back of my mind, and

The ouroboros as depicted on King Tut's burial shrine.

I had to investigate further. Down the rabbit hole I went, exploring this esoteric and ancient symbolism.

The ouroboros represents the concept of eternity and endless return, as well as the unity of the beginning and end of time, creating an eternal cycle. This cyclical nature of our universe is one of renewal. As life dies it decays into the ground and grows again as new life. From the death of a solar system springs forth another. I touched on this a bit during my last blog article on the possibilities of a universe parallel to ours running in reverse time. Has our ancient symbolism always shown us what our science is now discovering ... or rather, rediscovering?

Not only do we see this iconography of the ouroboros in ancient Egypt, but we also see it in ancient Hindu traditions. In their depiction, a tortoise supports elephants upon whose back the Earth rests. All of this is enclosed by the serpent Asootee.

However, the most recognizable representation of the ouroboros is probably that of the 1478 drawing by Theodoros Pelecanos. This drawing is contained within a manuscript Pelecanos produced now known as the *Parisinus graecus 2327*, which includes copies of texts from the Eleventh Century and other works of unknown origin, and is held within the Bibliothèque Nationale in France. The ouroboros drawing happens to be one of these copies but not from the Eleventh Century – it is much older, and is from a lost alchemical tract by Synesius, a Greek bishop of Ptolemais in ancient Libya, c. 373 – c. 414 AD. Welcome to the rabbit hole.

Synesius of Cyrene

In 393 AD at the age of 20, Synesius traveled with his brother, Euoptius, to the city of Alexandria in Egypt, where he became an enthusiastic Neoplatonist and disciple of the legendary philosopher, Hypatia. Some years later in 398, he was chosen as an envoy to the imperial court in Constantinople but returned to Alexandria in 403 where he married before moving to Cyrene in Libya in 405. Although Synesius later became a Christian bishop, he maintained Neoplatonism roots and studied alchemy. His letters to Hypatia are the earliest known references to a hydrometer, a device used for measuring the relative density of liquids and is still used today. In fact, I use a hydrometer to measure the specific gravity of my wine during the winemaking process.

It certainly sounds like Synesius had quite an interesting life, but what does that have to do with the ouroboros aside from the fact he created an illustration of it? When we research and explore, we look for connections.

The famous destruction of the Great Library of Alexandria dates back to 48 BC, a casualty of war when Julius Caesar found himself trying the survive a civil war between Cleopatra and her brother, Ptolemy XIII. Under siege, Caesar set fire to Ptolemy's fleet in the

Hypatia as depicted by Jules Maurice Gaspard in 1908.

Alexandrian harbor, which gave him the upper hand, but this action had dire consequences. The fire spread into the city and consumed the Great Library.

All was not lost, however. The Great Library had a "daughter library" nearby in the Serapeum, a temple dedicated to the deity Serapis, which housed some remaining documents. The Serapeum endured for another four centuries, containing the largest collection of books in the city of Alexandria during that time, until it was destroyed by Theophilus in 391 AD.

During its time serving as the de facto Library of Alexandria, the Serapeum saw rise to Neoplatanism beginning with the work of Plotinus in 245 AD when he came to Alexandria from Lyco (which could either refer to the modern Asyut in Upper Egypt or Deltaic Lycopolis, in Lower Egypt). Over the next 145 years, Neoplatanism would see itself branch off into different sects: one version taught at the Serapeum which was more religious in nature and influenced mightily by Iamblichus, the philosopher from Syria who was the biographer of Pythagoras, and a second version purported to be truer to the original teachings of Plotinus. This second version was taught at the "Mouseion" in Alexandria, an emulation of the Hellenistic Mouseion that had once included the Library of Alexandria, and was headed up by Hypatia's father, a mathematician named Theon. Hypatia succeeded her father as the head of the Mouseion, and her school was allowed to endure even after the destruction of the Serapeum. Enter Synesius.

Synesius wasn't someone who just sat in Hypatia's classroom and quietly took notes. He developed a strong enough professional relationship with her that they often corresponded via letters after he left Alexandria, and it is from these letters that we've come to know as much as we do about Hypatia's life. Synesius's significant interest in alchemy led him to write a commentary on Pseudo-Democritus, those alchemical works which were attributed to the philosopher Democritus but were actually compiled by anonymous Greek authors.

All of this to say ... When we look at this drawing, we are looking at a piece of the lost Library of Alexandria, something that survived the ancient world and multiple destructions of knowledge centers. It is still with us today because Synesius recorded it around the Fourth Century AD and Theodoros Pelecanos decided to make a copy of it just over a thousand years later. There is much that was lost when the Great Library was destroyed, but this is a piece we can hold onto, and it's an important one as we continue to dive into the Connected Universe. While so much knowledge and wisdom has been lost over the millennia, the universe has left us some clues to help pick up the pieces, and while the original Great Library of Alexandria is no longer with us, its scant survivors are there to help us.

Exploring Ancient Ireland

July 28, 2022

To say the country of Ireland is charming is an understatement. It truly is as magical, mysterious, and lusciously green as everyone says it is – and more so! My Ancient Mysteries of Ireland tour from Mysterious Adventures Tours kicked off on July 1, although I got into the country on June 30 and took in some of the Temple Bar area as well as the National Leprechaun Museum – yes, one truly exists. And it was really a nice warm up for the tour that was about to take place, learning about some of the culture we'd be experiencing and raising a pint of Guinness to kick off the next week and a half.

(Note: You'll find the full 2-hour, 24-minute video travel blog within the Connected Universe Portal member site.)

The official first day of the tour took us up to the notorious Hell Fire Club (not of *Stranger Things* fame), the old hunting lodge built on top of an ancient cairn that witnessed all sorts of sordid depravity by those politicians and influencers of the Eighteenth Century who wheeled and dealed within its confines then partook in various taboo sexual rituals. Rumors of black magick, animal sacrifices, and more

The notorious Hell Fire Club.

are said to have occurred there.

A real treat, however, was the "fairy woods" leading down from Montpelier Hill (the name of the hill upon which Hell Fire stands) and exploring the luscious green landscape within it. Some of my favorite photos from the entire trip are from the sojourn into the forest. The five of us on this little excursion got a bit turned around on our way down the hill and almost walked off in the wrong direction until a woman with her dogs got us pointed the right way. Fortunately, the bus was still waiting for us!

We capped off Day 1 with a quick visit to Moore High Cross. Tucked away through a crevasse in a stone wall, this granite monument rests in the ruins of a small abbey. Of note, we tried our first experiments with dowsing rods here and, as expected, once nearing the cross (which really serves as a granite obelisk like something out of Egypt), the rods switched directions with the change in energy.

Getting lost in the fairy woods.

Day 2 was a busy day packed with tours of three castles -- Rock of Cashel, Cahir Castle, and Blarney Castle. Ok, Rock of Cashel isn't technically a castle, it's an ancient monastery permeated with legends of St. Patrick, but it does resemble and sit prominently on a hill like a castle, and it was the traditional seat of the kings of Munster for hundreds of years before the Normans invaded.

Admittedly, thanks to bartenders Malikae, Meghan, and Francis at the Hayes Hotel the previous night, I was a bit "off" that morning and neglected to film any video (I also forgot half my wardrobe at Hayes, and our amazing bus driver, Eddie Doyle ran back to get it while we toured Rock of Cashel). But it had definitely been a fun night as evidenced by Natalie, Sarah, Lynn, Ann, Jenn, and myself even if I had woken up four minutes past the time we were supposed to report down to the bus! The smiles on these tours and friendships we make are what it's all about!

Following Rock of Cashel, we spent some time at Cahir Castle,

The Rock of Cashel.

which unfortunately kind of got forgotten on this tour. It's really a wonderful castle with plenty of history (and hauntings, of course), cannonballs lodged in its walls, and more, but it really got overshadowed by our final stop of the day, Blarney Castle. Blarney was easily one of my favorite stops (if not *the* favorite stop) of the whole tour. I was so pleasantly surprised by what we explored there, and we could have easily spent an entire day touring the grounds. As it was, we only had a couple hours to make something of it.

What really surprised me about Blarney were the gardens, which were absolutely amazing. Sure, I had heard that Blarney had gardens and a stone circle, but I wasn't prepared for how vast the gardens really were. Not only did it have a stone circle, but it had a dolmen, waterfalls, lush vegetation and plant life, a wooded tunnel, a boardwalk, manicured gardens, a lake, and on and on. We only got to see a fraction of what was there – and that was we before we even got to the castle!

The infamous Blarney Castle.

Yes, several of us did take the time to go up and kiss the Blarney Stone. With our limited time, it was a commitment to make in having to forego exploring some of the garden area, but we were treated with extra exploration of the castle. Kissing the Blarney Stone isn't just climbing up to the top and giving the stone a smooch. Along the way, there are chambers of the castle to explore as you climb up the long, narrow spiral staircase (this would never fly in America with our fire codes). And on the way back down, there is even more of the castle to explore! Again, we could have spent an entire day there, and as it was, we returned to the bus late to a rousing mock cheer.

Day 3 was another jam-packed day, starting at Charles Fort and the legend of the woman in white. The placement of the fort along the water is extremely picturesque, and we had quite a charming storyteller for a guide. What I find fascinating is how the details of legends change over time, and in the video travel blog within the member area of the Connected Universe Portal I provide two renditions of the fort's ghost story – one told by me on the bus and the other told by the guide. Now, I will be the first to say that the story told by the guide would certainly be the more accurate telling, since it's coming straight from the historic location. The version I told was from a variety of articles written about the old fort, so really coming down second hand. Having just given a presentation on the nature of legends back in June, the small changes in the story were of interest to me. Of even greater interest is that recently they had discovered a couple of skeletons in a cave down the bluff from the fort which may actually play into the true story of the jilted lovers and the commander who mistakenly killed his daughter's new husband.

Following Charles Fort was a quick stop at Ballynacarigga Castle. This was locked, so we couldn't venture inside, but we did get a glimpse of a sheela na gig carving on the side which is iconography that has been used to ward off evil spirits but has also been used for fertility.

The last part of that day, however, was a moment I'd been waiting on for a long, long time – stepping into Drombeg Stone Circle. In our field, one generally expects to feel some sort of energy at a location like this, which I did, but I was even more taken aback by the resonance I could actually hear with my own ears. It reminded me of the sound dampening alcoves in the structures outside the Step Pyramid at Saqqara in Egypt. I was not surprised, however, at the action of the dowsing rods, as they spun in place for a moment before definitively pointing outward toward the standing stones. Others in the group had some fantastic personal experiences there as well, and the amazing view of the countryside and sea beyond capped off what was certainly a top highlight of the tour.

If exploring creepy old castles and abandoned churches is your thing, then our first stop the following day is certainly for you. Templemichael Castle and the nearby church were a real treat,

The ancient and mysterious Drombeg Stone Circle.

especially as a late addition (much of our original itinerary changed following the COVID fallout). We had the place just to ourselves and crept through the overgrowth into the 12th Century ruins that are rumored to have once been a Templar stronghold. We were never quite done as the castle led to a tower which led to other out buildings – so much to explore!

Our explorations at Templemichael were followed by a surprising trip to St. Declan's Monastery in Ardmore. It wasn't so much the monastery that was surprising -- although that was quite fine – as it was our spontaneous excursion to the Ardmore beach. It was Independence Day back home in the United States, and what's the 4th of July without a trip to the beach?

Day 5 was a rather thematic one – we were going to jail! We spent the morning touring the Old Cork City Gaol and the afternoon exploring the rather extensive Spike Island. In some way, the old Gaol reminded me of exploring haunted prisons back in the United States, and I was impressed with how much they embraced their

Remnants of the White Star pier where the Titanic *last docked.*

history. Throughout the building are mannequins of various prison guards, officials, and prisoners all well-detailed to the actual physical descriptions of the people they were portraying. It really helped to give a voice to these people who would have otherwise been lost to time.

We had to take a boat ride out of Cobh to get to Spike Island, which was a nice change of pace from the bus – although we all loved Eddie and his bus! The old prison/fort is a massive complex with quite an extensive history, including a lost monastery that had been wiped out by the Vikings. The view across the water from there, like from Charles Fort, was absolutely fantastic.

As an added bonus, back in Cobh are the remnants of the pier that was the final port of call for the *Titanic*. While it was built in and left from Belfast, there were a couple other ports in Ireland it stopped off at before heading out to open waters and meeting its fate with the iceberg. Cobh was the final stop.

We began the next day in Glanworth with all intentions to visit the castle there, and we somehow missed the entrance. We pretty much walked right by it and up the hill without even realizing we had passed it. From atop the hill we were blocked by an electric fence that was keeping a herd of cows in a field, so onward we went to visit an old abbey just a few paces up the road and a nearby cemetery. Of interest in Glanworth is the old stone bridge that is the narrowest bridge still in operation in Europe. It is just barely wide enough for a car, and as we crossed, and a car approached we had to squeeze against the side of the bridge to ensure our feet wouldn't get run over!

From there we ventured on to Desmond Castle – just in time! We nearly missed the last opportunity of the day to tour, and we sincerely appreciated our guide for going past time to show us around. I was also afforded the opportunity by the guide to unlock and open the massive doors that lead into the castle! The key and key chain were equally as massive!

Even though the day was getting on and it suddenly got cold and blustery, we still made our way out to Grange Stone Circle, the largest stone circle complex in Ireland. This circle of stones was much larger than Drombeg and it also includes a giant circle earthwork all around. Given the construction of the earthwork and the flat basin inside with the stones pressed up against the embankment, this would actually be considered a henge enclosure. I tried the rods here as well and was met with similar results as Drombeg – an initial spinning until transfixing outwards toward the stones. Given the breadth of the circle, however, I didn't hear any unusual sound resonance at Grange like I had at Drombeg.

Day 7 was split between two amazing castles -- Charleville and Leap. Both are considered to be amongst the most haunted castles on the island, although we really didn't experience any hauntings while we were there. Instead, we had other amazing things happen.

Charleville is a truly beautiful castle that is fervently being restored. The entrance hall is magnificent, the accessible rooms are

Interior of Charleville Castle.

truly breathtaking, and there are mysteries that linger throughout this building that has Masonic origins. The two towers were of great interest to me. Without a lot of time toward the end of our visit, I managed to squeeze in another dowsing rod test. In the center of the Red Room tower one of the rods pointed north and the other pointed west (toward the other tower). In the center of the Masonic Library tower one of the rods pointed south while the other pointed east (again, toward the other tower). Samantha, the Charleville caretaker, also showed me with her pendulum how it spins counterclockwise in the center of the Library while it spins clockwise in the "Red Room." What this tells me is that the concept of duality, "As Above, So Below," is built right into the architecture of the building. We also see it in the black and white floor tiles of the entrance hall, which are original to the castle.

When it comes to Leap Castle, the idea of the Bloody Chapel and a possible elemental roaming the premises have prompted a

The legendary Long Room at Trinity College.

large number of people to fear what may be lurking in the shadows there, but most of us on the tour found Leap to be an immensely peaceful location. Nothing jumped out of the oubliette murder hole or morphed out of the stone walls to "get" us. We spent a delightful evening exploring the castle and its rooms and then were later blessed to get a sample of Sean Ryan's music and his daughter's dancing. (She's a professional Irish Riverdancer.)

That was really the final day for our primary tour. We had a last day in Tullamore which we used as a free day. Many people went shopping for those final Ireland souvenirs while others of us continued to explore. A couple of us found ourselves walking for miles down the Grand Canal Greenway to scope out other castles, ruins, and old stone bridges. That evening, we had a magnificent goodbye dinner in downtown Tullamore and we shared with each other our favorite moments from the tour, some of which were described above.

Many say Leap is the most haunted castle in Ireland.

We found ourselves in Dublin early the next morning as most from the tour had flights to catch back to America. However, some of our compatriots stayed on in the city a little while longer to do a little additional touring. Compelled to see the Long Room at Trinity College, also known as the Jedi Library, I made one final little discovery -- the busts of William Shakespeare and Sir Francis Bacon sitting right next to each other. That might not sound like much ... unless you're interested in the theories that while there may have been a man from Stratford-Upon-Avon named Shakespeare, he almost certainly wasn't a playwright. Of those theories of who may have actually written the Shakespeare works, Sir Francis Bacon is one of them. Hmmm ...

That, essentially, wraps up the Ancient Mysteries of Ireland tour! These have just been some really brief highlights of a truly remarkable time we had traversing the countryside on the Emerald Isle. I've pieced together a 42-minute recap which can be found publicly on my YouTube Channel, but the full 2-hour, 24-minute travel blog can be found within the Connected Universe Portal member site.

Real Time Travel: What Does it Look Like?

August 8, 2022

Article Notes: The Stacked Time Theory presented in this article became the primary basis for my book Travels Through Time *and permeates throughout much of my research. Observing time as an object is how many theoretical physicists believe beings in other dimensions observe our dimension and reality of time and would be able to move about it at will much in the same way we can manipulate three dimensional objects. If one keeps this principle in mind, it should be easier for one to negotiate the principles of real time travel. Or ... just watch the film* Interstellar *a few times.*

"Everything is solidly there, whether we call it past, present or future ... We invent time to explain change and succession."
– J.B. Priestly, *Man and Time***, 1968**

What is time? How do we define this elusive thing we call time? We've, generally, been taught that time is like a river, flowing endlessly in one direction. We are caught up in its current and can only proceed downstream within its rushing waters. This "river of time" that we're stuck in, however, flows as a river not because of the water but because of the banks that are holding the water in place. If we were to remove those banks, time would spill out in all directions, flooding the plains until it came to a standstill and was simply just ever-present. We would no longer be rushing downstream with it but would be able to easily wade through those waters to any point we'd wish. What those banks are and what the mechanism is that's holding them in place we don't know, but they control the flow.

Although this is a nice analogy, and perhaps it got the reader thinking a little, I generally don't regard time as a river at all. Time doesn't really exist, after all. Time is merely a human construct to describe our reality and to try to bring some order to this world in which we live. What we describe as time helps us to differentiate the seasonal changes of our planet, to help us know when it's appropriate to plant and harvest crops, and to help us get to the office at the right moment so we don't upset our bosses.

Just weeks before his death in 1955, the famed theoretical physicist Albert Einstein wrote, "The distinction between past, present, and future is only a stubbornly persistent illusion." I wholeheartedly agree with this and have addressed similar concepts when I've discussed the idea of the simulated universe, which is beyond the scope of this article (see "Shadows in the Matrix" in my book *A Walk in the Shadows*). But one pertinent quote from that discussion in my book comes from Gregg Braden, a best-selling author and speaker on consciousness:

"The Sanskrit word maya actually means illusion. This is a fundamental concept in the Hindu tradition. ... They tell us that it is under the illusion, under maya's influence, that the soul identifies with the body to the point where we cannot tell ourselves as separate from the illusion of this physical world."

The quote continues on, and while I'm not going to get into

Illustrating Stacked Time Theory during a 2015 video on YouTube.

details about the simulated universe in this particular piece, it is does address an ancient culture discussing the illusionary nature of this world and that the universe as we know it is not as it seems. (I discussed several cultures in the recent *Connecting the Universe* class within the Portal member site and released later as a podcast.)

Many years ago, a thought about the nature of time struck me, and I started toying around with the idea that time is actually all concurrent, all existing at once, eventually calling it "Stacked Time Theory some years back. Imagine that every moment that has ever occurred, is occurring, and will occur in a specific location are all stacked together in one extremely tall pile of photographs – a living picture captured every second, if you will. All of these captured photos are still living and on-going within that tall stack without knowledge that the others in the stack are also living and on-going. The time slips we have talked about in some of my other work (see the Versailles time slip, the "Conjuring house," and the Doppelganger Effect) would be when two of these moments in the stack of photos vibrate or resonate at the same frequency and overlap for a moment, as if they're echoing into each other. Real time travel in this scenario would be the ability to go to a location and move up and down this stack of moments at will.

Although I formulated this theory on my own, throughout my years of research I've come to realize that this idea has many similarities to Albert Einstein's theories about the space-time continuum. It was quite eerie, in fact, when PBS ran a documentary on Einstein and used an example of taking photographs of falling dice to illustrate the "block universe" of his space-time continuum. What influenced me to jump down this rabbit hole, however – no offense to Einstein – was the film industry.

Ever since I was a young kid in the early 1980s, I've loved the movie *Somewhere In Time*, starring Christopher Reeve and Jane Seymour, based on the novel *Bid Time Return* by Richard Matheson. In this heartbreaking story, Reeve's character has journeyed to a hotel on Mackinac Island where he is drawn to the historic portrait of a beautiful woman. He desires to meet her and wills his consciousness from 1980 back to 1912. In order to do this, he acquires clothes and other items from the era to use the power of his mind and convince himself in his 1980 hotel room that he is actually at the hotel in 1912 at the exact same time the woman is there. With his consciousness, he was able to jump from one photo in the Mackinac Island stack to another. Sure, it's a fictional story, but I believe when we finally discover the secrets of time travel it will be more of this nature, rather than something mechanical, to make these journeys. Time travel will have more to do with meditation, the interconnections of the universe, and consciousness than a Delorean and a flux capacitor. We'll also be able to use the Earth's energy and sites of power around the globe to aid us in these meditations and take us on these journeys as they may have once done so in ancient times.

I began this article with a quote from J.B. Priestly who wrote the fascinating *Man and Time*, a study about the way humans look at time and what "time" may actually be. Richard Matheson used concepts from this book in *Somewhere in Time* and actually

Spatial observation, rather than time, of a town. Google Earth image.

referenced it in the *Bid Time Return* novel. In many areas, Priestly explores the fascinating concepts ancient cultures presented about time and how the universe worked, including the Egyptians, Greeks, Australian Aborogines, and more – much of which is far too in depth for this article (you can find me talking about it on the *Connecting the Universe* podcast … and within the Portal) – and I like what he has to say about how we've come to view time these days: "We are worse than those ancient peoples who believed that behind all change and succession was a special god, more real than they were. At least they ended with a god who could be worshipped and might be placated, whereas we are trying to measure and analyze a ghost container."

But perhaps his best analogy is this: "Our spatial and temporal experiences simply refuse to be as widely separated as the scientific philosopher's Space and Time. Let us say I travel by car, at 60 miles an hour, across the five miles of the Little Puddlefield district. I see a church, two farms, four bungalows, and an inn successfully within five miles; I have a Time relationship with this region. On the next occasion, I fly over it in a jet plane on a clear day, look down and see all at once the church, the two farms, the four bungalows, the inn, and what was in Time is now in Space. The difference in ordinary experience is simply between two modes of travel."

This takes us back to my original illustration at the beginning of this article where Priestly's road becomes our river and his aerial view from the jet plane becomes the still sea of water the river expands out to if we remove its banks. It's perspective. You could also think of it like the film *Interstellar* and the tesseract in five-dimensional space Matthew McConaughey's character, Cooper, interacts with. Here, he was able to view the physical representation of every moment in time of his daughter's bedroom. The filmmakers did an admirable job of tackling this concept by presenting time as a three-dimensional object to the viewers – every moment presented as a cube connected to each other moment. When the camera was pulled back this became a top-down view of an intricately connected web of moments, their version of all the water at once from our former river or Priestly's jet plane viewpoint.

The question then becomes how to willingly access those moments if they're all concurrent. In so many of our science fiction movies it is some sort of machine teleporting us from one year to another – whether that's a car, a pod, a telephone booth, or some other contraption. In *Interstellar*, it took using gravity from the fifth dimension (we'll get deeper into dimensions another day) to encode a watch and send a message. In *Somewhere in Time*, it was the ability to fool oneself into existing in a different year and willing the consciousness back in time. Again, I believe real time travel will be **more** of the latter than the former, and mastering such an ability will take patience and work. Perhaps, the ancients knew better how to maneuver through different periods of time and when we feel energy at stone circles such as Drombeg or Stonehenge and see stargates depicted at Abydos, Hatshepsut's Temple, and more that these are faint remnants of a knowledge they had in traversing space and time.

In Episode 6 of *The Shadow Dimension* docuseries, researcher Mary Marshall has a fantastic quote in which she states, "We are starting to learn that both the past and the future influence the present. It starts to create a picture for us, in that, we may be experiencing ourselves."

When it happens, perhaps we won't be discovering time travel, but rediscovering it.

Stargates of Ancient Egypt

October 3, 2022

Autumn begins to settle into northeastern Ohio, more specifically the Cleveland area, with crisp air and overcast skies to look forward to until snow and the bitter chill of winter's kiss encompasses *The Land*. While the frigid air may cause most to look past winter to the spring beyond, I'm especially looking forward to February 7. Why? That's because I will once again be stepping off an airplane in Cairo, Egypt, where I will enjoy the warm blanket of the desert heat for the Stargates of Ancient Egypt Tour. At that time of year, the temperatures will be an ideal 75 – 80 degrees. What do we expect to find?

In June 2021, I was sitting next to Mohamed Ibrahim on a flight from Cairo to Aswan as we embarked on the middle leg of the Return of the Kheper Cycle Tour, a tour that celebrated the dawn of a new cycle of life with exclusive two-hour access for just our group inside the Great Pyramid of Giza on the summer solstice. It was absolutely amazing. In my hand as I sat in my airplane seat was a copy of Christopher Dunn's book *Lost Technologies of Ancient*

Mohamed Ibrahim and I outside the Red Pyramid at Dahshur in Egypt.

Egypt. Mohamed and I began to talk, and I revealed to him that, like Dunn, my father was a machinist, which launched us into a discussion about some of the greater mysteries of ancient Egypt and the type of technology they likely had at their disposal to create many of their mesmerizing structures. As our flight neared Aswan, Mohamed said, "I would like to do a tour with you. Let's talk after this one." Thus, was established the kernel of what has now become the Stargates of Ancient Egypt Tour.

What's a stargate? When we think of the word "stargate" we usually think of the 1994 movie of the same name or the various *Stargate* television shows that have been produced. Yes, the idea is to use some sort of portal to travel from one point in the universe to another – or even just across our own planet somewhere.

In modern times, theories concerning wormholes were first introduced to the scientific community in the early Twentieth Century, although the nomenclature was different. Albert Einstein's theory of general relatively had not been immediately embraced, and Austrian physicist Ludwig Flamm had been reviewing another physicist's solution to Einstein's equations when he realized alternative solutions were possible. In 1916, Flamm proposed a "white hole," or a black hole that has been, theoretically, reversed. With this possibility available, a space-time conduit could connect the entrances to black holes and white holes.

By 1935, the theory of general relativity was firmly entrenched, and Einstein, along with physicist Nathan Rosen, used the theory to elaborate on Flamm's idea to propose the idea that "bridges" crossed through space-time. If one could bend space and time, these bridges could connect two different points to create shortcuts across the cosmos. This would greatly reduce the amount of time and distance between these points, making it a much more effective means of travel through space. When we refer to wormholes today, we are referring to these Einstein-Rosen bridges, and it is believed that many of these entrances which can be readily accessed by intelligent life are our stargates.

So how does that apply to our exploration of ancient Egypt in February? I don't want to give it all away, but allow me to give you a little taste while you sip your favorite autumn brew.

Hatshepsut's Temple

The layout of Hatshepsut's Mortuary Temple is absolutely fascinating, and if I had any influence into the design work of a stargate in an upcoming blockbuster movie, this temple would be my basis for it. First, we have to consider the long staircase one must climb up to the temple which leads straight back to the Holy of Holies. Alongside this beautiful staircase are two carved falcons which are the animal representation of the god (or neter) Horus; however, these falcons do not appear to be the original animals depicted on these sculptures. A closer examination of the stonework

The grand staircase of Hatshepsut's Mortuary Temple.

from these statues up alongside the staircase reveals the tail of a snake, the snake being an ancient representation of energy. It's difficult to say what kind of snake these statues may have originally been, but one theory is that they were originally cobras. In any case, it's the energy which concerns us, and that representation of energy leads straight up into temple and is pointed back at the Holy of Holies.

If one looks off to the left of the temple complex, there is a platform with a ruined collection of blocks atop it which is inaccessible to the public. These ruins are actually the last vestiges of a small pyramid. What is a pyramid doing here? If one ascribes to the idea that Christopher Dunn has put forth that many of these pyramids were once some sort of power plant or machine, then this pyramid off to the side may have acted like a generator we see standing off to the side of so many large buildings. But a generator for what?

We have a picture starting to take shape for us with the symbolism of energy alongside the stairs and a possible power generator off to the side, but it becomes more blatantly obvious once one has traversed up the stairs. On the left side of the doorway into

Above the warning sign for tour guide are our stargate hieroglyphs.

the inner courtyard we find the hieroglyphs designating "great stargate." As one ventures further inside toward the Holy of Holies, we also find hieroglyphs designating "stargate" alongside the entrance doorway. Humorously (at least to me), is a photo I took of this stargate designation directly above a sign telling tour guides not to explain anything inside the entranceway to the Holy of Holies. Pay no attention to the man behind the curtain. Wink, wink.

The public does not have access to the Holies of Holies, the innermost sanctum of Hatshepsut's temple. There is a gate before the chamber with two guards posted, but for a tip they will lean inside and take a quick photo for you. Why can't one get inside? What's so special to deem this area off limits? If one gets there early enough, as one of my colleagues has done before, you can grease some palms with some hard cash (I couldn't tell you how much) and gain access for a brief moment. What's inside is fascinating. On one of the walls is a unique cartouche with a field of stars within it, a blatant representation of access by the king (Hatsheptsut, although female, was still considered a king, not queen) having access to the stars – a stargate.

Abydos

Seti's Temple at Abydos has so many amazing things going on with it, but most people seem to only be interested in one feature: the hieroglyphs that look like modern machinery. True, what we see looks like objects today we would construe as an airplane, a helicopter, a tank, and more. Deterrents of this idea state that old hieroglyphs were plastered over while new hieroglyphs were chiseled in, and then the plaster fell out over time leaving us with a combination of overlapping hieroglyphs. That's an interesting hypothesis, and some of it may certainly have been plastered over, but if that were entirely true then we would see similar strange "modern-looking" hieroglyphs elsewhere, and we just don't. It seems these images were still intentionally created, and Mohamed Ibrahim does a much better job of explaining this in 2021's Egypt Travel Blog on the Connected Universe Portal (can also be found in the Ancient Egypt course as well). This controversy, however, has nothing to do with stargates.

As one ventures inside Seti's Temple, we find a large chamber with friezes depicting the ceremony of the djed pillar, a yearly celebration of the renewal of energies in Egypt. The djed pillar was a symbol of the backbone of Egypt, Osiris's backbone, and what's fascinating is that while we see many depictions of the djed pillar, trinkets and figurines carved into the shape of a djed pillar, even depicted as columns at Saqqara, no djed pillar has yet to be unearthed to our knowledge to show us what they truly looked like. This was an important part of Egyptian culture, and within this chamber depicting the celebration of renewal we find three smaller chambers labeled as stargates. With Osiris we have a story of ascension, and while we see a story of the ascension of the djed pillar in the chamber outside the stargate chambers, the function of a stargate itself is to ascend to some other location or world.

Other fascinating aspects of the Abydos complex include one of

Raising of the djed pillar in the Hall of Osiris.

the largest known lists of Egyptian kings, which fails to include several famous kings such as Akhenaten and Tutankhamen, the archaic and far older Osirion behind the temple, the mysterious depiction of the Flower of Life symbol completely out of time and place, intricately placed light shafts, and more. The Abydos complex is a very important one, and that it may have once housed stargates makes it all the more fascinating.

These are just a couple examples of stargates scattered throughout the ancient structures of Egypt, more of which we'll be exploring during our Stargates of Ancient Egypt Tour in February. We also see the symbolism depicted at Karnak and other temples, and there are fascinating stories about stargate activity coming out of Zawyet El Aryan, the remains of a pyramid complex near Dashur closed off by the Egyptian military and referred to by some as "Egypt's Area 51."

Mysterious Triangles of the World

November 23, 2022

Article Notes: This is another one of those articles that originally started as a Haunted Road Media Learning Short on YouTube, got posted as an article on the old mikericksecker.com website, and then got reposted as an article on the public side of the Connected Universe Portal.

Triangle areas of the world are vortices of energy which build up from the Earth's core and cause strange phenomena to happen, such as unusual weather patterns and interdimensional portals. The most famous, of course, is the Bermuda Triangle ... we'll get to that one in a few minutes. Airplanes and ships travelling through these triangle areas report equipment failures and compasses running wild as well as extraterrestrial sightings. Some of the most bizarre disappearances in history happen in these vortex areas ... let's take a brief look at some of the most popular hotspots.

The Alaska Triangle

The Alaska Triangle is an area of Alaska from Juneau to Anchorage to Utqiagvik (formerly Barrow) which is known for strange disappearances, anomalies, and supernatural activity. In any given year, 500 – 2,000 people go missing in Alaska, a total of 16,000 since 1988. Like the Bermuda Triangle, the Alaska Triangle seems to harness the Earth's energy grid to create a vortex of mystery and a possible portal into another dimension, affecting planes, boats, people and more.

I've appeared on a handful of episodes of *The Alaska Triangle* on the Travel Channel, and the show covered a number of strange occurrences and disappearances, including missing airplanes and ships, UFO sightings, paranormal activity, and cryptid sightings. (Since the original publication of this article, I've also published the book *Alaska's Mysterious Triangle*.)

The Missing Douglas story is particularly interesting. This was a Douglas C-54D airplane which took off from Elmendorf Air Force Base in January 1950 and disappeared without a trace. The weather called for mostly clear skies, and there was no reason to suspect anything was wrong with its final radio contact at 1:09 PM. However, at the very edge of the Alaska Triangle, near Snag in Yukon Territory, Canada, it disappeared. No wreckage or survivors were ever found.

During the search operation, cryptic radio messages were received, but it was difficult to discern the message they were trying to convey. Many believed these messages were from the crew of the missing Douglas C-54D. Yet, just as quickly as the transmission started, they stopped. If the plane had slipped into a portal into another dimension could those messages have been transmitting back through the portal since sound travels on a different wavelength and frequency than light?

Even when I lived in Alaska during the early-to-mid 90s, crazy

Exploring the Alaska Triangle in 2019.

activity happened when an engine fell off a plane taking off from the Anchorage airport. Fortunately, no one was hurt, but local citizens were shocked when the engine crashed into the parking lot of a local supermarket and shrapnel fell into people's homes.

Of course, the most notorious Alaska Triangle disappearance is that of the plane carrying United States House Majority Leader Hale Boggs, Alaska Congressman Nick Begich, aide Russell Brown, and pilot Don Jonz in 1972. In an effort that spanned an area of 325,000 square miles and more than 3,600 hours of search time, nothing was ever found.

Bridgewater Triangle

The Bridgewater Triangle lies in Massachusetts and roughly covers the area between Abington, Freetown, and Rehoboth. Cryptozoologist Loren Coleman coined the term after his research

Hockomock Swamp. (Bridgewater Public Library photo)

dating back into the 1970s revealed a concentration of supernatural sightings within this confined area of the state.

The central figure of the Bridgewater Triangle area is the Hockomock Swamp, once known as "Devil's Swamp" to Colonial settlers. Here, witnesses have spotted vicious dogs with red eyes, a pterodactyl-like flying creature, Native American ghosts traversing the waterways in canoes, and glowing lights throughout the trees. Reports of Big Foot activity also pocket the swamp.

Throughout the rest of the area which spans some 200-square miles, are other sightings of paranormal and extraterrestrial activity. One gentleman in 1990 encountered an extraterrestrial while walking his dog down a road in Raynham. While leisurely strolling along, the dog started whimpering and quivering as they passed under a streetlight. Up ahead on the road was a strange bipedal creature, standing about three to four feet tall, hairy with no clothes, large eyes, and it had a pot belly. The creature was uttering some cryptic words and beckoned the man to come; however, he turned and walked away with his dog instead. Later on, he deduced the creature was saying, "We want you. Come here."

Many local residents are also familiar with the red-headed hitchhiker along Route 44 in Seekonk. In this stretch of haunted road, a man with long red hair and a full matching beard has been spotted several times, but when motorists stop to pick him up, he disappears.

Lake Michigan Triangle

Known as the Bermuda Triangle of the Great Lakes, the Michigan Triangle spans from Ludington, Michigan, to Benton Harbor, up to Manitowoc, Wisconsin. Many believe the strange activity of the lake began with the disappearance of Thomas Hume and his crew of seven in 1891. They set sail in a schooner and were never seen again. If they sank, no wreckage of the boat ever washed up anywhere, nor did any bodies.

In 1921, the *Rosa Belle* was found overturned in the lake and all eleven of the crew were missing. The ship had observable damage that it had been struck by another ship, but no other ship reported any sort of accident, and no other wreck had been found.

In April 1937, Captain George Donner of the *O.M. McFarland* lied down to rest after navigating his ship through icy water but was never seen again. As the *McFarland* was nearing port, the crew went to wake Captain Donner as he had requested, but his door was locked. With no answer after they knocked several times, the crew broke open the door, but Captain Donner had disappeared and his whereabouts remain unknown.

In 1950, Northwest Airlines flight 2501 carrying 58 passengers vanished over Lake Michigan and the plane was never found. Just before it disappeared from radar, the pilot had descended the aircraft to 3,500 feet due to, "a severe electrical storm which was lashing the lake with high velocity winds." Two hours after the final transmission from Flight 2501, two police officers reported

The mysterious wreck of the Rosa Belle.

witnessing a strange red light hovering over Lake Michigan for about 10 minutes before disappearing. The red lights have been reported in the area since about 1913.

The possible source of the unusual activity in Lake Michigan could be a ring of stones that was discovered under the lake in 2007. The stones rest under only 40 feet of water but seem to have a similar alignment to that of Stonehenge. With ancient sites of power known to tap into the Earth's energy grid, is this ring of stones from a lost civilization powering the lake to manifest this unusual activity?

Nevada Triangle

The Nevada Triangle stretches from Las Vegas to Reno to Fresno, California, and like its counterpart triangles is known for its many strange disappearances. Over the past 60 years over 2,000 planes have been lost in the 25,000 square miles of desert and mountains. This triangle area also includes the notorious Area 51, the military installation long rumored to be a hot spot for UFO sightings, strange phenomena, and conspiracy theories.

Some believe the extensive number of crashes in the area are due to unusual wind conditions and a phenomenon referred to as a "Mountain Wave" which is an internal gravity wave within the mountain range that increases with elevation. Military plane crashes and disappearances in this area date as far back as 1943, with modern pilots still having deadly problems in the area. This includes Steven Fossett, a record-breaking aviator, who disappeared in 2007. Although nearly $1.6 million was spent in search and rescue efforts at the time, it was a random hiker a year later who discovered remnants of Fossett's plane some 65 miles away from where he'd taken off.

Dragon Triangle

The Dragon Triangle is also known as The Devil's Sea or the Pacific Bermuda Triangle and spans from Japan to the Islands of Bonin and then deep into the Philippine Sea. Legends of the Devil's Sea extend far back into history with the "dragon" moniker dating to Chinese fables from around 1,000 BC which speak of dragons living under the water's surface who attack passing sea vessels.

An early account of trouble in the Dragon Triangle dates to the days of Kublai Khan, grandson of Genghis Khan, who lost some 40,000 crew aboard ships bound for an invasion of Japan in the late Thirteenth Century AD. In the 1800s, a mysterious woman sailing a strange vessel through the waters of the triangle was spotted, and the boat was described as being in the shape of a traditional Japanese censor for burning incense. It's not known where she was headed and, thought to be ghost-like, she was never seen again. Paranormal stories like this caused the Japanese to name the triangle area "Ma-No Umi," or "Sea of the Devil."

In the 1940s and 50s, scores of Japanese fishing boats and military ships disappeared in the Dragon Triangle in the area between Miyake Island and Iwo Jima, so in 1952, the country sent an investigative team aboard *Kaio Maru No. 5* into the mysterious

Circa 1200 – 1300 from China, the Searching the Mountains *silk scroll depicts many images within its extensive story, including the turmoil in the Dragon Triangle, complete with the spiral, the ancient symbol for portal.*

waters. Contact was lost, and long after they first set sail, remnants of the ship were discovered in the sea. It's unknown what happened to the 22 crew members and nine scientists aboard. Following this incident, the Japanese government declared this area of the Dragon Triangle dangerous for marine voyage.

Bermuda Triangle

Of course, the most famous of all of these triangle areas is the Bermuda Triangle. Covering 500,000 square miles of water, and probably as many stories and legends, the Bermuda Triangle extends from Bermuda to Miami, Florida, to San Juan, Puerto Rico. When Christopher Columbus sailed through this area during his first voyage across the Atlantic Ocean, he reported sighting a great flame of fire crash into the sea. This may have just been a meteor, but he also reported experiencing erratic compass readings while traveling through these waters.

The legends of the Bermuda Triangle really started to take shape in 1918 when the *USS Cyclops* went missing with its crew of 309 sometime after leaving Barbados. It was carrying manganese ore,

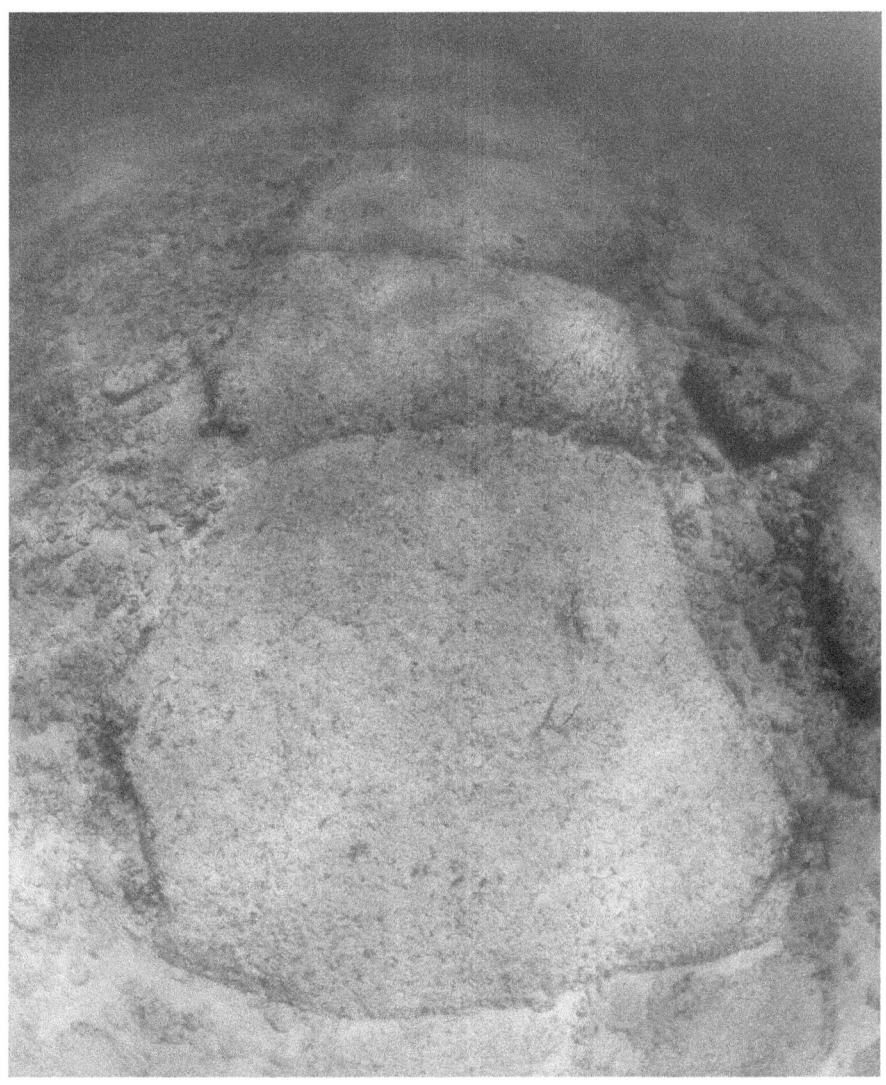
Was the Bimini Road part of a lost civilization?

and in a strange twist of fate, its two sister ships were both also lost while carrying metallic ore, but years later in the North Atlantic during World War II.

In December 1945, five torpedo bombers known as Flight 19 completely disappeared while on a training run. The Navy stated a navigational error led the aircraft to run out of fuel, but no remains were ever found. One of the search and rescue planes with a 13-man crew also disappeared.

In 1970, pilot Bruce Gernon flew into what he ended up calling an "electronic fog" in the Bermuda Triangle and traveled forward 30 minutes in time. Flying from Andros Island to Ft. Lauderdale, a flight Gernon routinely made, massive dark clouds that formed up ahead of Gernon's plane morphed into a spiral and swallowed the craft into the vortex. The plane's instruments began malfunctioning as bright white flashes illuminated the sky. When Gernon came out on the other side unscathed, the city of Miami was below him having traveled 100 miles in three minutes. Bruce Gernon's experience in Bermuda seems to have similarities to the missing Douglas airplane in the Alaska Triangle, safely traversing a portal while those in the Douglas, unfortunately, did not.

These are just a handful of the plethora of tales from this infamous vortex of strange activity. The Bermuda Triangle also contains the famed Bimini Road under its waters which some speculate may be the ruins of the lost civilization of Atlantis ... but that's a story for another time.

Part 2

Finding the Way

Notes on Part 2

This first set of articles is from the first days of the blog I now house on Substack. I was really just finding my way, trying to figure out what types of topics I wanted to cover and if there were going to be articles and topics that were a bit more candid. I was also trying to write articles for this blog every few days which I, ultimately, determined was quite challenging with my schedule, and I've now settled into a nice weekly routine.

There is one truly candid article I decided not to include here, although it is still live within the blog's archive, and that is the one when I met William Shatner for all of a minute at GalaxyCon in March 2024. It's so completely out of place, thematically, in comparison to the rest of the material here that I've decided to eliminate it within this text. For those who are disappointed, here's the bit of relevant text from that article:

"Over the past couple years with my appearances on *The UnXplained*, I've been asked several times if I've met

William Shatner. I've had to say, "no," up until now since, for production, they film *him* on an impressive studio set while the rest of us are filmed separately in a myriad of locations. For instance, I have filmed both in a private hotel lounge in New York City and in "Mike's Office" in the Fenyes Mansion in Pasadena, California, for this show. [I was gifted a photoshoot with him at GalaxyCon] so I could make it official that I met him. He's 93 years old, so there may not be too many of these opportunities left.

What happened, you may wonder? Well, if you've ever been to one of these before, you're probably familiar with how quickly you usually get ushered through. You really have all of a minute as you get lined up for the photo and they snap it – there's not much time at all for conversation. However, as I walked in, I did tell Shatner, "It's a pleasure to meet you. I'm on a couple of episodes of your show, *The UnXplained*." His response was a kind smile and, "Ah, yes," just before the photo was taken. Then, I was ushered right back out. That was it. It wasn't a ton of time, but I was absolutely appreciative of it, and you know what? I have to hand it to Bill Shatner. At his age and with all the money he has, events like this are certainly not things he really has to do. But he does them anyway, and that is a truly wonderful thing. I hope when I'm that age I'm still as spry as he is and getting out to events to greet the fans."

These articles led straight into the 2024 Stargates of Ancient Egypt Tour, and following the tour articles is when I really started to find my footing for the blog and what it was going to be.

As for the name of the blog, **connecteduniverse.substack.com,** why did I go with that instead of mikericksecker.substack.com? Actually, there is a mikericksecker Substack I had started a few years back, but this was originally meant to be a bit of a sports blog called "The Mike Zone." Having been an athlete in my younger days, it's a bit of a guilty pleasure for me to follow baseball (the sport I, primarily, played) and football (although I boycotted the NFL for 20 years when they moved the Cleveland Browns to Baltimore following the 1995 season). With everything else I have going on with writing my books, conducting research, filmmaking, podcasting, etc., I really just didn't have the time to keep up a sports blog, even though I quite enjoyed writing the couple articles I did there.

After I wrote a few articles for my Connected Universe blog, I ultimately decided I was going to ditch the sports blog, so I tried to see if I could just set up a forwarder from mikericksecker to connecteduniverse. This never worked, even after contacting Substack's support. Oh, well. In the future I may use mikericksecker as a blog for my fiction writing or something else. We'll see.

An Odyssey of Exploration:

Blogging My Adventures in the Connected Universe

February 24, 2024

Article Notes: This was the first article on the new blog site at https://connecteduniverse.substack.com, a simple welcome message as I devised the direction for the work. It would take me a few months to figure that out. The next book became Portals to the Stars.

I write, therefore, I should probably blog, too, right? Actually, I've been blogging off and on since before blogging was even a thing. I had realized early on that one way to get people interested in coming back to my website, which at the time featured a single book, was to keep periodically updating the content of the site with bits of news. Since my first book was a mystery novel, this included news snippets from the world of mystery fiction writing, including monthly features on mystery movies and computer games – and I did all of this by hand.

Yes, I had to keep adding page upon page and manually updating the links throughout the website because back then there was no such thing as a content management system. When PHP finally

My original website as it looked in 2004.

came along and revolutionized the way we published content, it was a godsend. I jumped on board with PHP Nuke, then Mambo, Joomla, and finally, Word Press in which my primary website is built today. Now, for blogging purposes at least, I'm jumping into Substack, and the Connected Universe Portal is built with Kajabi who specializes in the creation of online learning platforms. There's a small blog there, too, but those are more like full articles I've written.

This blog here is going to be more personal in nature, at least as far as the writing process goes. The series I'm currently working on, *Connecting the Universe*, is meant to bridge some of the more fascinating and esoteric aspects of our universe together. Originally, this was supposed to be one single work; however, last year when I was in Egypt a different thought suddenly came to mind. I had just finished a lengthy presentation on stargates, Atlantis, and other mysterious aspects of ancient Egypt, and we were on the tour bus headed to one of the temples when it hit me that *Connecting the Universe* was not a single book but an entire series of books covering these topics. But what to start with?

I had plenty of material already written on stargates, earth energy, time travel, Atlantis, ancient symbolism, supernatural activity, and more. After much deliberation, I decided to dive headlong into the nature of time and time travel. Here, I could start the series with a nice base from which to work, discussing the innerworkings of the universe, the fourth dimension of time we're typically bound within, how dimensions work, formally introduce my Stacked Time Theory, and give us a place to jump off from heading into the other works. *Travels Through Time* not only discusses the nature of time and time travel, but it also slips into the areas of ancient symbolism, modern science, supernatural activity as time-related events, dreams and premonitions ... well, I'm kind of giving you the back cover bullet point list of what's in the book. Essentially, it shows how all of these different areas which we're going to explore in the *Connecting the Universe* series are related to one another and does so in a way that's fairly easy to follow. While there's both a lot of science and metaphysics within the book, I use a lot of pop culture references to make it easier for the casual reader to follow.

So, where to next in this series? Originally, I thought I would go straight into the stargates of ancient Egypt and Egypt's connection to Atlantis. I'm extremely passionate about that topic and is why I'm now hosting the Stargates of Ancient Egypt tours with renowned Egyptologist and Tour Guide Mohamed Ibrahim. However, there's a bit more research I need to put together on that, specifically at the Temple of Hathor in Dendera, and logically, if we're starting with time as our base for the series then we need to work our way up to the stargates. Thus, the next book in the series will be my work on earth energy.

I previously explored the energy and magnetism of the earth, telluric currents, and what we commonly call ley lines in my book *Alaska's Mysterious Triangle*, but that was just an introduction to those concepts in order to set up what that particular book was really about: the strange phenomena that occurs in Alaska. This new book I'm working on will cover the Earth's energy much more in depth, will explore more triangle areas of the world, the "vile vortices," ancient sites of power, vortex areas, and more. This will be far more than just an expansion on the work I've done in Alaska.

This blog will highlight the process of producing that work as well as other areas which interest me in my overarching area of research – which is kind of everything. You'll find here additional detail, opinions, and insight on some of my Mike's Morning Mug posts, feedback on hot topics, insight into my adventures and travels, and more. It will almost be like an introduction to what I've included within the Connected Universe Portal, but a bit more in a freeform nature and comes from my keyboard rather than the video camera.

I welcome you to this great expedition, this odyssey of exploration into the Connected Universe, where our adventure to uncover the mysteries of the cosmos becomes a journey into unlocking our true potential.

Travels Through Time *had just won a book award when the blog started.*

Where to Start the New Book?

Triangles, Megaliths, Supernatural Activity, UFOs ... Oh, My!

March 3, 2024

I try to get some bit of writing done each day. Some days I'm able to get more done than others, and there are some occasions in which I find a groove and just keep going. That happened last year when I got deep into *Travels Through Time* and the words just seemed to jump out from my keyboard. On one particular night, I was tossing and turning in bed, unable to fall asleep when I decided to get up and see what I could do with the book. I wasn't necessarily thinking about the book in bed, but it just seemed logical that if I was going to be up anyway, then I may as well get some work done even if my ability to write well late at night is usually pretty spotty.

At about 3:00 AM, I was finishing up the chapter "Ancient Perspectives on Time" with a piece on the Australian Aboriginal Dreamtime when the following suddenly flowed out of me:

"This is so very different **than** the modern way we view time today, a constant ticking away to our next appointment, to the alarm clock waking us for work in the morning, to the bus or plane we need to catch. It drones on, almost inescapable, an invisible bondage to a master we created of a slavery we don't realize we're within – tick, tick, tick. Somewhere deep within, passed down from our ancient ancestors and still marked in our DNA we realize something is wrong with the world, there is a greater understanding we've lost, something that scratches at our minds, but we can't soothe the itch with the answer. It's elusive to us. Instead, we keep plodding along to the beat of modern civilization, a crooked cadence that has spanned generations, following the path we simply know, that's been passed down to us and those that came before us, because the truth has been lost over the millennia, ironically … to time."

    I would love to get into that kind of zone again with this next book. As I stated in the last blog, the *Connecting The Universe* series started off as a single work, so I already have some material for this next edition. These materials consist of the original script I put together for my "Triangle Areas of the World" video I produced on YouTube some years ago, a document I started compiling on ancient stone circles, and a large piece I started writing on the Earth's energy grid. I also have plenty of reference materials in my book *Alaska's Mysterious Triangle* and several of the *Connecting the Universe* livestream classes in which I covered phenomena in hotspot areas around the globe. I also did some background work on Ivan T. Sanderson and his concepts of the "vile vortices" when *Ancient Aliens* came calling to have me talk about this subject. So, where to begin?

    There are certainly a lot of jumping off points here that I could tackle since I don't usually write my books in any particular order. I will write each section or chapter as I feel inspired to do so, which is a trick I've carried over from my fiction writing (my first book, *Deadly Heirs*, was a mystery novel) and helps prevent writer's

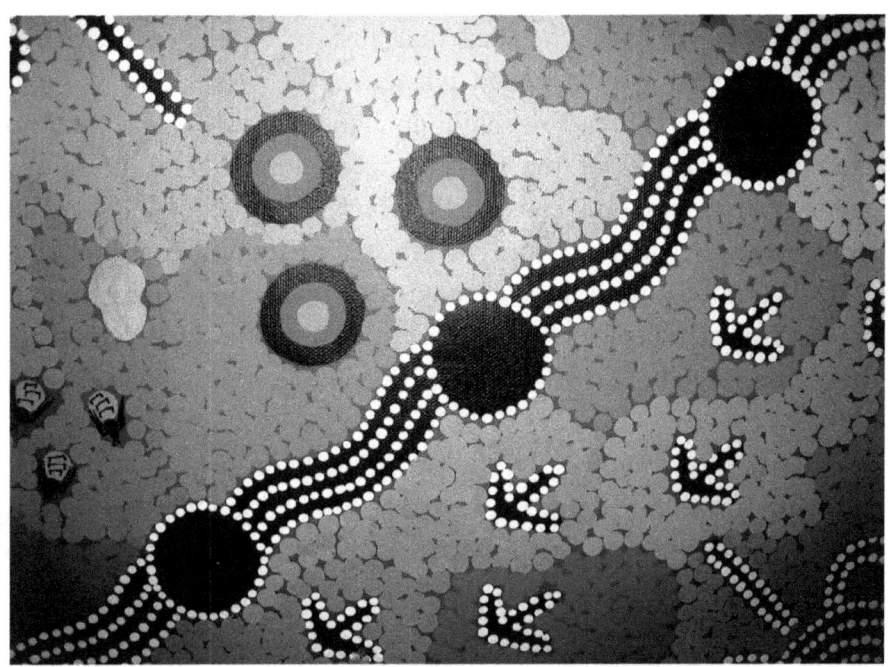

Aboriginal artwork of the Dreamtime. Alan Levine photo.

block. If I get stuck in an area, then I'll simply move on to another and come back around when my mind is clear on the one that stumped me. Eventually, all of the parts become a whole, and I'll sort of "glue" them together with natural transitions.

I've begun work on the triangle areas of the world since I already have plenty of material here and should get me rolling into a nice groove from which I can build some momentum. My initial thoughts on this piece are to break many of these down and have an entire section of the book be on this particular subject. In other words, I'll have a Part I, Part II, etc. and the various triangle areas like Bermuda, Alaska, the Dragon's Triangle out in Japan, etc. will each be their own chapter. This doesn't mean I'll work exclusively on these areas, however. As other subjects come to mind or I stumble across important information during research phases, I'll crack open a document and work in other areas, but triangles will be my initial focus for now.

We also need to consider that just recounting the strange phenomena that has happened all across the world due to these unusual energetic hotspots isn't enough. We will also want to examine the "why" of the matter and explore the source of the energy that has not only caused all sort of phenomena to occur from strange disappearances to supernatural activity to UFO sightings and more but also caused ancient peoples to build monolithic sites of power at these locations. What knowledge about these locations did they possess that we've lost to time and are now re-discovering today?

This is why writing is such an adventure to me. It's not just about throwing some words on a paper and regurgitating facts and figures with a few names and dates; it's about the stories behind these events. More to come …

The Juggle is Real!

A Little Bit of Everything to Start the Week

March 5, 2024

Some people say, "The struggle is real," when concerning challenges they may be facing, but for me I say, "The juggle is real," because it seems I'm always juggling a thousand different tasks on a daily basis. Ok, perhaps it's not a thousand ... perhaps it's 996 1/3 things I have to do each day, but it sure is quite a lot.

Following a day (Sunday) which began by posting a Morning Mug video to the Connected Universe Portal and was followed up by working on the new book and blogging about the process, I spent a sizable chunk of my Monday working on video clips I'm extracting from my Phoenix MUFON presentation video. In early December, I had the honor of speaking before the Phoenix, Arizona, chapter of MUFON about my latest book, *Travels Through Time*, and they professionally recorded the entire thing and provided me with a copy. I was extremely impressed! (They also hired professional photographer Chris Loomis who captured the photo below, as well as several others). With this footage now in hand, I will be featuring a couple of these clips on a new "Presentations"

Photo taken by Chris Loomis.

page on my website, another part of this week's juggle as I continue updates out there.

Of course, with a social media presence across multiple platforms, I couldn't just leave this to simply posting the clips on the new page. I also had to create versions of these clips to post on Facebook, Instagram, and TikTok as well. (Ok, I'm on Twitter-X and Threads, too, and some people consider YouTube to be a social media platform.) So, after creating the different formats and captioning them, I got them uploaded to all of these platforms.

Now, Monday was an unseasonably beautiful day here in the Cleveland, Ohio, area, so I also spent a substantial chunk of time outside working on the yard and getting it into better shape following the winter weather — which we may still have some of (this is Cleveland, after all). I had to take advantage of the good weather while it was here, and it was refreshing to get outside and get some fresh air. Self-care is important. (As of this writing, we had thunderstorms today which cooled everything back down and made everything wet, so the yard work was a good call.)

Not only did I take care of some outside work, but I'd been meaning for a while to reorganize my computer area for the last month, desiring to streamline my setup ever since I stepped away from my 30+ year IT career at the beginning of February. Reorganization and streamlining is good for peace of mind and freeing the brain from clutter while working on all of these different projects. And, thus, it was done.

With the new computer setup now in place, I took to continuing the work on the new "Presentations" page on the website, but in this line of work one must stay on his or her toes. At 6:00 PM Eastern on Monday evening, the Hauntlanta paranormal convention announced that I will be returning there as a guest this September 19 - 22. So, of course, I had to post that wonderful news across my social media as well. And then for good measure, not long after that, I reminded all of these platforms that we're coming down to the wire to sign up for the Stargates of Ancient Egypt Tour this April. And now, you've been reminded, too.

This seems like a lot of jumping around, for sure. Like I said, the juggle is real. However, it's wonderful to get a lot of items on the checklist crossed off — and I do keep a list. Part of that new computer setup was taking the monitor out of the "studio" for Wednesday night's *Connecting the Universe* and setting it up as an extra so I can follow that list while I'm working, making the tasks at hand more prominent. Not to worry ... I will move the monitor back for our Wednesday night livestreams.

As I wrap up this little random blog, I'll dive into completing the artwork and copy for the next *Connecting the Universe*, this one featuring UFO hotspots. Fortunately, I have a template for this and a virtual assistant who will schedule these sort of posts out to the social media platforms, but then I'll plunge right into putting together the material for the show (as well as the members-only after show for TCUP subscribers). That might sound like I'm creating massive amounts of work for myself when I should be concentrating on writing a new book, but here's the genius of it: you can bet a good portion of that material I put together on UFO hotspots will make it into a book on earth energy. I don't have to juggle everything.

UFO Hotspots and Earth Energy

A Relationship Between Two Strange Phenomena

March 9, 2024

Article Notes: This article was inspired by Ancient Aliens *asking me to participate in the episode covering the 37th parallel and the "UFO Superhighway." I will do this sometimes – write about in a blog or discuss on an episode of* Connecting the Universe *the topics I've been asked to cover on a television show. Of course, I don't mention the television connection at that point since I'm not allowed until the episode airs, but those paying close attention will see the connections. The notion of the 37th parallel's connections to UFOs was postulated by Chuck Zukowski, and he had a season of his own television show,* Alien Highway, *which covered a few of the cases. My good friend, Heather Taddy, also starred on that show. Unfortunately, Chuck elected not to participate in the* Ancient Aliens *episode.*

This past Wednesday, our *Connecting the Universe* "interactive class" covered UFO hotspots and the relationship between energetic hotspots on Earth and the more pronounced UFO activity in these areas. This is a topic I am absolutely going to cover in the new book and really could be its own separate book, altogether. Thus, it will likely be a very large section of the work. Let's take a closer look as to what I'm referring to.

Before we dive into the UFO phenomenon, let's first answer the question, "What is a hotspot?" A hot spot is any location that seems to have significantly more activity – of whatever you're investigating – than other locations around the globe. This is beneficial to recognize if we're investigating a type of phenomenon because (I'm going to quote myself here from an episode of *Ancient Aliens*), "If we're trying to solve a mystery, you want to go to a location that has the most clues. And these are the locations that would have the clues to connect our ancient past to our modern reality." If UFOs, paranormal activity, Big Foot, etc. are what you're researching, you're going to want to go to the locations that seem to have the most reported sightings. That would be a basic "hotspot."

When it comes to a hotspot of Earth energy, which seems to be attractive to all these phenomena, we need to start in the very center of our world: the Earth's core. The Earth's core is a ball of molten iron that's spinning, and as that iron spins **it** creates a magnetic field that emanates out from the planet. This is quite beneficial for us because it protects our planet from the solar wind and mass coronal ejections the Sun bombards us with. However, as that magnetism rises up from the core and passes through the Earth's mantle and crust it interacts with a variety of different metals and minerals. Depending on what it interacts with and in what quantity those metals and minerals are in, this can create anomalous magnetic activity in a much more localized area on the surface. This is how some of those strange "vortex" areas around our planet are created.

This notion isn't something mystical. For example, I included the following in my book *Alaska's Mysterious Triangle*:

> "A geographical survey of Alaska in 1965 by the United States Department of the Interior discovered as many as five different areas of distinct magnetic character in just the

100,000 square miles they surveyed (Alaska is 663,300 square miles large). In their interpretation of the magnetic data, the report stated:

The magnetic profiles show numerous anomalies caused by variations in magnetization of the rocks, principally the mafic and ultramafic varieties, but also some granitic and metamorphic rocks. This magnetization is a combination of that induced by the present earth's field and the remanent magnetization – the latter tending to be largest in the mafic volcanic rocks. In some cases the direction of the remanent magnetization is reversed to give a negative anomaly. Several of these negative anomalies that cross basaltic dikes or serpentine bodies can be seen on profiles from the southern part of the area. Narrow step anomalies on the magnetic profiles are caused by rocks at or very near the surfaces, whereas some of the broader, smoother anomalies are probably caused by rocks at considerable depths.

In other words, there are a significant number of different types of anomalies occurring in the region due to the geological structure of the Alaskan ground and the stone within it down to significant depths. These anomalies are also exacerbated by the Earth's magnetic influence, field, and currents upon these types of rocks and minerals within the area known as the Alaska Triangle."

Past episodes of *Connecting the Universe* and a handful of videos on my YouTube channel have covered a variety of these locations across the world, including the American Southwest, ancient Egypt, and the Alaska Triangle (and other triangle areas of the world), but this time around on Wednesday I decided to touch on a cluster of UFO reports from the American Midwest. Let's take

Google Earth Map of a cluster of UFO sightings and activity in the Midwest.

Wreckage of Mantell's P-51 Mustang in 1948.

a look at a few of these.

Mantell Incident in 1948 (Fort Knox, Kentucky)

In January 1948, Kentucky Air National Guard pilot Captain Thomas F. Mantell crashed his P-51 Mustang and is widely considered the first pilot to have perished while chasing a UFO. The weather was nice that day for winter, about 49 degrees with only a few scattered clouds. His squadron of four was just on a routine training mission out of Marietta, Georgia, to Louisville, Kentucky, when the tower personnel at Godman Field in Fort Knox asked them to divert to investigate an object that had been seen over their airfield. What happened after that is shrouded in mystery and conflicting reports.

What we can gather is that the object was teardrop or ice cream cone in shape with red lights and was very large – about 250 – 300 feet in diameter – and it was very high in the sky. The pilots approached the craft, but we're unsure of how many, whether that was three or four – some reports even say five even though there were only four pilots and one of the four had continued on to Louisville. Mantell kept climbing in altitude, but the other pilots were unable to because they were either ill-equipped for the oxygen requirement or had to re-fuel, depending on the report. In one report, Mantell's wingman, Clements stated that Mantell had disappeared at about 25,000 feet even though he could still see the object. He had to turn around and refuel, and when he returned to the skies, neither Mantell nor the object could be found. What happened to Captain Mantell in the sky is unknown, but the wreckage of his plane was later discovered scattered across a mile of land in Franklin, Kentucky.

The "official" explanation was that Mantell was chasing a secret balloon, which sounds eerily reminiscent of the excuse given for the Roswell incident. I have an even bigger problem with this excuse with the Mantell incident than Roswell because of the sheer number of people involved. For one, these were trained military personnel, and the ones in the air were pilots. You can't tell me they don't know what a balloon looks like. Secondly, it wasn't just the four pilots that would have had to have misidentified this, but you had the air traffic controllers at Godman Field misidentify it, their commanding officers that would have authorized them to radio these pilots, plus the commanding officers of the mission who would have had to have authorized the rerouting of their pilots. None of that makes any sense. We'll never know what happened to Thomas Mantell, but he wasn't chasing a balloon.

Cape Girardeau (April 12, 1941)

Six years before the Roswell crash, in July 1941 at Cape Girardeau, Missouri, Reverend William Huffman of the Red Star

Baptist church was summoned to the site of an accident by local law enforcement in order to read the last rites over the victims of the crash. He was shocked when he discovered this was not an ordinary vehicular crash but what he was praying over were three small gray beings unlike anything he had ever seen before. Two were dead and the third was dying. The military was beginning to take over the scene as he conducted the last rites, and they confiscated all the crash material and the bodies.

Here we have another military crash retrieval that predates what we call the modern UFO era, so when we start having Congressional hearings and the big "reveal" that the United States has recovered extraterrestrial craft, well ... this is something we've actually been talking about for a long time. However, it's nice that it's finally being read into an official record and is starting to be taken more seriously.

Hopkinsville, KY (August 21, 1955)

This one is a controversial tale (aren't they all?) but it is in the same general regional area as these others. On the evening of Sunday, August 21, 1955, Elmer "Lucky" Sutton, was visiting his mother, Glennie Lankford, and three younger half-siblings at the farmhouse he'd grown up in, about eight miles north of Hopkinsville. He was joined by his wife, Vera, a couple of their friends, and several others from the family, for a night of playing cards.

The strangeness of the evening started with Billy Ray claiming he'd seen in the sky a rainbow-colored object with streaks trailing behind it. He was generally laughed at by the others, but Billy Ray convinced Lucky to go outside with him to have a look around. At first, they didn't see much of anything, but suddenly an unusual glowing object began approaching them from the woods. As it neared, they realized what they were looking at was a short, humanlike creature, with large eyes, two legs that seemed to float rather than walk, and two arms raised as if in surrender. Lucky screamed, and the two men ran inside, slamming the door behind them. They then grabbed rifles and started shooting at the being from the house.

There's a lot more to this story, including neighbors who heard the gunshots, but they – and the whole family – took their story to the police and the headlines followed.

Piedmont, Missouri (February - April 1973)

Between February and April 1973, Piedmont, Missouri, and the area surrounding it, suffered a rash of UFO and UAP sightings. The first of these sightings was witnessed by the coach and several members of a local high school basketball team. As they were driving, they saw flashing lights in the sky, about 50 feet off the ground about four or five feet apart. They watched these flash red, green, amber, and white for about five or ten minutes until the object moved off.

Strange lights were seen by others in the area for quite some time with a number of these being either around or even in the waters of Clearwater Lake. Just recently, Missouri Governor Mike Parsons signed legislation in 2023 declaring Piedmont and the surrounding area the UFO capital of Missouri.

About 45 years later, I was driving down Interstate 44 one night heading westward to Oklahoma to visit a couple of my kids when I suddenly noticed something in the sky running parallel with the highway. These were two long, vertical red lights that were nearly pacing me. I kept looking up, then took a peek back at the road, looked back up, looked back at the road ... for about a minute until – zoom! It suddenly zipped away off into the night sky. My mouth agape, it dawned upon me, "I think I just saw a UFO."

Southern Illinois (January 5, 2000)

On the evening of January 5, 2000, a V-shaped UFO was spotted over several towns throughout southern Illinois to the east of St. Louis, Missouri, but what's fascinating about this is the number law enforcement officials who witnessed it.

The initial sighting was called in by local Highland business owner Melvern Noll who stated the object looked triangular in shape, about the size of a football field, had several decks, and had red lights underneath.

The police reports contained the following:

Lebanon police officer Ed Barton: Very bright light that kept changing colors.

Shiloh police officer David Martin: Saw something in the sky but not sure what it was.

Millstadt police officer Craig Stevens: Huge object, kind of 'V' shaped.

Nearby Scott Air Force Base was contacted, but they denied having anything in the sky.

Cahokia Mounds and Adjacent Area

Right down the road from the Southern Illinois sightings is the Cahokia Mounds National Monument which contains the largest pyramid north of Mesoamerica, Monks Mound. Visitors say the energy is palpable, and having visited the mounds a couple times myself, I can certainly say that is the case. This was a sacred site to the people who lived there, and at the height of its civilization (1050 – 1150 AD) it had a larger population than London at that time. This

Monks Mounds at Cahokia National Monument.

work on the Earth's energy will certainly delve into why the ancients would have built such large monuments on these types of locations, whether that be for healing purposes, sacred rituals, astronomical alignments, or entering into altered states of consciousness. We'll even cover what some would call highly speculative in that they were using these sites to open up portals or stargates – but that is for another time. (For sone additional background on Cahokia, please watch Episode 5 of *The Shadow Dimension*.)

Just up the road to the north is Alton, Illinois, which is considered by many to be one of the most haunted small towns in America with its central figure being the Mineral Springs Hotel right along the Mississippi River. Along with the energy of running water directly to the west, the historic section of Alton is buffeted by limestone bluffs, giving this area fascinating natural energy. Just to the north of town set into one of these bluffs are the Native American Piasa caves, named for the mural of the Piasa bird painted on the side of the caves. In the native Illini tongue, Piasa is supposed to mean, "The bird that devours me."

On his famous expedition with Louis Jolliet in 1673, French explorer Jacques Marquette noted the depiction of painting on the

Piasa Bird Mural and caves just north of Alton, Illinois.

bluff as:

"As large as a calf; they have horns on their heads like those of a deer, a horrible look, red eyes, a beard like a tiger's, a face somewhat like a man's, a body covered with scales, and so long a tail that it winds all around the body, passing above the head and going back between the legs, ending in a fish's tail. Green, red, and black are the three colors composing the picture."

While that original painting no longer exists, the current reproduction we see today was based on the description and sketches that have survived from the 1800s.

The Piasa bird has some similarities to thunderbird legends we find elsewhere, and I've already discussed in previous works like *Alaska's Mysterious Triangle* how some of these sightings could have very well have been modern airplanes that passed through some sort of portal and were named these types of birds because that's the only context the indigenous tribes of the time had for these types of craft they saw in the sky. Yes, you could attribute any ancient UFO sighting to these types of avian legends as well.

I'm not quite done here yet. Some years ago, the story of a modern UFO sighting just even a little further north, past Grafton along the Illinois River beyond the convergence with the Mississippi, was related to me and featured on an old episode of either *Inside the Upside Down* or *Beyond the Shadows*. I would have to dig for it, but this was witnessed by several people about 15 or 20 years ago and hovered in the air for several minutes. So, this watershed area is certainly a hotbed of activity, and we haven't even talked yet about the reports of rampant hauntings throughout the region or the fairy sightings further up the Illinois River.

Some readers may have wondered why I haven't mentioned anything about ley lines yet. We'll get to that down the road and we'll discuss the differences between ley lines and telluric currents as well as how they're related. We'll save that discussion for another time, but if you must know, I certainly discuss it in my book *Alaska's Mysterious Triangle* since that book investigates this same type of activity up in the Great White North.

Shadows, Ireland, and Wine

Shadow Dimension Updates and Preparing for St. Patrick's Day

March 13, 2024

Article Notes: As of this writing – or compilation of writing – The Shadow Dimension: Beyond the Shadows *is in its final stages of post-production. It's been a long road with a lot of delays for a variety of reasons, but I will be happy to announce soon that as of autumn 2025, the work is complete.*

Like I said last week, the juggle is real. One of my long-standing projects that keeps moving on and off the backburner is the long-awaited follow-up to 2021's series *The Shadow Dimension*. Still currently running on streaming platforms like the Roku Channel, TubiTV, and Filmzie (among others), *The Shadow Dimension* was a passion project to dive into the heart of paranormal shadow-related activity and to see if there was any correlation between that type of reported phenomenon and locations that have reported portal activity. Having to navigate the logistics of COVID-19 was a challenge (it was filmed during 2020), but I was able to get enough filmed and produced to release a six-part docuseries. I was quite

Investigating the woods behind the Hinsdale House, New York. The Shadow Dimension: Beyond the Shadows *ventures from New York to Egypt to Alaska.*

proud of the accomplishment.

Ever since then, I've been promising a second season which has long been in postproduction – I filmed the interviews for it back in 2021 – but the long wait is finally going to come to an end this year. Along with everything else I have going on (as highlighted in my "The Juggle is Real" post), I've also been bringing a second *Shadow Dimension* closer to reality, although it will not be released as another six-part season series. Those who have been following me for a while may have heard me mention during a recent airing of *Connecting the Universe* or in one of the Mike's Morning Mug videos on the Connected Universe Portal that the next *Shadow Dimension* will be a full-length documentary, approximately 90 minutes long. Some of you will likely recognize the film's subtitle: *The Shadow Dimension: Beyond the Shadows*. I've teased a few clips in the past (again, check some of the Connected Universe content), and you can expect more of that over the next couple months.

Speaking of *Connecting the Universe*, we have a great *Edge of the Rabbit Hole* episode coming up, featuring my good friend and psychic medium, Rob Gutro. We've had Rob on several times over the years – I've lost count as to how many – and he's going to return this time to chat with us about historic haunted locations throughout Ireland, a St. Patrick's Day special. This is going to be fun since I hosted a tour there myself almost two years ago. Rob recently explored there himself and will be offering insights from his perspective as a medium. We'll be chatting about some amazing locations like Blarney Castle, the Rock of Cashel, the old Cork City Gaol, and more. I'll provide a video recap of our 2022 Ireland tour below, but be sure to tune into the interview with Rob since he visited several places we didn't. Ireland will certainly play a role in the upcoming book about earth energy with a special look at the stone circles that dot the landscape. I was most particularly drawn to Drombeg Stone Circle which has a distinct "bubble-like" effect when standing in the direct center of the ancient standing stones. Yes, it's an acoustical effect when you talk, the sound waves from your voice reverberating off the stones back at you, but imagine thousands of years ago when the stones were in their full glory (and all there) how chanting in that circle must have felt.

We also learned of a triangle area in Ireland while we were there, a phenomenon for which more and more areas are starting to become recognized – Alaska, Lake Michigan, Bridgewater, Falkirk, just to name a few. I've mentioned this in brief a time or two during *Connecting the Universe* and have recently begun featuring it during my presentation on triangle areas of the world along with a video clip displaying the interesting dualistic energetic properties of Charleville Castle. There will be more on this soon, and, oh ... stay tuned for information about another Ireland tour I'll be hosting in the not-too-distant future.

Another creative endeavor in which I enjoy is wine making, and I spent Monday evening this week at my parents' house where my dad has an area of his wine cellar set up for us to craft our vintages. He got me into this hobby about 15 years ago, and it's been wonderful to be able create something I enjoy tasting over a nice meal or with a plate of wine and cheese while watching a movie. I'm currently in the process of making a batch of Sauvignon Blanc and just got done bottling the Merlot. While I have an absolute passion for all of the research and writing I do, it's good to have other hobbies and creative outlets as well. I often get asked if I will be selling any of this wine at the events I speak at, but unfortunately, I can't sell any of it without a liquor license in whichever state I may be (but that doesn't mean some other arrangement can't be made).

My mother also set us up with a huge loaf of her annual Irish soda bread, so the week is definitely off to a good start!

Mammoths and Creating New Life Forms

Are Our Scientists Playing God?

March 15, 2024

Mike's Morning Mug has been a combination social media post and video blog that I've been producing for well over 10 years, and I'm now adding this feature to this new blog here. I've always had a grander vision for this feature other than the near-daily sharing of a news article and the weekly video blog expounding on some topic.

Yesterday, I posted a video Morning Mug on the Connected Universe Portal discussing two articles I recently posted on my social media, one on the continued work to clone and resurrect the long-extinct woolly mammoth and another on research being done in creating new life forms in the lab. With both of these I've posted the question "should we" and harkened back to Jeff Goldblum's quote from *Jurassic Park*: "Your scientists were so preoccupied with whether or not they could, they didn't stop to think if they should."

Let's first take a look at the woolly mammoth story, which is a project that has been in the works for a few years. The article I posted was from *LiveScience.com* (although you can find the information in several locations), and it tells us, "Scientists at the company Colossal Biosciences have derived induced pluripotent stem cells from elephants, which they say could boost efforts to resurrect woolly mammoths."

I'm not going to get into all the intricacies of induced pluripotent stem cells from Asian elephants and how those can be integrated with mammoth DNA, but when I posted this article as a Morning Mug on X (formerly Twitter), MammothAI, which is a cryptocurrency developed specifically to help fund this research, responded with the following: "Closer than you think!"

This is a topic we covered in brief in the first season of *The Alaska Triangle* television show, and I also included it in my book *Alaska's Mysterious Triangle*. The section in the book primarily addresses whether there may actually be some mammoths still wandering about in the remote far reaches of the great white north, a distinct possibility given how vast the land is up there, but the last couple paragraphs dive into this genetic project:

"Other scientists, however, are concerned about the conservation of endangered species. Love Dalén, professor of evolutionary genetics at the Centre for Palaeogenetics in Stockholm who works on mammoth evolution, remarked about the effort, 'If endangered species have lost genes that are important to them ... the ability to put them back in the endangered species, that might prove really important. ... I still wonder what the bigger point would be. First of all, you're not going to get a mammoth. It's a hairy elephant with some fat deposits. ... We, of course, have very little clue about what genes make a mammoth a mammoth. We know a little bit, but we certainly don't know anywhere near enough.'

Here's something else to consider. If we create genetically-engineered mammoths that are, essentially, just a hairy elephant that looks like the woolly mammoths of old, and we introduce them out into the wild, what would happen if they encounter a lost pocket of

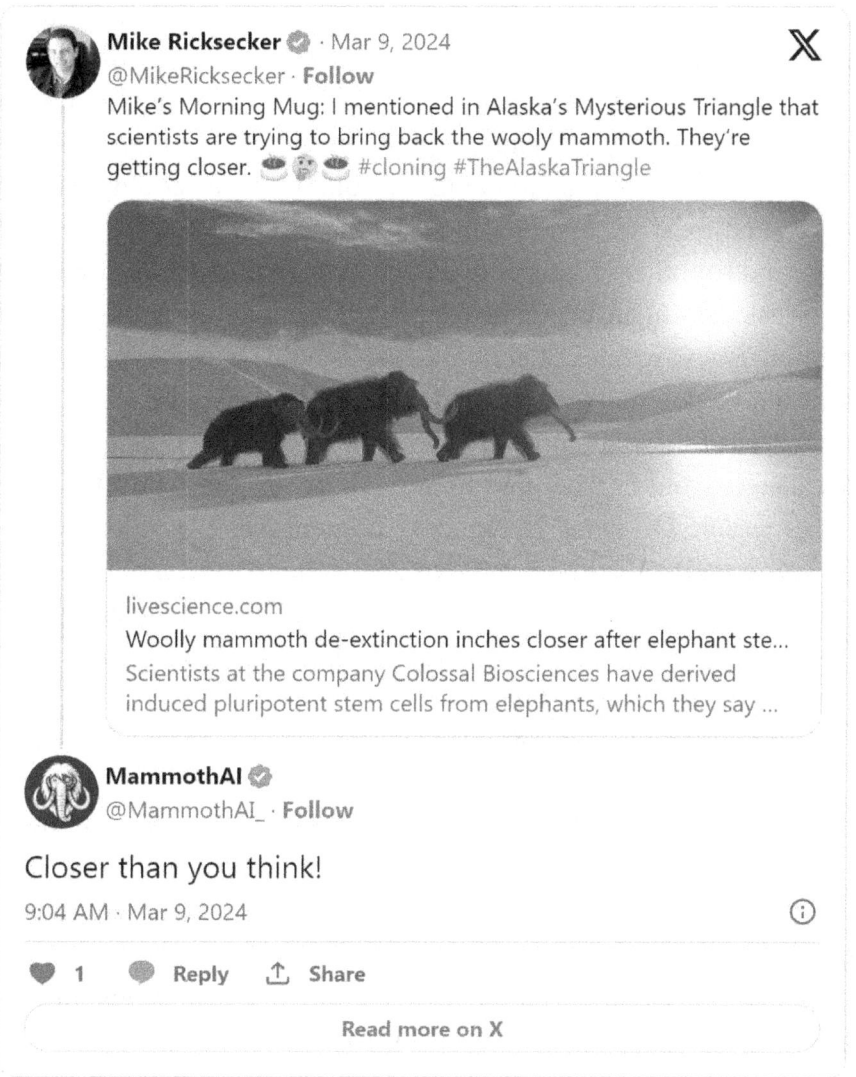

true mammoths? Would interbreeding between these two create an even different type of hybrid, one that's part-pure woolly mammoth and part human-engineered? What would something like that look like or act like?"

Another point to consider that I didn't really touch on in the book but has come up in conversations and interviews since the publication – there's a reason the mammoths became extinct to begin with. For as much as humans have done in recent years to damage the planet, the loss of the mammoths was a very natural extinction that had very little to do with humans even though our ancient ancestors did interact with these beasts. About 13,000 years ago the planet and environment had changed enough and reduced the mammoth's natural habitat to the point that they could no longer thrive and exist. The same thing has happened for thousands and thousands of other creatures that once lived in this world. If we were to be successful in bringing back woolly mammoths, are we just creating a new species of animal (and it would be a *new* species) that it would be doomed to fail and die? Would we only be able to keep a handful of these mammoth hybrids in a zoo for people to gawk at because it wouldn't be able to survive out in the wild? It sounds rather cruel. Or what if the development went in the opposite direction and we inadvertently created some sort of uncontrollable killer monster that began running rampant across the landscape and destroying everything in its path? In other words, yes, what if this really became *Jurassic Park*?

And that brings us to our next article ... the progress by scientists of actually creating an entirely new life form in the lab. Again, you can find this reported in several places, but in an article published by *Futurism*:

"In interviews with the *Washington Post*, scientists say they've created an RNA molecule that made copies of other types of RNA, which gets its experts ever closer to creating the conditions for early Earth life in a lab.

The Salk Institute for Biological Studies scientists worked from the theory that before there was DNA or proteins, RNA existed as the initial ingredient in the so-called 'primordial soup.'

As part of their research, *WaPo* reports, they created a lab-made RNA molecule that accurately copied others and resulted in a functioning enzyme. Now that the institute has done that, it's poised to study the earliest evolutionary stages of life in unprecedented ways."

Are wooly mammoths the first step to Jurassic Park*?*

So, it's not new life just as of yet, but this is another step taking us in that direction. I've previously explored this type of research when discussing artificial intelligence and the growing of brain organoids in the lab. The original purpose of these experiments was to combat Alzheimer's and dementia, but in 2019, this brain organoid research team published a report that they created human brain organoids which produced coordinated waves of activity, resembling those seen in premature babies. The waves continued for months before the team shut the experiment down. Two years later, brain organoids were developed with "optic cups" with retinal tissue that responds to light.

When you start combining these types of research together – creating early building blocks of life in the lab and growing brain organoids with working brain wave activity with a set of quasi-eyes that respond to light – at what point do we produce a human-generated new life form? Would a new life form produced in this manner have a consciousness?

In the video version of this Morning Mug on the Connected Universe Portal I also ask the question if we've been down this road before, if humans were previously a genetic experiment by some

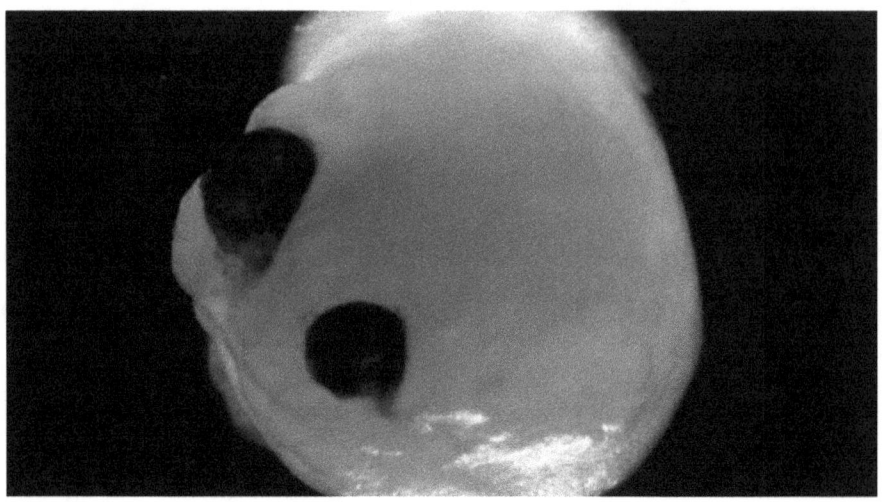
Human brain organoid with optic cups.

other race of beings. There are stories like this concerning the Anunnaki, that they altered our DNA to create humans as we are today. Or, if we're in a simulated universe, is it something that is more organic and biological in nature, not a computer but a genetically produced universe in which our species is but one of a series of biological experiments, each creation in turn *eventually* becoming the creator?

I'll dive more into these questions in written form at another time, but all of this should cause us to pause for a moment and ask the question: *Should we?*

The Mandela Effect and Paradoxes

Inside Time Travel Enigmas

March 21, 2024

Article Notes: Much of the material here on the Mandela Effect and paradoxes can be found in my book Travels Through Time, *and paradoxes was covered earlier in Part 1 in the old blog archives. What you'll find new here is the bit on resonance and how it related to stone circles and pyramids.*

How do earth energy hotspots influence high strangeness across the globe? We looked at that a bit in last week's blog entry on UFO hotspots and how UFO activity seems to be attracted to these types of areas on our planet. However, UFOs and UAPs are certainly not the only type of unusual phenomena witnessed at these locations. Over the course of this research, I'm going to be exploring quite a lot of these types of activities, whether that's UFOs, timeslips, bigfoot, hauntings, strange disappearances, and more. I already have covered these quite a lot in my previous works. *It's all connected.*

This week's *Connecting the Universe* covered the Mandela Effect and paradoxes, two types of phenomena that I discuss in my time travel research and my book, *Travels Through Time*. What does that have to do with a book I'm writing on earth energy and its effects? Again, it's all connected. And yes, I did reference these two phenomena briefly in my blog post on meeting William Shatner since my own significant Mandela Effect experience involved him.

Time travel, time slips, interactions with other dimensions and space-time, at its core, comes down to energy, frequency, resonance, and vibration. That's almost a straight quote from Nikola Tesla who said, "If you want to find the secrets of the universe, think in terms of energy, frequency and vibration." However, it's something I've been saying off-the-cuff for years during my interviews and presentations on this subject matter. I've thrown in *resonance* to this as well since resonance is when objects naturally vibrate at a definitive frequency – two of Tesla's words included in that definition. For instance, studies conducted in the 1990s and published in a paper by J.M. Randall, R.T. Matthews, and M.A. Stiles of Silsoe Research Institute's Bio-Engineering Division showed that the overall range of resonant frequencies of standing humans "was found to be from 9 to 16 Hz and independent of mass, height and mass to height ratio." The range changes a bit for someone who is sitting, **but** the point is there's a *range* of resonant frequencies, and each individual human differs as to what their resonant frequency may be.

In the circles I frequent, we talk at times about "vibrational level," the energy frequency that surrounds and permeates every cell in our bodies. It is different for everyone since this personal resonance is a reflection of one's thoughts, feelings, and beliefs, and I believe it allows everyone to experience other aspects of this universe, or what some might deem supernatural, in different ways. When we enter into these various hotspots of earth energy around the globe, that personal resonance, that frequency upon which we operate, is altered. It's altered even greater in and around ancient sites of power like stone circles and pyramids, and if we remembered how to harness that and control it – I say *remembered* because I believe it's a lost art the ancients once knew – then achieving feats like entering other dimensions or other points in time would be achievable.

When these interactions become achievable, then the results of those interactions would permeate like ripples (or like the butterfly effect) from the moments in time in which something may have been altered. This is where the Mandela Effect and paradoxes come into play. I'm not saying someone went back in time to change branding, such as the spelling of Froot Loops – that's extremely trivial. But some small change in the far past may have caused other outcomes to have occurred, and some people remember the original variations. Let's take a deeper look at this.

The Mandela Effect

The "Mandela Effect" is named after Nelson Mandela, the South African anti-apartheid activist who became the country's first Black head of state who passed away in 2013. The "effect" part of it is due to the fact that when he passed away, millions of people from all over the world thought he had already done so decades beforehand. How is that possible? Quoting my book, *Travels Through Time*:

> "Postulated by writer and researcher Fiona Broome, the Mandela Effect occurs when a large number of people remember certain facts in our society today as having been quite different in the past. In Broome's case, as it was with so many others, they remembered Nelson Mandela passing away while he was still in prison, possibly from the tuberculosis, but he'd also had prostate surgery in prison as well. Common themes for this effect are generally centered on pop culture or branding, such as the spelling of Oscar Mayer hot dogs and bologna which many people remember

as M-E-Y-E-R even though the television commercials even had a jingle spelling out the brand name. Do you remember the Fruit of the Loom branding with a cornucopia behind the fruit? Many people around the world do, although their brand artwork does not actually have a cornucopia. Did Curious George have a tail? Some remember him with a tail, but the lovable monkey in children's books does not. What were the lyrics to the song Mr. Rogers sang when he walked into his home and changed his shoes? There was a recent film in 2019 on Fred Rogers starring Tom Hanks which is titled *A Beautiful Day in the Neighborhood*, the lyric most people remember Rogers singing, but the producers must have been victims of the Mandela Effect because the actual lyric is, 'It's a beautiful day in this neighborhood.' A simple internet search on this phenomenon will reveal scores of these types of oddities ranging from the status of the Lindbergh baby case, to the Evil Queen's mirror in *Snow White*, to Mona Lisa's smile. Do you remember the villainous gremlin in the 1984 movie *Gremlins* having the name Spike or Stripe?"

I've had my own Mandela Effect experience centered around an old movie called *Sole Survivor* and William Shatner. Yes, my recent photo op with him was the inspiration for diving down this rabbit hole this week. It's not an account you'll find on any of those Top 50 lists of Mandela Effect occurrences (unless it's been added there in recent years due to me discussing it and including it in my book), but that has only helped legitimize it in my mind. I'm not going to copy and paste the entire account here out of *Travels Through Time* like I did with the above paragraph, but I'll go ahead and link the video here in the post. Yes, it's the same one I included in the Shatner blog post, but for ease of access, here it is: https://youtu.be/_GY8xDhWUU8

What could have caused this discrepancy with this particular film that I, my mother, and many people from across the globe that remembered it was an old back-and-white film from the late 1950s or early 1960s? Again, I believe this was the result of a paradox playing itself out. Perhaps, somewhere along the stack of time, someone went back and changed something that resulted in historical alterations that many people recall in the original context. I'm not saying someone went back in time to intentionally alter the film *Sole Survivor*. Again, that would be rather trivial. However, when changes occur in a certain moment in time there are ripple effects that extend outward that are unforeseen. A time traveler could have come into the picture and inadvertently thwarted the original black-and-white production. Perhaps there was a car accident that killed a producer, maybe there was a fire that burned the original script, perhaps the writer's path in life took a different turn and he got involved in Hollywood later rather than sooner. There are any number of possibilities.

As those who move through the stack of time come and go, there are residual consequences for their presence, and while seemingly subtle in most cases, they leave their mark. Why do some people remember the original variation and others don't? That is certainly one of the more mysterious elements of this phenomenon.

Paradoxes

So, I don't have the space here to dive into all the different kinds of paradoxes that have been proposed over the years, but we'll conduct a brief overview here. Even my chapter on paradoxes in *Travels Through Time*, while rather lengthy, is just a smattering of these perplexing mindbenders. However, I will take this one straight from the book, because it's just so darn fun:

Transitive Property of Equality

If x=y and y=z, then x=z

If 3 + 6 = 9 and 4 + 5 = 9
then 3 + 6 = 4 + 5

"Many theorists in the scientific field disregard time paradoxes, such as in the Novikov Self-Consistency Principle (the concept that if an event would cause a paradox or some alteration to the past, then the probability of that event occurring is zero), and cling to a belief that if something creates one of these mind-benders then it can't truly exist outside of science fiction storylines. Some even suggest various paradoxes like the Grandfather Paradox, if one could ever truly exist, would actually break the universe. Typically, these theorists get hung up on the mathematical elements of a logic problem, and since it can't be resolved in what might be considered a rationally acceptable solution, the whole thing must be thrown out. Consider the following paradox:

Cheese has holes.
More cheese = more holes.
More holes = less cheese.
More cheese = less cheese.

From the result of this basic mathematical logic problem which uses the Transitive Property of Equality (if x=y and y=z, then x=z), we are able to deduce a solution that makes sense mathematically but doesn't make sense to the context of our subject: cheese. How could more cheese equate to less cheese? This is certainly self-contradictory. Sure, this may seem trivial and a bit of a trick of words, and some may casually dismiss this point because of that, but it proves the results really only pass muster if they fit nicely within the context of our preconceived prejudices.

If the third line above stated 'More holes = better cheese' and therefore 'More cheese = better cheese' there wouldn't be any cause for alarm and the whole thing might simply be dismissed as personal opinion. However, since the final piece of this basic math transition gives us a contradictory statement of words, it can't possibly be true. Yet, it is, personal opinion on cheese aside."

I've provided some rather sizable chunks out of *Travels Through Time*, which was not my intention, but I did cover these topics in great detail there, and a review of the material is certainly helpful as we move forward in this research. Paradoxes exist because of our viewpoint of the universe and how we believe it's supposed to function based on the narrative and science we've put into place thus far. Most academics are going to disregard the conundrum of the cheese problem above as a trick of words because they don't want to consider how the math breaks down when presented with real-world logic.

Grandfather Paradox

The Novikov Self-Consistency Principle was postulated in the 1980s by Russian physicist Igor Dmitriyevich Novikov to try to explain that while time travel is possible, time paradoxes are forbidden because, mathematically, the probability of the event creating the paradox would be zero. Here again, we have an academic relying on math to try to explain concepts that are beyond the mathematics of the third dimensional space in which our fourth dimensional consciousness resides. Ironically, two other physicists debated with each other about Novikov's theory – Kip Thorne and Joe Polchinski – and Polchinski developed his own paradox to disprove Novikov's ideas. However, Polchinski's paradox was just the Grandfather Paradox in disguise using a billiard ball and a wormhole rather than a time machine and a grandfather. This always amuses me when I talk about it.

Polchinski's Paradox Illustrated

I'm not disregarding the work many of our physicists and mathematicians have achieved – we're able to achieve some absolutely amazing things these days because of their accomplishments. We have computers and cell phones, advanced cars and airplanes, and we're able to study and explore the cosmos unlike we've ever done before with rocket ships, satellites, and deep space telescopes. However, for many of them, they can't think outside the box of our current dimensional space, and they keep much of their work inside the comfort of the 3D realm. Yet, when they peer out into the deep reaches of the universe, they keep discovering unexpected phenomena – but that is a topic for our next blog (and Morning Mug).

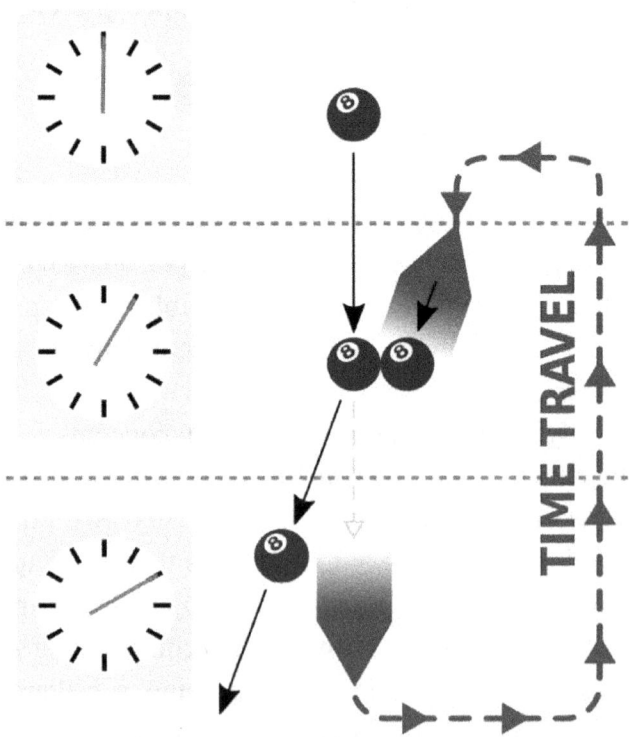

Archive of the Connected Universe: Volume 1

Discovering Lost Locations with Ancient Documents

How Much Truth Do Our Ancient Documents Contain?

March 24, 2024

Article Notes: Show me an ancient map, and I'll show you secrets hidden in plain sight.

I was quite intrigued last week when I posted an article for my daily Morning Mug in which researchers from Greece's National Research Foundation and the Ministry of Culture admitted that one of the documents they were using to help locate ancient shipwrecks was Homer's *Iliad*. I don't claim to be a scholar of the *Iliad* or Homer's other works like the *Odyssey*, but I know enough that these were largely considered to be myths until 1871 when the ancient city of Troy was finally discovered. Up until that time, the city had been considered by most academics to be a work of fiction, a setting Homer created for some of his epic tales, much in the same vein that most scholars still consider Atlantis. Thus, I opined on this matter in my latest Morning Mug video on the Connected Universe Portal.

Why is modern humanity so arrogant to believe that we know

better than ancient peoples who lived thousands of years ago? They would have known their cities and regions and people much better than we do today. They were right there in the middle of the action. Were some aspects of these tales embellished? Of course they were. We do the same thing today depending on the writer's perspective and the message he or she is trying to convey. We must consider in any of these ancient works that there are going to be grains of truth – and much larger grains than we previously imagined.

I love going to the original source material when I'm writing. Those who have read my books will recall in many chapters in which I've quoted, not some scholar's opinion on an ancient work, but I've quoted the ancient work itself. For instance, in *Travels Through Time*, I quote directly from the most illustrious copy of the *Egyptian Book of the Dead* (aka, *The Book of Going Forth by Day*), *The Papyrus of Ani*, while discussing the ancient Egyptians' thoughts on the nature of time:

> "You shall be for millions on millions of years, a lifetime of millions of years. I will dispatch the Elders and destroy all that I have made; the earth shall return to the Primordial Water, to the surging flood, as in its original state. But I will remain with Osiris, I will transform myself into something else, namely a serpent, without men knowing or the gods seeing."

Of course, in my upcoming work I will be making substantial use of these kinds of documents, and I do have a particular affinity for ancient maps. In my book on strange phenomena in Alaska, *Alaska's Mysterious Triangle*, I made use of the famous Piri Reis map fragment from 1513 which mostly depicts the Caribbean, the coastline of South America, and Antarctica. How in the world did I manage that? Everything is connected, hence The Connected Universe, and I was drawing parallels to Alaska and Antarctica.

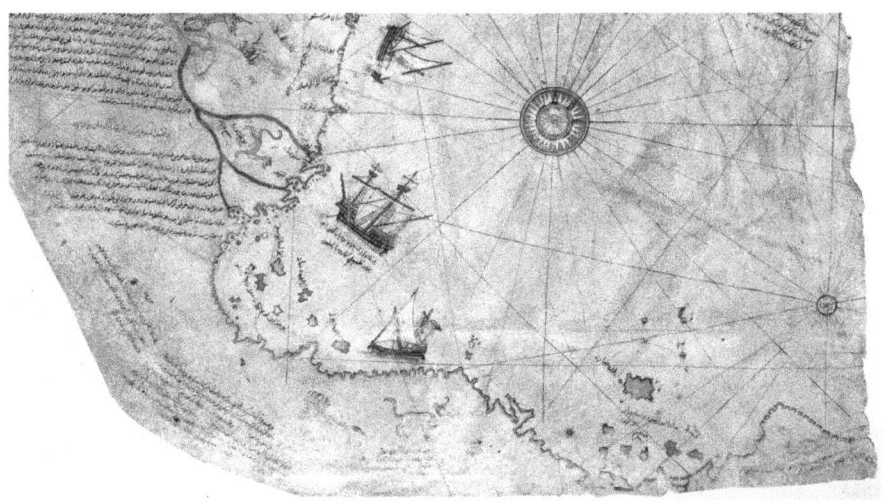

Bottom portion of the 1530 Piri Reis map fragment depicting Antarctica.

With the upcoming book on earth energy, I will be doing the same again. The poles of our planet are significant, and there's been a tremendous amount of scientific research in Antarctica in recent years. We'll look at pole shifts, neutrino research, UFO sightings, and Ivan T. Sanderson's vile vortices, of which the South Pole is one.

Of course, there's the controversy of Antarctica being included on ancient maps since our current historic narrative is that Antarctica wasn't discovered by modern seafarers until 1820. However, along with the Piri Reis map, the 1590 *Orbis Terrarum* by Petrus Plancius also included Antarctica as well as *Nova Totius Terrarum Orbis Geographica ac Hydrographica Tabula* by Henricus Hondius II in 1630. Then, the continent suddenly disappears from record for nearly 200 years. These were, essentially, compendiums these map makers constructed, combing the works of previous cartographers into works that were more accurate and complete for the age. The ancient cartographers from which they drew up these maps knew something the contemporary Europeans of the age did not. The original sources, at this point, have been lost to time, but I believe we need to consider that there is truth within these documents and

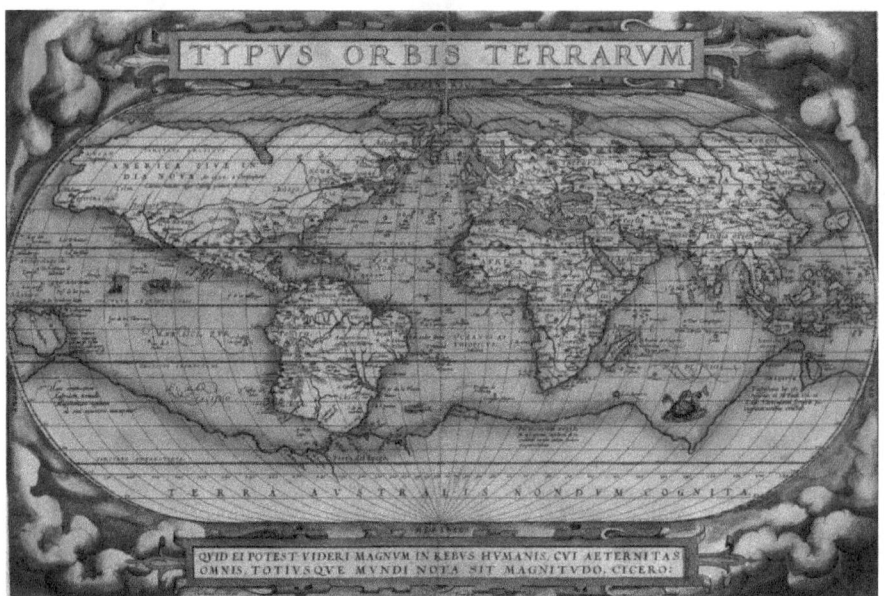

The 1590 Orbis Terrarum by Petrus Plancius.

they should not be disregarded as myth or random "doodles" (as the Antarctic land mass on the Piri Reis map is generally considered by modern academia).

Oh, and one final comment about my recent Morning Mug video on this subject … it contains a rather adventurous tale in which my friend Luis and I got a bit lost in Baltimore in 2003 with only a "Bird's Eye View" map of the city from 1869 to help guide us. How well did that fare for us? Perhaps better than you think!

Time Travel: Consciousness or Physics?

A Mike's Morning Mug on Black Holes and Time Travel

March 28, 2024

Article Notes: The Morning Mug video I made public is called "Black Hole Time Travel? Inside Real Time Travel and the Fourth Dimension" and can be found on the YouTube channel.

Should we master a black hole or master the dimensions?

While I was traveling on Monday, there were several people who reached out to me regarding a recent article that was published about time travel and that astrophysicist Ronald Mallett had solved the equation using black holes. I was a bit bemused because I've been familiar with Mallett's work and his theories, which I actually addressed in my book *Travels Through Time*, but as this article began filling my inbox from multiple sources, I decided I ought to address it. So, I did what I don't normally do: I made one of my Morning Mug videos for the Connected Universe Portal public and opined for a good 20 minutes on the topic with selections not only out of my book, but also out of *The Time Machine* by H.G. Wells and an article about the recent breakthroughs of researchers at the University of Cambridge. I won't rehash everything I said in the video here. That would be redundant, but there are a few points I do wish to emphasize. First of all, I do not disagree with Mr. Mallett and his theories that we could use a black hole to travel through time. Space and time bend around a black hole due to the massive tidal gravitation forces around it. The problem is in the feasibility of humanity actually using a black hole to be able to accomplish the task. The video above quotes most of the opening to the "Real Time Travel" chapter of *Travels Through Time*, but I'll provide just one of those paragraphs here:

> "Of course, there are some logistical problems to all of this. First of all, the closest black holes to Earth, Gaia BH1 and Gaia BH2 are 1,560 light years and 3,800 light years away from us, respectively. We're not getting near those any time soon. Secondly, in order to get that close to a black hole and be able to successfully navigate away from it, you would have to be traveling near the speed of light – and faster than the speed of light if you accidentally slip past the event horizon – in order to get away from it. Finally, the gravity of the black hole is so strong that you and your craft would likely have been stretched out in a grueling phenomenon called spaghettification, stretching you out flat like pasta and, essentially, destroying the craft and killing you. So, the idea of using a black hole as a natural time machine really is not feasible."

Ok, we can rule out actually using a black hole to accomplish time travel by humans, but Mallett suggests creating a machine using similar characteristics to how a black hole operates, such as the gravitational forces produced by spinning, and create a machine based on these properties. The article cites him being influenced by

The Time Machine by H.G. Wells. The problem in that, other than trying to produce this machine with black hole-like properties (we've already connected extremely small black holes with a wormhole in a quantum environment) is that Wells's time traveler uses properties of *other dimensions* to travel through time and not the physics of a black hole. It's his explanation of how dimensions work that start the book in the very first chapter:

> "The Time Traveller proceeded, 'any real body must have extension in four directions: it must have Length, Breadth, Thickness, and—Duration. But through a natural infirmity of the flesh, which I will explain to you in a moment, we incline to overlook this fact. There are really four dimensions, three which we call the three planes of Space, and a fourth, Time. There is, however, a tendency to draw an unreal distinction between the former three dimensions and the latter, because it happens that our consciousness moves intermittently in one direction along the latter from the beginning to the end of our lives.'"

If you've been following my work, whether that's been watching or listening to the *Connecting the Universe* podcast or, perhaps, you've read *Travels Through Time*, the above ought to sound a bit familiar. From **the** "Stacked Time Theory" chapter:

> "Along the x, y, and z axes, the first dimension is length along the x-axis. This is really, quite simply, a line. When we add in the y-axis, or height, our second dimension becomes a flat plane. Think of a piece of paper, although, technically, a piece of paper does have a very narrow depth side along the z-axis to give us our third dimension, or 3-D object. A better example would be a cube which has all of these, equally – length, width, and depth – which gives the

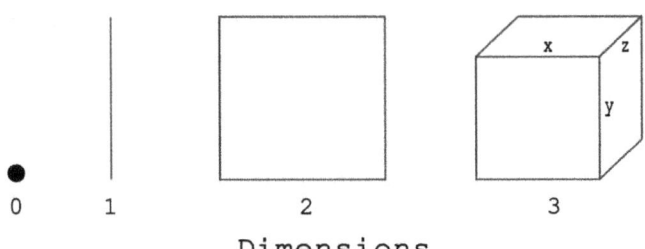

Dimensions

cube volume. The fourth dimension, as believed by many scientists and theoretical physicists, is time, the dimension in which we live and exist, and knowing an object's position in time is crucial in trying to determine its position in the universe. There are six more dimensions beyond time which are not immediately perceptible to us but still have a direct influence on us and our reality. That gives us 10 dimensions, but some include an eleventh dimension before the first, also known as dimension zero, which is simply a point."

Ironically, I did not at all reference *The Time Machine* when I wrote *Travels Through Time*. I had only vaguely remembered the story from my early childhood when a *very* abridged version of the book was read to one of my classes. That sounds like sacrilege when one is writing a book on time travel, but I had so much other material and research at my disposal that I didn't go back to Wells's work until just recently.

I also state in the "Stacked Time Theory" chapter, "Time travel will have more to do with meditation, the interconnections of the universe, and consciousness than a DeLorean and a flux capacitor," but I think I'll use this more thorough quote from the "Real Time Travel" chapter:

"Thus, I harken back to Matheson's *Somewhere in Time* and Richard Collier willing his consciousness from one point in time at the Grand Hotel, 1980, to another point in time in the stack, 1912. I believe if we can quiet our minds enough, shut out the chaos of the world, put ourselves into a meditative state, and truly believe we are at another point in time – not believe we will travel there, but believe we are already there like the practitioners at the medicine-less hospital believing the woman was already healed – then we can project our consciousness to another point in time and experience that time as if we are truly, physically there. We could do this to the past or we could do this to the future, anywhere up and down the stack. As we meditate on this and put our mindset into one that we are actually there in whatever year and day it may have been, then our own personal resonance, frequency, and vibration will tune itself to the resonance, frequency, and vibration of that moment and take us there. I believe, in good practice, this is something we can achieve and is most likely something the ancients knew how to do within their stone circles, temples, and stargates – we will be rediscovering lost knowledge. ...

That powerful energy of the universe is within us all, because we are all a part of the universe, we are all connected to it, to each other, to time and beyond. The DeLorean and flux capacitor will become a dinosaur concept, the fanciful ideas of whipping around a black hole a vague musing for aging physicists, for we will have the technology for time travel where we have always had it – within ourselves."

I won't delve into examples of time slips throughout history to illustrate the point – that would be too cumbersome for today's blog post, but many have been witness to two moments in time resonating at the same frequency to get a glimpse of each other. The key to fully traveling to these moments would be to not only find that frequency, but to also harness it and hold on to it. Those who are outside our fourth dimension, those in the fifth dimension and beyond, aren't encumbered by that challenge, and all time is available to them as a whole object. Every moment – past, present, and future – are available to those in higher dimensional spaces.

Christopher Nolan's film *Interstellar* explored this, and actually combined theories about black holes with theories of interdimensional travel when the protagonist, Cooper, ended up inside a tesseract (a representation of fourth-dimensional space from the fifth dimension) in which he could observe every moment *ever* of his daughter's bedroom in order to find the correct one so he could send a message back in time. The concepts represented were pretty darn close to what I've been calling Stacked Time Theory.

So, which is correct? Is time travel possible via black holes or via the consciousness through interdimensional manipulation? They're both correct. I just believe the more readily accessible means of time travel is the consciousness – something we have with us at all times – rather than out in the depths of space.

Revisiting the Alaska Triangle

Challenges of Writing About a Mysterious Topic I've Already Covered

April 2, 2024

Article Notes: In early 2024, I was still intending for the second book in the Connecting the Universe *series to be a deep dive into earth energy, how ancient civilizations harnessed it, and the unusual activity that is usually experienced at these locations. It made sense that would be the next topic as a follow up to* Travels Through Time. *When in Egypt in late April, however, as what always seems to happen when I'm in Egypt, I decided to pivot and instead write* Portals to the Stars, *my deep dive into stargates. Within that book are the chapters called "Energized Earth" and "The Stone Circles" where some of that information currently resides, but I will, eventually, write the full volume which will also include information on triangle areas around the world.*

How much more strange phenomena is at my disposal to unveil about the Alaska Triangle? Honestly, one of the challenges I face in writing the new book is in deciding what to include about this peculiar region of the world. Of course, there is plenty of unusual activity that occurs in the Great White North, but my book *Alaska's Mysterious Triangle* already covered the subject matter at length. What do I pull from that book, what new material do I include, and what do I leave on the cutting room floor even if it's interesting and relevant?

I have an entire section I am dedicating to triangle areas of the world, including the Bermuda Triangle, Bridgewater, Lake Michigan, Nevada, the Dragon's Triangle near Japan, a triangle area I learned about during my 2022 Ireland tour, and more. When we discuss the energy of the earth, vortices, and strange areas of magnetism around the globe, what we call "triangles" are some of the most notorious areas of strange activity on the planet. So, the coverage of the Alaska Triangle is certainly necessary, but I'm not just going to copy and paste entire swathes of text out of the old book and put it into the new one.

Of course, I have to cover some of the basics, such as the Alaska Triangle consisting of an area from Juneau to Anchorage to Utqiagvik (formerly Barrow), the fact that every year 500-2,000 people go missing in Alaska (and more than 16,000 have since 1988), and that a 1965 geographical survey by the U.S. Department of the Interior classified some of the magnetization in the region as "negative anomalies." However, when it comes to the strange activity of the area, much of which many would describe as "supernatural" in nature, well … let's just say *Alaska's Mysterious Triangle* covered missing people and airplanes, extraterrestrials, paranormal activity, cryptid encounters, government cover-ups, and more. Let's take a glimpse at what I'm looking to cover in the new book:

Missing Airplanes

Honestly, there are two stories here that I'm absolutely going to have to cover again: the missing Douglas Skymaster in 1950 and the

Flattop Mountain where we filmed The Alaska Triangle *in 2019.*

Boggs – Begich disappearance in 1972. Both were extremely high profile, especially the latter since the House Majority Leader at the time was involved, and Nick Begich's son has both spoken out against HAARP and, like his father, run for congress. Unusual electromagnetism certainly has an effect on a plane's navigational equipment, but the fact that so many planes go missing without a trace in this region is cause for concern. Surely, some have a logical explanation to their disappearance, but when you examine the fact that these were two of the largest search and rescue operations *ever* in U.S. history, that other planes have gone down in these areas and were easily found, and still more than 70 and 50 years later, respectively, not a trace of either plane has ever been discovered, you have to ask yourself *where* did they go?

If they passed through some sort of portal like Bruce Gernon did in the Bermuda Triangle – and I just recently talked to another pilot who conveyed a similar story – then we have to ask ourselves where they may have gone. While it may be conjecture to say they could have traveled to the distant past through a portal, it could more readily explain some of the thunderbird legends of old. Indigenous tribes of the time would simply be relating these planes in their own context, which would be some sort of large bird. It also gives us a bit of a bootstrap paradox – how could our colonial ancestors have learned about these thunderbird legends from indigenous people hundreds of years ago if planes from the future had not already traveled into the past?

UFOs and Extraterrestrials

Again, this is a subject in which I'll have to write more about something I've already covered: Captain Terauchi and Japan Airlines Flight 1628 in 1986. However, it's not just the most important UFO encounter in Alaska; it's one of the most important UFO encounters in the country. Not only was there a media frenzy about this encounter that involved JAL 1826, Anchorage Air Route Traffic Control, the U.S. Air Force, and United Airlines, but the FAA, CIA, FBI, and a science team appointed by the Reagan Administration all got involved. The CIA silenced the final report, but years later, FAA Division Chief John Callahan went public with what really happened. I could have just as easily included this story in the "Government Cover-Ups" chapter of *Alaska's Mysterious Triangle*.

Since publication of the book and the renewed interest in UFO and UAP activity by the government, there is plenty more to dive into here. In some respects, Alaska has received a boon of renewed interest in this type of activity, the most prominent of which would probably be whatever was shot down and landed in the Beaufort Sea in February 2023. Was it a UFO or a surveillance mechanism by a foreign power? We still don't know since it was, reportedly, never recovered.

Paranormal Activity

Interest in paranormal activity in Alaska **seems** to have also increased. The television show in which I participated, *The Alaska Triangle*, did a fair job of bringing some of these stories to light. Admittedly, when I was researching out the book, most Alaskan ghost stories were relegated to a couple paragraphs on an obscure website. Fortunately, I had visited a couple of these locations when I filmed up there in 2019, such as the Historic Anchorage Hotel, which probably has some of the more colorful stories of the region. What I discovered was that many of these locations shared in a similar tale – a husband or boyfriend went off to work the gold rush, the wife or girlfriend turned to prostitution when money ran out, and upon returning after being gone for months, the man turned to violence after discovering what happened to his partner. In some form or another, this incident certainly occurred, but did it occur at multiple locations across the state? Perhaps. Or, perhaps not.

Cryptid Encounters

Alaska is loaded with a large variety of various cryptids, whether that's sasquatch, strange sea creatures, the ircenrraat, or some other legendary creature. I've probably received more feedback on these phenomena than any other since publication of *Alaska's Mysterious Triangle* with a particular focus on the kushtaka (or otter man). The lore of this creature is very similar to wendigo legends of the Great Lakes region – the kushtaka lures its prey out into the forest and either devours the person or turns him or her into another kushtaka. I've been in active communication with Native Alaskans who have given me a bit more insight into these encounters, the creature's origins from the Tlingit legends, and where people still encounter these creatures today. Even the more accurate spelling, before it was anglicized, has been passed on to me: kóoshdaa káa. Many thanks to Dave Kanosh!

Black Pyramid

Ok, I take it back. *This* one has received more interest than another other since publication: the Black Pyramid (aka the Dark Pyramid). Honestly, this proposed megalithic structure that is supposed to reside underneath Mt. Denali is extremely mysterious, and information is limited. There are only a few people who have come forward to speak about it over the years, and the two most prominent were both featured in the premier of *The Alaska Triangle's* second season. Technically, the episode ran before publication of *Alaska's Mysterious Triangle*, but the book was already set to print, so there will certainly be some more information that I've learned about this than what was in my first take.

I'll be honest, though. The gatekeeper on this is Linda Moulton Howe who is the one that collected the reports from the scant number of people who have come forward about this subject. The television show did a flyby of the area in a plane and discovered an area that had once, clearly, been occupied by humans, but no one got boots on the ground – or under the ground – to capture a photo or any video footage of this structure. Unlike the Great Pyramid of Giza which stands very prominent in the Egyptian desert for us to speculate about its intended function to our heart's content, we have no visual of the Black Pyramid at all other than a seismic reading from 1992. At this point, we only have anecdotal stories to rely upon – but that's nothing new in this line of work.

Of course, there are other topics I will include in the new work regarding the Alaska Triangle. These are just a taste of what I will be discussing, and you can see how the accounts I've already written about are already extremely intriguing. What more will I include in the new book? You'll have to wait and see.

Anticipating the Solar Eclipse

What this Rare Phenomenon Means

April 5, 2024

We won't see another one of these until 2044 – when I turn 70. That's a long time between eclipses, so I'm absolutely going to savor this one, and I'm right smack dab in the middle of the prime path residing here in the Cleveland, Ohio, area. Our ever-changing weather forecast currently has us at sunny and in the 50s on Monday, which will be absolutely perfect (although I wouldn't mind it being another 10 degrees warmer than that). Get ready to soak in that eclipse energy! What do I mean?

Cultures across the globe throughout history have expressed myriad eclipse legends over the millennia, and our modern society has plenty of its own ideas as well, even if some of those concepts do have roots back to those from thousands of years ago. When we had a solar eclipse back in 2017, I put together the following "Top 10 Solar Eclipse Legends" video. It's a bit rough, but there is certainly some interesting lore within it.

Today, there are generally two ways in which our world will

examine this rare event: physical and metaphysical. The physics world will examine the impact the eclipse will have on the amount of solar energy that will reach the Earth, such as NASA's Jet Propulsion Laboratory which will teach students to measure lux before and during the event. Using an interactive eclipse map and setting their devices at the correct angle, students will use a lux meter to measure the brightness of the Sun at specific times and record these on a data sheet. Elsewhere, experts debate as to how much impact the eclipse will have on power grids since solar power generation will temporarily drop to zero – it's a little challenging to harness solar energy when the Sun isn't available.

As for the metaphysical community, well, there are almost too many concepts to account for here, whether it's a sacred time to sit and reflect or one that ushers in new beginnings, but I'll briefly touch on a couple things. Some metaphysical traditions teach that eclipses are portal openers to higher frequencies and states of consciousness, and the change in vibration can be witnessed by the odd behavior in animals leading up to an eclipse. This Earth-Moon-Sun alignment can activate the pineal gland, the third-eye, which has long-thought to be a connecting link between the physical and spiritual worlds. If there's ever a perfect time to meditate, this just might be it.

The energy of an eclipse is believed by many to be an amplifier of thoughts and intentions, so if you do meditate (I'm going to watch with the special glasses, but I'll meditate earlier in the day) set those intentions before entering into the meditation. Astrologers have been pointing out that this April 8 eclipse is occurring in the sign of Aries, which is a sign of fresh starts, innovation, and courage. So, this is almost a double-dip since eclipses are viewed in many traditions as a time of introspection, transformation, and powerful new beginnings. If you've been looking to try something new in your life, the Great North American Eclipse of 2024 could be your starting point since this kind of solar phenomenon is also believed to accelerate events.

For me, however, what I'm looking forward to most of all is I'm going to spend the time with people I love. My daughter is coming in from Oklahoma for her birthday on Saturday, and we'll be there together with my parents and my sister's family, witnessing something together that we likely won't all see together again (although, I hope so). Life gets busy, and I have a thousand different things on my plate with all the projects I have underway, but we have to take advantage of these moments when we can, because suddenly those opportunities won't be there anymore.

Oh ... and, you know, this would also be a good time to watch *Ladyhawke* again.

Silver Circle in the Sky ... and Heart

Final Thoughts on the Solar Eclipse

April 10, 2024

We've put away the special sunglasses, all the photos have been posted, and we've returned to our regularly scheduled programs, but the image of the Great North American Eclipse of 2024 will remain embedded in the minds of the generations who witnessed it (and, no, not just because some tried to sneak a peek without the glasses). I've taken a couple days to decompress, to ponder it all, and relive in my mind those glorious four minutes of complete totality here in the Cleveland, Ohio, area. Sure, there will be other eclipses, and I could travel the globe somewhere to witness totality again, but it won't be like this one again.

I mentioned in my previous blog post that my daughter, Arielle, came to visit from Oklahoma (as well as her fiancé, Tyler). We also celebrated Arielle's birthday, which was on Saturday, so it was an entire extended-weekend celebration for multiple reasons. At my sister's house where we had a cookout and watched the eclipse take place, plenty of family was present, and my niece and nephew ventured out one of second floor windows of the house and onto the garage roof with a few of their friends to view the event – not because it offered a better vantage point, but because they were kids being kids.

While the anticipation grew and we caught glimpses of the moon slowly creeping over the Sun, we got caught up in conversation with friends and family, invited a random Amazon delivery man up for a burger while he worked his route, and talked to a new neighbor who had just moved in from Frederick, Maryland, where I had previously raised my kids for 11 years many moons ago – such a small world. It was really that last 20 minutes, however, when we really started to notice the changes of the environment around us. It grew darker and cooler, and the way the light scattered across the landscape was almost unnatural. It just didn't seem quite real with the way the shadows were cast in the dim glow.

When just a sliver of the Sun was still visible, we were finally able to cast off the sunglasses and view the eclipse with the naked eye, although it still pretty much looked like a giant ball of light without the eyewear. But once that moon locked into place over the Sun and all went dark above us, there was a collective, "Whoa," amongst us as we stared at the silvery glowing circle in the heavens. It was truly a surreal moment, and even with all the amazing photographs that were taken, there is no way to truly capture that image that hung above us for those four short minutes. How fascinating it was that 96 million miles away we could see with our own eyes massive prominences – what many of us were calling solar flares at the time – erupting from the surface of the Sun, powerful jets of gas far larger than the size of the Earth. For me, while I was completely awestruck at the time, I also felt a wonderful peace throughout the experience as world grew quiet, almost reverent of the moment, as a silver shimmering circle brandished itself in the sky where our Sun should be.

Photo of the April 8, 2024 solar eclipse taken by my daughter, Arielle.

In true 2024 fashion, however, we did all clamor for our phones to try to capture this amazing moment – my daughter got the best photos, so I gave up trying and just grabbed hers. A shot that I could have gotten with my phone that I wish I would have was the 360-degree sunset all around us along the horizon. That was pretty wild, as well, with its reds and pinks and oranges cascading off the faint clouds that almost threatened our day, but the true spectacle was hovering directly above us, and I wanted to take that in for as long as I could. Once the moon moved out of totality and the first rays of sunlight burst forth from beyond, there was another collective cry from the crowd, this time an, "Aww …," and the photo trading began. Again, Arielle captured the best images from our group (my niece, Emily, got some good ones, too), and the dialogue quickly shifted to replay mode.

Perhaps our rituals in 2024 are a bit different than rituals from

Cuneiform tablet: A Ritual for the Observances of Eclipses

thousands of years ago – we're eating burgers and drinking beers out in the driveway while an ancient cuneiform tablet from Mesopotamia described their eclipse rituals as:

"As the eclipse begins, the ... priest shall light the torch, and attach it to the altar ... As long as the eclipse lasts, the fire upon the altar thou shalt not remove. A dirge for the fields thou shalt intone; a dirge for the streams that the water shall not devastate, thou shalt intone ... As long as the eclipse lasts, the people of the land shall remove their headgear; they shall cover their heads with their garments."

Yeah, we didn't do that. Although, instead of lighting torches the streetlights did turn on. So, two days later, guests having traveled back home and back in our regular routines, what does this all mean?

Well, it certainly doesn't mean a celestial dragon devoured the Sun like the ancient Chinese used to believe (their ritual was to bang on drums and pots to frighten the dragon away). I believe it's quite personal for everyone, and when some traditions tell us that it's a transformational time, I believe that. That's not to mean that, all of a sudden, my life is completely different, but when you witness something you've never seen before in your life it changes you. Let me give an example.

I've always been a big baseball fan. In fact, the biography on my website and in my press kit used to include that tidbit in the last line. I grew up playing baseball, lettering in high school, and even though my life deviated from the path of playing longer that I wanted, I was a diehard Boston Red Sox fan. The day after the eclipse, amazingly enough, at Fenway Park in Boston, the Red Sox celebrated the 20th anniversary of the 2004 curse-breaking team that won the World Series for the first time in 86 years. There had been some absolutely heart-breaking losses the team had endured over the previous couple decades, and the absolutely magical run the team went on that October, becoming the only baseball team to overcome a 3-0 series deficit in the postseason, was truly amazing. That they did it in the American League Championship Series against their archrival New York Yankees who had long caused them so much suffering, the team to which they'd sold Babe Ruth and started the so-called curse, could not have been written any better. Following that, they swept the World Series against the Cardinals, and the final game in which they secured the championship was played under a lunar eclipse. Why do I bring up all of this baseball lore?

Well, that's not the only World Series the Red Sox have won since then. The championship they won in 2007 was a strong team that, essentially, legitimized 2004. The 2013 team with a cast of colorful characters sporting wild beards was a hoot and came in the wake of the Boston Marathon bombing. The 2018 team was a powerhouse that just annihilated everyone that came in their path, probably the best all-around team in modern Red Sox history. However, none of them will ever be that 2004 team which, in many ways, were those other three rolled up into one – fantastic colorful characters that were a powerhouse. However, none of those other three took us on that magical ride that the first one gave us.

Pre-game at Fenway Park's "Pesky Pole" in 2004.

That 2004 season, I was there for both the Opening Day and final season games in Baltimore, and I went on a road trip with my friend, Luis, and son, Collin, up to Fenway Park that August to catch a game in which Hall of Fame pitcher, Pedro Martinez, tossed a shutout. In fact, that final game in Baltimore was a meeting of members from a Red Sox chat room I had been a part of for the previous five years, and it was fun. The "Damon Disciples" were in full force that day (Johnny Damon fans dressed up like Jesus since he'd grown out his beard and hair) and the lineup manager Terry Francona put together that day was all in fun (catcher Jason Varitek leading off?) since the

Red Sox had already wrapped up the wild card spot for the postseason. During that October, I'd crank up a Red Sox/Boston themed playlist that featured a lot of Dropkick Murphys, "Dirty Water," and more.

Long story short (too late), the other three championships the Red Sox have won this century, although all fantastic in their own right, can never be what that first one was. It was a complete experience. It changed me. And that is the way I feel about this solar eclipse. I could witness another eclipse of totality – perhaps make the trip up to Alaska in 2033 – but it will never be like this one was. That I got a chance to be with so many people I love over these past several days has been fantastic, and that we got to share in something we will likely only see once together in our lifetimes is truly amazing. (For the record, when the next one comes through Ohio in 2099, I intend to still be around … when I'm 125. However, I will have to travel a little southwest for that one for 100% totality. The next total eclipse, specifically, in Cleveland will be in 2444. I have a sneaking suspicion I won't be here for that one.)

When and if I ever see another solar eclipse in totality the situation will be different, it will never be like this one was. I will still enjoy it, and I will certainly appreciate it, of course. So, I suppose all of these words and the foray into some baseball stories was my way of saying – I will absolutely cherish what a rare and wonderous moment those four minutes on April 8 had been.

The Call Back to Egypt

Previewing the Stargates of Ancient Egypt Tour

April 12, 2024

What is the draw to ancient Egypt? In a few days I will be setting out for my third Egypt tour in the past four years. It is becoming a yearly pilgrimage as I have been co-hosting the "Stargates of Ancient Egypt" tour along with Egyptologist and tour guide Mohamed Ibrahim who has been operating a class act operation for more than 20 years. This is the second incarnation of the Stargates tour, and I'm greatly looking forward to exploring new locations and discovering new secrets at places we've already explored. Once again, throughout the tour I will be uploading a daily video blog to the Connected Universe Portal which you won't find anywhere else. What might we find along our travels?

Giza Plateau and the Pyramids

The pyramids on the Giza Plateau are not only the most iconic structures in Egypt, but they are some of the most iconic structures in the entire world. That we get to venture inside them continues to be awestriking, no matter how many times we enter, but the special treat is when we have the Great Pyramid of Giza all to ourselves for two hours. During this time, the entire pyramid is open to us. Typically, the public will climb the Grand Gallery up to the King's Chamber, but for us, we're able to also explore the Queen's Chamber and climb down into the Subterranean Chamber. To me, the smoking gun of the Great Pyramid being some sort of machine lies in the Queen's Chamber, so it's important that we get a chance to explore it. And, of course, there's the Great Sphinx.

Saqqara

Saqqara is a vast site that includes the Step Pyramid, the Serapeum, and miles and miles of tombs and tunnels. Every time we visit here there is always something new Mohamed shows us that I hadn't yet previously seen. Last time it was one of the other shafts that is built exactly the same as the shaft upon which the Step Pyramid was built. For what purpose were those shafts built, and how many more might also be hiding out there in the desert?

Bent Pyramid and Dahshur

The Bent Pyramid at Dahshur is an absolute gem, and it is the most difficult climb into any of the pyramids – but it is absolutely worth it. This building is certainly some kind of harmonic resonance device with its myriad corbeled structures built within it, which include tall shafts and smaller variations of the Great Pyramid's Grand Gallery. Adjacent to the Bent Pyramid and the Red Pyramid, which lies just to the north, is a military site known as "Egypt's Area 51." The remnants of two other pyramids rest on this property, and it is rumored that there is an actively working stargate within the installation.

The Bent Pyramid at Dashur, inside of which are mysterious corbeled structures.

Alexandria

We will be venturing to the fabled city of Alexandria this year, which is a city I have not yet toured. Another one of the ancient wonders once stood here – the Great Lighthouse – and, of course, the famous Great Library. I would have loved to have visited both when they existed. There is now a massive modern library which was built in honor of the ancient one, and modern excavations and underwater explorations have revealed much of the old city.

Luxor

Depending on the schedule of the river boat and the day we'll be flying south to Upper Egypt (yes, you read that correctly, Upper Egypt is in the south – it's based on the flow of the Nile River), we may fly into Luxor from Cairo or fly into Aswan. The entire Luxor area is riddled with temples, which is where we get the name Luxor from: when the Arabs took over in the Seventh Century, they thought the temples were palaces and called the city Al-Uqsur, their term for "the palaces." Prior to that, the Greeks called it Thebes, after their own great city, and Homer actually called it "Hundred-gated Thebes," referring the many temple entrances. The ancient Egyptians, however, called it Waset, which meant "place of great power." The Luxor temple itself boasts a Muslim mosque built on top of a Christian church which was built into one of the corners of the ancient Egyptian temple.

Karnak

Massive. There is so much to see here, and if you're looking for stargate symbolism, during our last tour it became a scavenger hunt within the group, and [multiple people from the group] found several stargate symbols here. The site also contains massive obelisks, a broken one of which used to lay on its side, and if you sneaked behind it and knocked on it with your knuckles, you could hear and feel the reverberation from the energy of all the quartz embedded in the granite. Unfortunately, they have now propped up this broken obelisk upright onto a cement slab, which just looks awkward.

Hatshepsut's Mortuary Temple

This temple is the absolute epitome of a stargate. I gave a brief

Hatshepsut's Mortuary Temple. Perfectly designed as a stargate.

overview of it in my book *Travels Through Time* which I will include here:

"At Hatshepsut's mortuary temple outside of Luxor, we find a massive staircase that stretches upward into the temple, which is built into the cliff face, and is the beginning of a direct path into the Holy of Holies. The sides of this staircase are flanked by sculptures of falcons, representing the god Horus, but on closer inspection, one can see that these falcons have snake tails that lead all the way up the staircase. It is believed by many that these falcons were once snake heads, possibly cobras, re-carved in ancient times when the temple was repurposed. Back in Chapter 1, we discussed how the serpent in the ancient world was a symbol of energy – life energy, healing energy, universal energy. To the southeast side of the temple are the remains of the base of a small pyramid – there is almost nothing left. Engaging in the debate on whether Egyptian pyramids were power plants or not is beyond the scope of this book, but whether you believe it was a power plant or that it was harnessing electrical energy from the telluric currents of the earth, it was there to power the temple. As one walks up the staircase, into the courtyard, and into the barque hall for Amun, each entrance that is passed through is marked with the hieroglyphs for "stargate," or *saba*. The barque hall, literally means transportation for the god, but there is more beyond, although the next chamber, the Holy of Holies, is blocked by a set of Egyptian guards. If one arrives early enough before the crowds and offers a large tip to these guards, entrance might be granted – but you didn't hear that from me. Inside the Holy of Holies is a cartouche full of stars, the ultimate symbol of passage to the cosmos. So, here we have an amazing setup: the symbolism of energy along the stairs, each entrance adorned with the stargate hieroglyphs, the cartouche full of stars within the most sacred room of the whole complex, and a pyramid powering it all. This lost esoteric symbolism and history is why I have joined forces with Egyptologist Mohamed Ibrahim to host an annual "Stargates of Ancient Egypt" tour."

Valley of the Kings

These are the great tombs of nearly 500 years-worth of New Kingdom Pharaohs, including the infamous tomb of King Tutankhamun. There are 65 known tombs, many of which are elaborately painted with amazing pieces of artwork, hieroglyphs, and friezes, but nearly all of which were plundered by grave robbers. It's believed Tut's tomb became lost during a mudslide from a torrential downpour, preserving it from thieves. We usually visit three or four of these burial sites during our visits.

Temple of Hathor at Dendera

Everyone wants to know if the Dendera "lightbulb" was really an indication that ancient Egyptians had electricity and incandescent lighting. I certainly believe they did things to harness the energy of the earth for a variety of purposes, but this is not an incandescent

Discovering stargate symbolism at Hathor's Temple in Dendera.

lightbulb – in fact, there are several of these "lightbulb" depictions throughout the complex. It symbolizes a creative energy, and I don't have the space to dive into it all here, but those that have been following *Connecting the Universe* on the Connected Universe Portal will be familiar with the video clip I've provided with Mohamed explaining the nature of this. This temple also contains an amazing blue ceiling depicting the night sky, an ancient Zodiac wheel, and on our last adventure we discovered many more symbols of stargates than originally believed.

Temple of Seti at Abydos

There is so much going on at Abydos that I don't know if I have room for it all. That we usually have to incorporate both Dendera and Abydos in a single day is almost a disservice to each since there is so much to experience at both locations, but travel logistics make this a necessity. Sure, there are the mysterious hieroglyphs on one of the lentils in the entrance hall, but those seem to have overshadowed so much more that is going on at this location. The temple is loaded with esoteric symbolism – 72 columns, 7 chapels, 3 stargate rooms just in the primary structure. The antechamber to the three stargates contains 10 of its own smaller pillars and a beautiful depiction of the raising of the djed pillar, the backbone of Osiris and of Egypt. The famous King's List hall is here, and behind the temple is the mysterious Osirion, a far older structure which contains carvings of the flower of life.

Aswan

The granite quarry at Aswan is where so many of the obelisks and statues originated from, and it's still a mystery as to how they were able to transport many of these downriver some 500 miles to the ancient sites in lower Egypt. Sure, they probably used the Nile, but how did they lift some of these pieces that weighed upwards of 1,000 tons? And what kind of boat or barge did they place them upon that would account for the massive amount of buoyancy needed to float these things downriver and then the ballast needed to keep the boat in the water properly when not loaded with these huge pieces of granite? At the quarry, among other things, we'll visit the Unfinished Obelisk, the massive 1,200-ton behemoth that was abandoned in situ and question how they could have possibly tried to carve these things with just stone and copper tools traditional history tries to tell us. Also in Aswan, we usually visit the Nubian Museum which has a number of amazing artifacts and is where the Napta Playa stones were moved to preserve them from vandals.

Temple of Philae

This is a beautiful Temple of Isis which had once been on an

The Temple of Philae from the water on approach.

island in the Nile and is now on an island in what has become a man-made lake due to the installation of the Aswan High Dam in the 1960s. The entire temple was moved from one island to another or otherwise it would have been submerged. Upriver to the south, the same was done with the temple of Abu Simbel, cutting the monument into pieces and moving it higher up the hill. The construction of the dam, while it provides electric power to a growing population, unfortunately, greatly altered the flow of the Nile. However, Philae is still a wonderful temple to visit, and some of my favorite water photos come from here.

Cairo

Usually, on the backend of our tour when we return to Cairo is when we visit the Egyptian Museum in Cairo which houses many amazing artifacts, including King Tut's mask. While many of Tut's artifacts remain at this museum, much has been moved to the new Grand Egyptian Museum which is still awaiting its long-anticipated full opening. Tucked away in one of the corners of this museum is a sarcophagus which was abandoned mid-construction when the lid that was being cut off the underside broke, but it shows us that ancient Egyptians did have large circular saws at their disposal. Depending on the time we have available to us, we may visit other museums as well, such as the Civilization Museum which contains the royal mummies.

In between it all, we will visit a large variety of markets, restaurants, and shops throughout the region. We'll taste local foods, be shown how papyrus was made, alabaster carved, and make selections from essential oils and spices. Again, I'll be featuring all of this in the video blogs on the Connected Universe Portal.

So, why am I so drawn? As you can see, there is a ton to explore and experience, and what I've mentioned above is just scratching the surface. So many of the mysteries of our ancient past come out of Egypt, and it's been a life-changing experience each time I've made the pilgrimage there. You should join us one of these years!

Archive of the Connected Universe: Volume 1

Part 3

Stargates of Ancient Egypt

Notes on Part 3

The Stargates of Ancient Egypt tour has become an annual pilgrimage to one of the most ancient and mysterious parts of the world, one in which we routinely make new discoveries during our explorations, many times right as we're simply showing our guests the secrets hidden in plain sight. For instance, during our 2023 tour at the Temple of Hathor in Dendera, we made an amazing discovery in the middle of our guide Mohamed Ibrahim describing a set of stargate glyphs he'd been pointing out to guests for a good seven years. As described in my book *Portals to the Stars*:

> Back in Dendera, the room with Nut and Geb is loaded with stargate symbolism of a bit of a different sort. Here along the interior wall that holds the entrance doorway, we find depictions of gates with objects like the djed pillar placed within them, and stars displayed over the top of the gates. Each gate has a different number of stars, and Mohamed was telling us about these gates in 2023 when we

suddenly made more discoveries, "This object is, what do we call it? Gate. Now, we can see five stars, and the symbol djed. But we also see different symbols, and many stars here … this is like the address of where you want to go, or the name of the place, or the name of the way."

He proceeded to show us more of these symbols on the wall on the other side of the doorway when something caught my eye around the frame of the window in the wall, and I said, "Hey, Mohamed. Does that go around the side?"

He stepped back and leaned his head into the window frame which was partially blocked by security fencing. "Ah, we didn't see this before. This is too much."

Excited, I headed out the door and exclaimed, "It keeps going!"

The Stargates of Ancient Egypt tour in 2024 would have no shortage of discoveries, as you will see in the following pages in this particular section. During this time in Egypt, I wrote a (somewhat) daily travel blog, and the Connected Universe Portal contains the video travel blog version which is far deeper and more extensive.

I've thoroughly enjoyed every tour I've been a part of in Egypt, and have made many lifelong friends along the way, but this particular group really connected on multiple levels, and it became a truly magical tour. It's also where I met Kate.

Getting the Hard Part Out of the Way

Egypt Tour Day 0: The Travel Day

April 16, 2024

What's the most challenging aspect of touring the world? For me, it's the travel to and from the destinations. Some airlines do a nice job of trying to make your experience with them as enjoyable as possible, but let's face it. Everyone hates dealing with TSA at the airports. And that's probably putting it mildly. However, as I type the beginning of this, I am sitting in a small wine and cheese bar in Charles de Gaulle airport, so there are certainly some perks, as well.

This past weekend, I essentially spent two days traveling en route to the Stargates of Ancient Egypt tour I'm hosting again with Egyptologist Mohamed Ibrahim. Between each leg I experienced massive layovers – 10 hours in Boston and 8 hours in Paris – spending more time waiting around for flights than actually flying. I actually prefer longer layovers, something in the two-hour range works pretty well, because it allows for some flexibility should a flight be delayed, and sometimes I can relax with a meal. As it so

With 8 hours, finding a place to sit and write at Charles de Gaulle airport in Paris

happened with this journey, flight times got modified after I had purchased tickets and, suddenly, what were already long layovers, turned into massive ones. Well, it's all part of the adventure, as I like to say. But that does make traveling this time a bit of a challenge.

I have a hard time sleeping on airplanes, and since the Boston-to-Paris flight took off at 11:35 PM on Sunday evening, this was the flight to attempt catch a few winks. However, they provided a full dinner service at 1:00 AM, cutting into the near-six-hour flight, and then a few hours later provided a breakfast service. Give it up for AirFrance for being on top of the food (as well as wine and champagne), but that really only gave me about a three-hour window to sleep. Um, have I mentioned I have a hard time sleeping on planes? I just can't get comfortable. Whether it's my arm falling asleep from propping up the pillow, my legs getting cramped, or – seriously – my butt hurting on the seat, I will only get about three and a half minutes of shuteye before I wake back up and make some sort of adjustment. I'm a total train wreck (that's putting it mildly)

About to take off on the last leg to Cairo.

attempting to sleep on airplanes.

Getting into Cairo just after midnight capped off the flying for this leg of the adventure, but there was still the matter of getting through the airport and to the hotel. One of the many things I love about doing tours with Mohamed is that he and his team have this down to a science. When you descend the escalator after disembarking the plane, one of his team members is standing right there with a sign to greet you and, literally, walk you through everything. This includes travel visa, baggage, customs, and out to the tour bus to take you to the hotel. At the hotel, you are greeted by another one of Mohamed's team members to assist you in getting checked in. It's a very seamless operation, and I absolutely appreciated this the first time I toured Egypt – and I still do.

And yeah, I was pretty ready to crash at the hotel after the extra-long travel, although my travel was not nearly as long as another person on our tour, Lisa, who was flying all the way in from Hawaii and had several long layovers like I did. It's worth it, however, for experiencing the Egyptian adventure that awaits us!

(Going forward during this tour, I will be posting a daily blog, as much as I can since, once we get on the Nile River cruise, the internet connection can be a bit sketchy. This will include the written blog here along with some photos, but the full video blogs will be posted to the Connected Universe Portal, which will be a much more immersive experience of our tour here. You can still view the 2021 Egypt Tour travel vlog there as well.)

Like Visiting Old Friends

Egypt Tour Day 2: The Giza Plateau

April 17, 2024

Article Notes: What happened to "Egypt Tour: Day1"? Well, there really wasn't much to report. The official Day 1 of the tour is the welcome meeting and dinner. This is where we all met in a conference room at the hotel in the early evening to discuss a few particulars about the tour and then went out for dinner. The dinner was quite lovely and held this time at a restaurant right on the Nile River which looked out over the water.

How has my relationship changed with the structures on the Giza Plateau now that I've been here several times? This was a question posed to me by one of the guests on the Egypt tour, Stefanie (who, ironically, is from the same area of Switzerland from which the Ricksecker's originated). I quite enjoyed this question and answered it like this: "It's like visiting old friends." Seriously, it really is.

I've always had a calling to Egypt which I, generally, date back to watching the *Mysteries of the Sphinx* documentary special featuring John Anthony West, Robert Schoch, and Charlton Heston

Hello, Giza, my old friend. (Sphinx & Great Pyramid, 2nd pyramid to the left)

back in 1993 (which can still be viewed on Gaia TV); however, I suspect it dates back further than that. Indiana Jones, anyone? Jonny Quest? Perhaps it's my sense of adventure. Whatever it is, I've always wanted to explore this land and its many magnificent structures. But now that I've been here several times and have gotten over that sensation of being overwhelmingly awestruck, what does it mean to me when I visit these locations?

    I liken it to visiting old friends. There's now a pleasant comfort when I visit as a warm smile broadens across my face when I gaze upon its magnificence. It's familiar and greets me with open arms as I amble up the hill and soak in the monumental visage of the Great Pyramid (this is typically where we start since the ticket booth and entrance are right there). We have an understanding with each other, unspoken but ever-present. The structures on the plateau are going to continue to stand there, massive and mysterious, for thousands of more years, and while I'm around in this lifetime I'm going to marvel at them, learn as much as I can, harness as much energy as I

Fantastic tour group this year for Stargate of Ancient Egypt (Saba Tours photo).

can, and introduce others to their grandeur.

The Giza Plateau is more than just the three major pyramids and a Sphinx, however. There is a reason the ancient Egyptians built at this specific location right down to where each block was placed. Why did the Egyptians build the second pyramid where it currently rests when a few feet further to the west it was flatter and would have been easier construction? Why were the casing blocks of each pyramid different – the Great Pyramid completely white limestone, the second pyramid half limestone, half granite, and the third pyramid completely granite? There was a method to their genius madness. There are so many tunnels and shafts throughout the plateau which only thicken the web of mystery – and we haven't yet found them all. And that ancient, ancient Sphinx – what is it hiding? The entire plateau is teaming with mystery, even amongst the gusts of wind today.

Likely, we won't ever discover all of these secrets for several generations, if ever. Traditional research has thwarted those who are looking outside the box for the real answers as to what the Giza plateau is all about. It's not about tombs and creating a behemoth of a monument for a single body in each pyramid. That's just totally nonsensical, and we'll see details of that when we venture inside the Great Pyramid for two hours, just ourselves, toward the end of the tour.

I believe these old friends of mine are encouraging me to unveil the handful of secrets I've deciphered but are simultaneously smirking at me as they hold back some of the deeper secrets for which our world isn't quite ready. "Show them the path, Mike, but they have to explore for themselves."

I'm continuously passing on what I know so that future generations may pick up the mantle and carry it forward. These old friends on the Giza Plateau aren't going to simply spell it out for us. It's a journey for each of us to take, to embrace the knowledge that is available to us, that is meant just for us as we venture into this sacred area of the world and pass it on.

The group with us this year on the Stargate of Ancient Egypt Tour is amazingly like-minded, very intuitive, and open to learning this esoteric knowledge that Mohamed, Ahmed, and I, in part, will share, in addition to discovering and unveiling many truths on their

Egypt Video Travel Blog Day 2: Giza Plateau

Egypt Video Travel Blogs (April 2024)

Like Visiting Old Friends
Egypt Tour Day 2: The Giza Plateau

April 17, 2024:

How has my relationship changed with the structures on the Giza plateau now that I've been here several times? This was a question posed to me by one of the guests on the

The Stargates of Ancient Egypt tour video travel vlog of the Giza Plateau

own. What we've explored so far is just the very tip of something far greater, and I can't wait to explore more with this amazing assemblage of people from all over the world — Costa Rica, Scotland, Switzerland, and several parts of the United States are all represented. There is so much more to bring to light!

Discovering More Ancient Secrets

Egypt Tour Day 3: Alexandria

April 18, 2024

Article Notes: Later, in the article on "Discoveries and New Theories in Egypt" we'll cover a time slip incident from Drem, Scotland. What in the world is a story from Scotland doing within an article about Egypt? You'll have to wait for that, but it was during the bus ride back from Alexandria during a conversation with Katherine Swinn that we made a connection between the time slip covered in my book Travels Through Time *and a "triangle area" in Scotland.*

Where in the ancient world would I like to travel back in time and visit? There are many — very many — but Alexandria is certainly near the top of the list since it simultaneously housed the Great Lighthouse (one of the seven wonders of the ancient world) and the Great Library, a building I could have gotten lost in for days, perhaps months, and they would have needed to send in a search

What did we discover on the ceiling of the catacombs

team to find me. So, it was great pleasure we visited Alexandria as part of this year's Stargates of Ancient Egypt Tour.

Our first stop was the labyrinth of ancient catacombs which have traditionally been attributed to the Roman era but could be far older. This was another Indiana Jones moment as we ventured down the spiral staircase around a long shaft that somewhat reminded me of Sintra Quinta da Regaleira, a Templar initiation well in Portugal, and connected with a vast network of corridors and chambers. Immediately stepping out from the shaft, there's a short hall which contains a scalloped recess on each wall. One of our guests, Stefanie, who has a career in music and sound, told me to stand in the middle and try talking. Interestingly, there was an acoustic amplification of my voice that played back at me through these. Keep that in mind.

Most of the tourists flocked to a central chapel which contained a variety of Egyptian friezes as well as statues in front of obelisks, but we saved that maelstrom for the end. Instead, we crept our way through myriad passages, exploring the chambers and strange recesses, and became astounded toward the end.

"Mike, we always discover something new on your tours!" Mohamed called out as I slipped into one of the chambers after having fallen behind while capturing some photos. This was a newly opened room in the catacombs, one Mohamed had not yet seen, and what he was pointing at was above our heads. There in red was a flower of life. We don't often see this design in ancient Egypt, although it has shown up in some surprising places like the Osirion behind the Temple of Seti in Abydos. That was the first surprise. The second was when we peered down into what's traditionally been defined as crypts and saw what, at first, appeared to be three different levels. But on closer inspection one could see that these deep crypts had a corbeled architecture to them, much like what we see in the Grand Gallery of the Great Pyramid. What was that kind of construction method doing here? So, we made multiple new discoveries at this location, and I'm strongly suspecting there is also a Templar tie-in to it as well. Give me some time on the latter.

After the catacombs we ventured to Pompey's Pillar, which is said to have been erected as a triumphal monument around 300 AD. Standing at about 26 meters and weighing an astounding 600 tons, this singular piece of solid Aswan rose granite is the only ancient monument in Alexandria still standing in its original location. How they moved this behemoth 800 miles from the Aswan quarries is anyone's guess. It rivals some of the biggest obelisks throughout the country with its sheer height and weight.

Our final visit this morning was to a historic Roman amphitheater which also had a section dedicated to the monument pieces from lost historic structures they've been pulling out of the harbor. The acoustics of the amphitheater itself were pretty amazing, and the reverberation reflected back at oneself when standing in the prime central spot was pretty surprising. In some ways, it reminded me of the type of resonance we observed at Drombeg Stone Circle in Ireland but in an even grander scale. What a day for acoustics!

Following that, we greatly enjoyed a late lunch, experiencing seafood on the Mediterranean with an amazing view of the sea. From where I sat, peering over Albert's right shoulder, I had a view of the Qaitbay Citadel which looks like a small castle. The significance of this is that building rests on the spot where the Great Lighthouse, one of the Seven Wonders of the ancient world, once stood. The lighthouse was massive, standing at more than 350 feet high, second only to the Great Pyramid at that time. The Great Lighthouse became a ruin after an earthquake in 1323, and many of the blocks from the building were used to create the citadel now standing there.

Across the harbor from the lighthouse once stood the Great Library of Alexandria which met its own fate in 48 AD when it succumbed to a fire. As fate would have it, the two infamous buildings only shared in each other's company for 200 years. A massive modern library has been erected at a location they believe is approximately where the original library stood, but there is no way to know for sure. That we got to have lunch within walking distance of each of these locations was absolutely an amazing moment for me, but I would still like to travel back in time to experience both of these in their full glory.

Pyramids, Tombs, and the Music of the Ancients

Egypt Tour Day 4: Saqqara and Dahshur

April 20, 2024

Article Notes: If you want to listen to Stephanie singing within the Red Pyramid, you can find clips of the moment on my various social media accounts such as TikTok, Instagram, and Facebook. The full account of it can be found on my Patreon and the Connected Universe Portal.

What a day! This one was so loaded with pure Egypt magic that we didn't get a chance to eat lunch until a little after 4:00 PM. Ok, maybe that's a little on the late side, but there is no denying we experienced quite a lot of what ancient Egypt has to offer. And I received a very vocal confirmation of one of my theories.

We began the day at the mysterious Serapeum at Saqqara, the underground nest of massive coffers that absolutely defy convention. The traditional narrative tells us that the Dynastic Egyptians somehow navigated granite weighing upwards of 70 tons

Gazing in upon a monstrous 70-ton box — all one piece.

down narrow passageways and placed them perfectly in even more narrow niches. Um, no. These things are so huge that the average human being can perfectly stand under the overhang of a lid.

At dinner, I put on my "guide" hat and posed the question to the group as we discussed the Serapeum, "How could they have done that?" This is a very intuitive group, and the general consensus was … soundwave technology that levitated the boxes into place. That's pretty much what I believe. And what were these boxes used for? Certainly not for Apis bulls (I call Apis bullshit). When they were discovered, they were empty. That story of a mummified cow being found in one? Those supposed remains have never been seen.

The Serapeum is quite a special location, buzzing with energy, a residual effect of how the system developed there worked — the boxes still retain some of it and can be felt as you approach. Are the boxes stargates? Regeneration chambers? Ancient batteries for the functionality of the entire Saqqara complex? There are many

At the Step Pyramid.

plausible theories, and I'm open to all of them.

Following that, we ventured further down the hill to a tomb to which I had never before been, the Tomb of Ty, a senior official from the 5th Dynasty. What fascinated me about this particular tomb was, not just the number of false doors it contained, but that the doors themselves contained hieroglyphs of a star and a house. Essentially, these were defined as portals to the star houses – essentially a type of stargate.

That was just a short detour. Soon we were off back up the hill to the area in and around the Step Pyramid, first to the Pyramid of Unas which contains an interesting sarcophagus that we're going to talk about in a later blog, and then we were diverted to the mysterious second shaft. To the south of the Step Pyramid lies an open shaft built nearly identical to the one under the pyramid, and with a special ticket we were able to venture inside. What's wonderful about this structure is that it gives us a close-up view of what they call "the vault" inside, a massive box at the bottom of the shaft that certainly looks much smaller from the balcony view inside the Step Pyramid. Exploring the box in this other shaft gives one a true impression that what we're dealing with is truly some higher intelligence for the age.

Those sites themselves – the Serapeum, Tomb of Ty, pyramid of Unas, the open shaft, the Step Pyramid – already make for quite a full day. But we weren't done. Remember, there was still a confirmation of one of my theories to be made.

Finally, there was Dahshur, the very first site I ever visited in Egypt, and a site I believe holds many secrets to the functionality of the pyramids. Here resides the Red Pyramid and Bent Pyramid, two structures that are dualistic in nature. The exterior of the Red Pyramid is rough and crumbling away while the Bent Pyramid's exterior still shines with the majority of its smooth casing stones still intact. The interior of the Red Pyramid is highly structured, each room like a mirror of the other, impeccably well-kept. The interior of the Bent Pyramid, however, is almost maze-like in its design, and it has undergone major restoration in ancient times. The king to whom the construction is traditionally credited, Sneferu, was actually the restorer of the structure — quite literally. That's what Sneferu means: "the restorer." Then take the colors of the two pyramids ... the dark red limestone versus the light beige Tura limestone. There's also a strong ammonia-like odor within the Red Pyramid while the Bent Pyramid is odorless. And then there's the obvious ... one is "bent" with an angular change occurring in the middle of the structure while the other has perfectly straight lines. These two pyramids were certainly built to be opposites of each other.

Both, however, served a similar purpose, it seems, since we find in both the corbel vaulted harmonic resonance chambers. I believe these were both massive sound devices. Mohamed believes the site has more to do with microwaves — and perhaps both ideas are

Unearthing the secrets of the Bent Pyramid.

correct. We don't have to limit ourselves. The vocal confirmation came from Stefanie, who works in the music industry and sang beautifully within the central chamber of the Red Pyramid. She, Pam, and I also performed a sacred "Om" in the chamber and immediately felt the resonance and energy reflected back at us. Yes, there was absolutely a sound component to these structures.

Another treat occurred in the Bent Pyramid when only four of us remained in the building, plus the chaperone, who offered for us to meditate in the primary chamber. This was an unusual offer since any kind of spiritual work within these structures is generally frowned upon, and we usually have to sneak doing it. Albert, Kate, Stefanie, and I jumped at the opportunity and greatly enjoyed the serenity in which to meditate. Personally, I felt a peaceful type of power surrounding me, almost like we had suddenly been encapsulated within a bubble. There is certainly still some energy being generated by the pyramid even if the acoustic component has been damaged over the millennia.

This was definitely a very full day, and while we were tired and hungry by the time we drove out of the area, there was also a feeling of fulfillment — at least for me, and others expressed the same. We're only on Day 4 of this grand adventure, and we've already covered a ton of ground with several new discoveries, and yet we have so much more to still explore.

Epic Site and a Haunting Stare

Egypt Tour Day 5: Karnak

April 20, 2024

Article Notes: What happened to "Egypt Tour: Day1"? Well, there really wasn't much to report. The official Day 1 of the tour is the welcome meeting and dinner. This is where we all met in a conference room at the hotel in the early evening to discuss a few particulars about the tour and then went out for dinner. The dinner was quite lovely and held this time at a restaurant right on the Nile River which looked out over the water.

It's almost too much. How can one try to explore everything Egypt has to offer when a site like the Temple of Karnak would take more than a week on its own? And if you want to be thorough, well … that would likely take a month or more. Karnak is seriously that huge. Can we expect to find stargates amongst the vastness?

Our day started early with a flight from Cairo to Luxor, an area named multiple times for its splendor. Its current name originates from the seventh century when the Arabs took control and called it Al-Uqsur, meaning "the palaces" because they believed the

Winner! (If I had a cosplay award.)

extraordinary number of temples with their beauty were actually palaces. Prior to that it was known as Thebes, the Greeks naming it for their own beautiful city of Thebes because they thought there was a striking similarity, and again, because of all the temples. Homer, the famous author of *The Odyssey* and the *Iliad*, called it "Hundred-gated Thebes," a reference to all of the temple gates. Is this at all a subtle nod to the stargates? The ancient Egyptians, however, called their city Waset, meaning "place of power," and it is that power that caused them to build so many mighty temples there.

Fortunately, the flight from Cairo to Luxor is only about an hour long, so the travel isn't too painful, and it gives us enough time to explore something significant after arrival. On a fun note, sitting behind me were a couple dressed as if they were from the 1920s and were funding an Egyptian expedition. If I had a "Favorite Cosplay" award to hand out, they would win it for this year. Or, perhaps they were time travelers popping into the future to see how the efforts of their expedition a hundred years ago may have paid off.

From the airport we drove straight to Karnak, the massive open-air temple that was once fully connected to Luxor Temple just over a mile and a half away. Mohamed's tour doesn't take us straight into the touristy area of the temple — we're not just tourists. We're exploring and discovering. To the left of the complex is a huge open-air museum of artifacts and structures, so after a brief introduction to the temple complex, we headed there. Right in plain site on shrines and doorways we see the hieroglyphs for Stargates

The long stare of Sekhmet.

emblazoned. We also learned the difference between Tefnut and Sekhmet who we visited after the open air artifacts.

The statue of Sekhmet is haunting. Tucked away in a small temple on the left side of the Karnak complex, Sekhmet's power emanates forth. Mohamed jokingly remarks that the headless statue of Ptah upon entering is due to Sekhmet, his wife, but it wouldn't be surprising if there isn't some sort of truth behind the humor. Sekhmet stands sentinel in her chamber, a silent stoicism permeating from the beautifully carved diorite. If the sun from the small skylight above catches her just right, her eyes appear to glow, creating an effect of pure power. Unfortunately, this was not the case when we arrived, but there was enough of a stream of light that several in our group were able to catch the ray with their hands for some wonderful photos.

From there we ventured to a part of the complex to which I'd never been: the Temple of the Seven Gates. Why is it called such? Earlier in the tour we highlighted the false doors in tombs that provided a way for the soul to travel between worlds. This gateway, however, was quite different since, for one, it was not in a tomb. Secondly, there are seven layers to the gate, seven dimensions through which the consciousness can travel. It's a powerful portal, and it's situated behind the primary Karnak complex where the general public throng simply was not visiting.

This allowed us to head into the primary Karnak complex from the backside, an area I'd not yet visited. There, Mohamed showed us a beautifully painted cartouche of Thutmose III being declared "Lord of the Pleiades" which is fascinating since he's also one of only a few kings we see associated with stargates. We also observed on a wall just outside the Holy of Holies an alchemical breakdown of the creation process of monatomic white gold. Some of the instructions have been chiseled away over the millennia, thus obscuring the method for making true transformative white gold cakes, but we can see there was certainly a process in place.

Enter random guy. As Mohamed ushered most of the group around the other side of the Holy of Holies, one of the temple chaperones got the attention of Kate to show her another room around the corner. Pam followed, and so did I to ensure they made it back to the group safely when they finished exploring this room. Inside on the left-hand wall was a scarab, the symbol of new life and beginnings, scorched black with the hieroglyphs on the other side of it chiseled away. As such, we have no idea what the full meaning of this writing may have been, but upon putting my hands close to the wall (but not touching) I could feel an energy emanating forth from it. There wasn't time to gather more information about this room,

The Seven Gates portal to ... where?

but it was quite interesting and noted for next visit.

At this point, we were pretty much on our way out of Karnak. We took a look at the massive 700-ton obelisk Karnak is known for, the stargate symbolism on the gateway behind it discovered last year, and we walked the row of columns which was much easier now that some of the general public had dissipated.

The rest of the day was, essentially, our own. We checked into the Jolie Ville resort, freshened up, and relaxed the rest of the evening as we prepared for the next day's explorations, one of my favorite days on the itinerary: Dendera and Abydos.

There's almost too much to explore at Karnak.

Discoveries and New Theories in Egypt

What the First Week of the Stargates Tour Has Taught Us

April 22, 2024

One of the things I greatly enjoy about returning to Egypt is always seeing and experiencing something new. That feeling is amplified when our tour guide, Egyptologist Mohamed Ibrahim, who is a native Egyptian and has been conducting the tours for nearly 25 years, also discovers something new. Last year we had an amazing moment at the Temple of Hathor in Dendera in the discovery together of additional stargate symbolism. It became like a scavenger hunt for our tour group, and many more symbols were found in Karnak and Abydos. That's one of the fantastic things about touring with Mohamed and Saba Tours. We're not just going through the motions of pointing out famous sites; we are constantly researching and exploring for new information. So, what have we discovered so far, and what does it all mean?

Flower of life in the Alexandria catacombs.

Alexandria

I previously wrote in brief about the discovery in Alexandria of the flower of life in the catacombs there. This was quite a surprising discovery since it is generally believed to be a "newer" ancient symbol, but yet we keep finding it in some truly extremely ancient structures. The most ancient location we've discovered its inscription is at the Osirion behind the Temple of Seti in Abydos, and we honestly don't know how old it is since the construction of the Osirion far predates the Temple of Seti.

We don't have enough time here to get into all the intricacies of the Osirion, but considering it is 40 feet further underground than the temple at the surface level, we could be looking at something that was built at least 10,000 years ago before the great cataclysm. Now, I'm pretty confident that the hieroglyphs on the lentil block above the flower of life are a more recent addition by the dynastic Egyptians. The rest of the complex is bare of hieroglyphs and are made with much larger blocks than dynastic Egyptians previously used. In fact, the construction technique reminds me quite a lot of the Valley Temple, which we've shown before to be prediluvian, constructed with material from the Sphinx enclosure and later restored with granite. We also don't find hieroglyphs in the pre-dynastic, prediluvian pyramids.

So, what of our flower of life in Alexandria? The room in which it was discovered would have been one of the earliest rooms constructed since it was near the front of the entire complex that had been chiseled out of the rock. So, this is quite older than most other areas of the catacombs. What we also find here, unlike other "crypts" throughout the entire structure, the "crypts" within this room plunge some 20 feet into the ground and have a corbel construction to them, like miniature versions of the Grand Gallery within the Great Pyramid of Giza. We also find this design in the pyramids at Dahshur which I go into more detail below. Thus, this room really helps us to date the catacombs complex far older than previously believed.

Purple Energy

An interesting phenomenon captured in some of the photos taken by the group is what we've been calling purple energy. This was first captured by Kate at the Great Pyramid which was like a soft glow morphing out of the pyramid, and then a purple halo captured by Lisa within the Serapeum around the box that was abandoned in the hallway. At this point, we can't say for sure exactly what it is and if there's any specific purpose for it, but it's something we've been keeping an eye out for ever since.

Confirmation at Dahshur

This was a big one for me. I pretty much described it in detail in the Saqqara — Dahshur post, but I'll sum it up here. One of my theories about the pyramids at Dahshur, the Red Pyramid and the Bent Pyramid, is that they are harmonic resonance machines. For what specific purpose were they built and how exactly they functioned, I can't yet say, but sound was absolutely a major component of the whole set up. They were also built with duality in mind.

Corbel ceiling in the Red Pyramid.

As an impromptu test, our resident music professional on tour, Stefanie from Switzerland (aka La Cheffe), sang a song she learned while visiting India within the primary chamber of the Red Pyramid. This chamber was constructed in a similar fashion to the other two within the pyramid, high vaulted corbel ceilings. The music rang out beautifully, and she was quite impressed with the acoustics to carry her voice. She knew it was meant for music. Now, I doubt it was meant for the specific music she sang — I suspect there was something at a specific **key** and at a specific frequency that needed to be performed, but this confirmed for me that this, indeed, is a harmonic resonance machine. Add in a sacred "Om" she, Pam, and I performed while there and a few similar things conducted at the Bent Pyramid, and I can say I'm pretty confident I'm on the right track.

Omm Sety's Room

I don't really have the space here to recap Dorothy Eady's story as Omm Sety, but the woman who believed she was a reincarnation

The unusual flat surfaces in the middle of the Room of Ships.

of an ancient Egyptian priestess and had an uncanny knack for knowing where the important places to dig around Abydos had been, had a favorite room in the Temple of Seti, the temple she was instrumental in helping to restore. This room is off limits to the general public and is kept locked. However, Mohamed knows everyone, and we were able to get into this room yet again (we got access last year, too ... I think the trick is getting there later in the day when the public is, essentially, gone). His friend, Mahmoud, the keeper of the keys, was a great help in discovering more secrets of this room at a temple rife with stargates.

As Mohamed got to chatting about why Omm Sety's room is known as the Room of Ships (there are friezes of ships all over the walls), Mahmoud made a comment about stargates and pointed up at the ceiling adjacent to the wall from which we entered. There, the ceiling extends higher and contains a window to the outside, but if one looks closer you can see how the ceiling suddenly slopes upward, but just in that middle section. Both the right and left sides are perfectly flat. This allowed perfect access to the outside world in a specific spot, so we mused about the idea of spaceships flying in and out of the room through this access point, one which may have been bigger before the restoration work.

For a time after that, the group became distracted playing with a beam of sunlight streaming in through one of the skylights above, but that's when Mohamed noticed something unusual about the columns in the room. As he looked up toward that ray of sun, it caught his attention that the base up the column near the ceiling didn't have its typical protuberance and was perfectly flat against the column. I looked up and, sure enough, he was correct. But something then caught my eye — the columns weren't perfectly round. Just as the capital was perfectly flat to the column, the column itself had a flat edge! This was strange, indeed. So, now we were seeing a perfectly flat space cut out to hold something specific or to create a smooth access or exit point via the ramp in the ceiling. I wanted to get a photo of this and discovered Ellie standing right at the center of the far wall — smart woman. She wanted to get the shot was well.

We chatted for a moment as we waited for the group to clear out of the way, it was time for us to move on, but then I noticed something peculiar. I politely asked Ellie if I could stand for a moment where she was, not to snag the first photo instead of she, but to get the proper perspective of the room and confirm what I thought I saw.

"Mohamed!" I called out. This was too good to be true. "Take a look at this." He joined us at the far wall, and he saw it the same as I when I pointed it out. The "straight" edge of the columns actually did not come down perfectly straight from the ceiling to the floor. Instead, they actually come down at an angle and make a "V" shape in the middle of the room! We may have previously had some mild musings about ships residing here earlier, but now we could see that, indeed, the middle of the room was nicely shaped to fit the hull of a ship!

There is going to need to be more follow up here. Next time I come I'll need to bring something to measure the angle — I can try from the photo, but I certainly didn't hold the camera the right way to get a proper measurement for that. (In fact, I probably need to stand on the bench against the wall, and I have a sneaking suspicion that would be frowned upon). Wild!

Drem, Scotland ... Say, what???

Ok, so this one has nothing to do with Egypt, but I'm including it here because it came up in conversation while on this tour, and it also pertains to my new book. Our new friend, Kate from Scotland, lives near Edinburgh and was showing me that there's a triangle area in the general region near where she lives. She's been experiencing what she calls portal activity in her home and was wondering how the triangle area pertains to that. When she showed me the map that included the Firth of Forth within the triangle, alarm bells went off in my head.

In my book, *Travels Through Time*, I delve into a time slip story

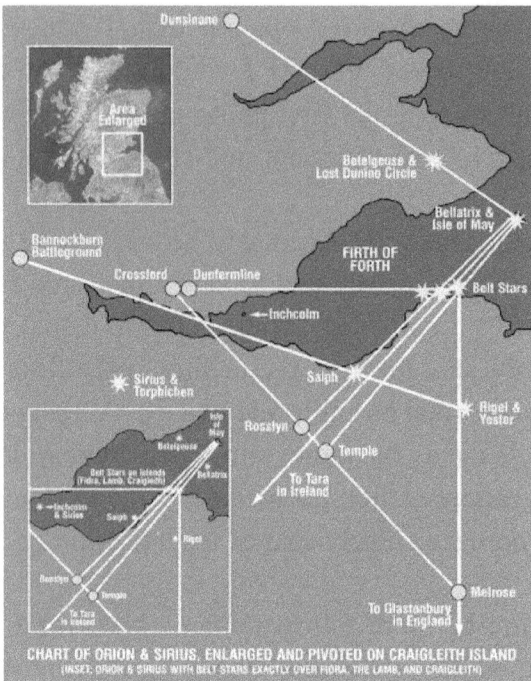

Triangle area Goddard flew through. (Jeff Nisbet map, mythomorph.com)

about a flight out of Edinburgh in the 1930s with Air Marshal Sir Robert Victor Goddard who got caught up in a storm and had to make course corrections when he spotted the Firth of Forth. From there, he looked for another recognizable point and spotted the abandoned Drem Airfield he had visited just the day before. However, when he flew over it was no longer abandoned, it was "a fully operational battle station" (*Star Wars* reference) and completely restored. Buildings had been repainted, there were unusual planes on the tarmac, and the maintenance crew members were wearing blue. Years later, these planes came into use and maintenance crews started wearing blue uniforms. Goddard had a time slip into the future.

Long story short (too late), Goddard's flight into the future took place in this triangle area. Once I mentioned Drem to Kate, she immediately recognized it, although she wasn't familiar with the story. The amazing discovery here is that I now get to use this bit of new information (at least new to me) in the upcoming book and that this experience occurred in a triangle area.

As you can see, it's been a pretty eventful tour so far, and we're only halfway into it. What other discoveries will we make over the next week? Stay tuned!

Best Day of the Stargates Tour?

Egypt Tour Day 6: Dendera and Abydos

April 24, 2024

This is always one of my favorite days of the Stargates of Ancient Egypt tour! Exploring Dendera and Abydos, while it is a long day because of the drive, is truly a magical experience. There is so much going on at both locations — and not just because these are both loaded with stargates. There are secrets of esoteric knowledge hidden deep within each, and we continue to make discoveries each time we return.

Temple of Hathor at Dendera

Hathor is a goddess (or, more appropriately, neter (nTr), as they're called in ancient Egypt — a force of nature) of healing, and the temple at Dendera is dedicated to her. Her iconography is displayed everywhere, most notably at the top of each column in the entrance hall. Although defaced long ago, each side of every column distinctly displays Hathor, and her depiction can be found all throughout the walls and ceilings of the temple, including a mid-

Temple of Hathor at Dendera.

level crypt in which I had not yet been. Located near the ceiling of the room next to the crypt in the floor that contains the infamous "lightbulb," this particular crypt shows us Hathor as a gateway. This is quite appropriate since on many occasions her likeness includes a gate on top of her head.

I asked Mohamed what was the significance of placing this crypt so high above the floor of the temple and he explained this was representative of mid-level consciousness. The temple is divided into three levels, each representative of a state of consciousness. There's the lower level or base consciousness — this is where we find the "lightbulb," or rather depiction of creation, the mid-level consciousness where we find the amazing blue painted displays on the ceiling where we find so much information about traveling the stars, and then there's the high level we find in the rooms on the roof of the temple which include the stargates and map of the universe.

I did accomplish one of my goals for this tour which was to catalogue all the stargate depictions from that room on the roof so I

Hathor and mid-level consciousness.

could try to interpret them for one of my upcoming books. While the next book is on earth energy, one of the books in the *Connecting the Universe* series will be covering stargates as well as the connections between ancient Egypt and Atlantis. If you've at all taken part in my special four-part Connecting the Universe special presentation, then you'll be familiar with some of the material I'm going to cover in this particular book.

The famed "Dendera Lightbulb" is a depiction of creation and base consciousness.

Dendera stargates and high-level consciousness.

There is truly a lot to explore at Dendera, and the energy of the location is of a special quality. I imagine that is why the ancients built the temple there and dedicated it to Hathor. They knew this was a place where people could come and experience her healing or one of her other qualities, such as fertility, the protection of women, or music.

Side note: We spotted our time travelers from the flight to Luxor at this temple in the mammisi.

Temple of Seti at Abydos

Two hours up the road from Dendera — I did mention it was a long drive, and to get to Dendera to begin with was already two hours — is the Temple of Seti at Abydos, another iconic ancient structure. We first had an authentic Egyptian lunch at a local's home, and then we started our afternoon adventure in a Temple of Ramsses which is just down the hill from Seti's temple. This is one to which

Temple of Seti I at Abydos.

I had not yet been, so I enjoyed getting to explore something new. This is a much smaller temple that is still undergoing some restorative work, but it was interesting to see, not a stargate, but a star door on a granite gateway entrance — and with this type of door think swinging saloon door. This is a slightly different variation and gives us an idea that there are different functions depending on which one you're passing through: stargate, great stargate, star door, and a place of destination in the star house.

Since we were coming into the Abydos complex from a different direction, we actually toured it backwards from the other times that I'd been there, which made for quite a different experience. Those that were unfamiliar with what this temple contains felt like there was a final treat saved for the very end when they got to see the hieroglyphs of what some think are modern machinery on one of the lentils in the entrance hall. But we're getting a bit ahead of ourselves.

We started with a look at the Osirion from above, but since we're a small group we didn't have the numbers (read: money) to get down inside of it. This is a temple that is 40 feet below the surface, a structure that is far older than the Temple of Seti, and is a site of

From the right, second line from the bottom, first four hieroglyphs: star door.

contention, meaning the purpose and function of it is hotly debated, not just in circles of alternative theories, but also in traditional academia. This general location (not necessarily the Osirion, specifically) is where the ancients believed the head of Osiris was buried, so the function of the temple is likely related to that, and we do have a good idea that this is why Seti built his temple there. Or did he repurpose something that was already there and added on to it?

The real treat was gaining access to Omm Sety's room, also known as the Room of Ships. This is a room that the general public does not get access to, but when you travel with Saba Tours, you have Mohamed Ibrahim who knows everyone and is good friends with the curator, Mahmoud. This is not the first time I have been in this room, but we did make new discoveries this time. I have detailed this in my last blog post on new discoveries, which is a subscriber-only post. I don't want this piece made available yet for public consumption. This will be revealed in that capacity in a more formal piece of work later.

Abydos is where Mohamed first found three stargates years ago, and last year we found two others in a room which includes an explanation of the use of white cakes before entering the stargate chambers. That we keep discovering new information every time we enter is a good sign that Abydos is extremely important in unlocking the secrets of the stargates — both of these temples are. And that is one of the primary reasons this day on the tour will always be one of my absolute favorites of the entire journey. What might we discover next year?

The Lord of the Pleiades

Egypt Tour Day 7: Luxor

April 26, 2024

What makes for a well-balanced tour? We had just completed a monumental day exploring Dendera and Abydos, but it was a long day with many hours occupied by driving in the bus to and from these locations. We were also staring the Valley of the Kings and Hatshepsut's Mortuary Temple in the face, two important locations that easily become a couple of the hottest in all of Egypt. Knowing this, Mohamed made sure to include a very light day in between the two with the only significant site to explore that of Luxor Temple. We also shopped for a spell in the Luxor markets and later had a presentation from Mohamed back on the cruise. So, first, what of Luxor?

Visiting Luxor temple during the day is a bit easier than at night since this is one of the Egyptian temples that gets lit up at night for tourists to come visit under the lights. It's pretty when they do that, and I've been there before in the evening, but the throng of people becomes a horde at that time. This time we explored during the day, and the crowd was … well, it was still quite a crowd.

Luxor Temple, April 2024.

One of the interesting facets of this temple is that it has been repurposed multiple times by a variety of cultures, six, specifically, but three drastically made their mark. Alexander the Great is depicted inside the walls of the temple in what we would call a scene in which he is cloned. (Seriously? Cloned? Yes. Check out the Day 7 video travel blog in the Connected Universe Portal for more information.) When Christianity began to filter into Egypt, the Copts (Egyptian Christians) built a church within the walls of Luxor Temple. The Romans left their Christian mark as well, but when Rome fell and the Islamic nations took over in the Seventh Century AD they built a mosque on top of the church. The mosque is still active, and I've been inside Luxor during the call to prayer. It's quite loud!

Inside, Ahmed showed the group how the practice of later kings claiming statues as their own was common place with how they positioned their cartouches on the sculptures. This makes it difficult to date these pieces, but we know they are far older than the Luxor Temple. Mohamed and I also had a nice little aside together as we examined two statues of similar design but very different quality. The craftsmanship on one was quite fine while the other appeared to be a weaker imitation of the first. How fascinating it is that the newer pieces are not as well constructed as the older ones.

As we ventured inside, we did find the depiction of a stargate but with some more specific information. This one also included "great Pleiades power" which is interesting since we previously saw Thutmose III in Karnak Temple being defined as "Lord of the Pleiades." And, of course, these two temples were connected. So, was Thutmose III using stargates to venture to the Pleiades?

We also took to the Luxor markets for a little shopping, and that became its own small adventure. I kept with Kate and Lisa as a bit of a chaperone and keep the group within the tour safety bubble, so to speak, and they ventured into a shop filled with small statues, primarily piled in heaps. Having stocked up on these sort of items on previous visits, I wasn't shopping, so I floated between the two ladies to make sure all was well. The one time I came back to Lisa she was haggling prices with one of the shopkeepers, and when I appeared she asked me what a fair price was for the objects she wanted. He was trying to get $50 U.S. dollars out of her, and I told her $30, which apparently, was what she had been trying to talk him down to. Nice telepathy! He had come down to $40 and didn't want to budge. I shook my head and said, "Nah, thirty," and Lisa started walking toward the door, employing the I'm-just-going-to-walk-away-strategy. "Thirty-five," the shopkeeper called after her, but Lisa kept going. She was going to get her statues for $30 — and she did! Once she was out the door the shopkeeper caved, "Ok, thirty! I'll go thirty!" Awesome! It was time to check on Kate.

Kate was in negotiations with another shopkeeper trying to get a couple statues down to 2,000 Egyptian pounds, which today is about $40 U.S. I had no idea where they started with this, but I tried helping the situation by telling her we needed to leave. We didn't really. We still had a little time, but Kate started backing out of the room and then asked me if I thought 2000 was a good price for the statues she was trying to get. I shook my head and said, "No, 1,500."

Baskets of spices at the market in Luxor near the temple.

The shopkeeper looked at me with a face that said, "You asshole," while Kate kept backing out of the room and saying, "Sorry, I have to go. I'll give you 2,000, but I have to go." The shopkeeper finally succumbed to the 2,000 Egyptian pounds.

    I've haggled before in the Egyptian markets, but I've never thought myself very good at it. Perhaps, because I wasn't the buyer and just floated around to take on the "bad cop" role I became a bit more useful in giving some small assistance to Lisa and Kate. In any case, it was fun, and aside from the alabaster shop we frequent outside of town, it was probably the most fun I've had shopping in Egypt.

Super Hot Stargates and Tombs

Egypt Tour Day 8: Valley of the Kings and Hatshepsut's Temple

April 28, 2024

Article Notes: The section here on the Valley of the Kings and the discoveries made there during this tour are fleshed out in more detail in the article "Evidence in Egypt of a Parallel Universe? Discoveries and New Theories in Egypt Part 2." I always say that every time we tour together we are always making new discoveries and connections, and this particular day happened to provide just that very thing.

How hot is hot? When I first toured Egypt it was at the end of June, and I was suffering from dehydration, so a visit to the Valley of the Kings in 120-degree temperatures wasn't exactly a stroll. I managed to keep cool inside the tombs, but when I laid down on the floor of the beautiful Ramsses V / VI tomb it seemed I was repurposing the complex for my own corpse. Someone might say, "Well, that's what it was built for." But was it?

The sarcophagus of King Ramses VI.

Valley of the Kings

The Ramsses VI tomb (we usually shorten it to this because his is the most complete and massive sarcophagus in the tomb) is the most ornate of the 65 in the Valley of the Kings and requires an extra ticket to enter — and it's absolutely worth it. Nearly the entire ceiling is painted a deep navy blue with hieroglyphs and characters emblazoned in a vivid gold color. Reds, browns, and oranges adorn the walls, displaying afterlife scenes in such a rich vibrancy that the paintings could be alive there with us in the tomb.

The most beautiful of these is on the roof of the final chamber containing the sarcophagi and, traditionally, depicts Nut, the goddess (neter, also nTr) of the sky in two forms: Nut of the Day and Nut of the Night. I'm not really going to debate that at all. Yes, clearly, we see one Nut stretched out with solar discs (Nut of the Day) and the other stretched out with stars (Nut of the Night).

Wall of the sarcophagus chamber with small rock outcropping on the right.

However, to think that's all we can decipher here is a bit shortsighted, in my opinion. I'm going to dive deeper into what I mean in my concluding "Discoveries" post, a follow up to my first one, when I've completed my coverage of the tour.

But what do I mean when I suggest the tombs in the Valley of the Kings may not have actually been built as tombs? Many who jump down this particular rabbit hole point out that there have been many occasions in which humanity has lived underground, and our planet is dotted with these refuges, such as Derinkuyu, many of which have been used by multiple cultures hundreds, or even thousands, of years apart. It does cause one to contemplate the possibility there may also be many in Egypt.

For me, I see it in the Ramsses VI tomb. Here is a massive hall so exquisitely decorated, so vivid in rich detail, yet for some reason, they couldn't be bothered to finish smoothing out a small section of wall to complete their artwork? What I'm referring to is the wall to the right side of the sarcophagus chamber. If you're looking for the "little alien" on top of the solar disc (nobody has any idea what that is) there is a patch of wall to the right which, if painted upon, would make that entire wall complete with art. However, it is left blank because there's a bit of stone jutting out from the wall. That makes no sense. This tomb served two generations and no one in that time could be bothered to smooth that out and complete the wall in a room they clearly wanted to make beautiful? Even the frieze above slightly paints into this outcropping — that bottom section is not smoothed out. This tells me the artists of this room were content to paint around this blemish and were not the builders. The builders, if they were intent on painting the walls, would have finished that small piece.

It makes more sense that the painters came along after the fact, discovered these long halls and chambers, decided to use them as tombs, and then decorated them according to their culture. If that's true, then who created the tombs and why? We need to move on now from the Valley of the Kings, so let's also include that bit for the forthcoming Discoveries post.

Hatshepsut's Mortuary Temple

There's no beating the heat on this particular day. You can wake up early to explore for a while before the furnace is cranked up, but at some point, you're going to feel the burn. The Valley of the Kings was pretty toasty during this year's Stargates tour, but we roasted at Hatshepsut's Temple. One of our group members had to tap out, and that's no slight on her part. None of us wanted to be out there very long, and this is a place I absolutely wanted to get back to and spend some time exploring since it's a perfect setup for a stargate.

Heading up into the primary temple complex are two falcon statues representing Horus, but if you look closely, these falcons have snake tails running all the way up to the temple and acting as

Hatshepsut's Temple in 2021. Too many people were there for a good photo of the temple in 2024. The stargate is all the way inside, straight up the stairs.

railings for the staircase. Snakes are representative of energy in the ancient world, and it's believed by some that the falcon statues were originally snakes, possibly cobras, and then modified later when the temple was repurposed. To the left of the complex are the remains of a small ancient pyramid almost completely in ruins, but if you subscribe to the idea that pyramids were used to harness the energy of the earth then this makes complete sense for our stargate. Continuing up into the temple we cross through two granite gateways, one marked as "great stargate" entering the inner courtyard and another as "stargate" entering the barque hall, a tall passageway that was supposed to be for the "transportation for the gods."

Beyond that ... well, when there is a crowd you can't get beyond that. I attempted asking one of the attendants there what it would cost to get past and step inside the Holy of Holies. His response wasn't that I couldn't, it was that it was too busy — these guys almost always have a price. However, I do know what is inside, and I've had colleagues share with me the imagery from there. On one of the walls is a cartouche full of stars, something we don't see

Did the pyramid that once stood here help to power the stargate inside?

anywhere else, and is really a perfect symbol for traveling the cosmos. So, like I said, the whole complex is really a perfectly constructed setup for a stargate. I detail this more in my book *Travels Through Time*.

The scorching sun was beating down directly on the temple as it always does, and we were melting, so I made quick work in showing the setup and, from there, Ahmed ushered us into a shady spot to show us the story of "Punt Land." This story of an expedition to an unknown distant land is controversial due to the flora and fauna displayed on the walls here. The traditional narrative tries to tell us it was somewhere in the Somalia area, but the coconut trees carved here tell us this was somewhere else. Somalia doesn't have coconut trees and other parts of Africa didn't start growing coconuts until about 500 AD. Hatshepsut's Temple dates back to at least 1500 B.C. That's quite a discrepancy.

We finally got out of the furnace and, after a quick visit to the

Colossi of Memnon, returned to our Nile Cruise and some well-earned showers. Sandwiched in between all of this was a visit to our favorite alabaster shop, Abo Elkomsan for Alabaster – their "introduction to alabaster" performance is legendary – and I may have purchased some again. You'll be able to watch that in the forthcoming video blog on the Portal. Whew! A day like this can wear you out quickly, but it is always so worth it.

The author learning how to make alabaster.

Exploring the Origins of Atlantis and Murder Pudding

Egypt Day 9: Edfu and Kom Ombo Temples

April 30, 2024

Article Notes: This return to Edfu absolutely helped inspire me to change directions with the second book in the Connecting the Universe *series. It was time for me to formally write about Atlantis ... as well as the stargates.*

There's almost nothing like the "A" word to get people riled up, whether that's traditionalists versus alternative history researchers or those factions with an alternative viewpoint of our distant past arguing about where the infamous capital city once stood. Very few agree on what exactly Atlantis was and where it stood, and even what I'm sharing here is controversial, but it's where I'm currently at with my research, and I'm pretty confident I'm on the right path. That said, this entry is not going to be an entire dissertation on Atlantis — I'm saving that for a bigger piece of work — but it will get some discussion since we find bits of the story on the walls at

The temple at Edfu where we find pieces of the "Atlantis" story.

the Edfu Temple. How so?

Let's back up a bit here. The last Stargates of Ancient Egypt tour didn't visit Edfu. We do try to provide a bit of a different experience from tour to tour so it's not redundant and those interested in returning can explore new things. Alexandria was a prime example of that — I'd never actually been before. With Edfu, I'd been there before, but it had been a few years, and I've researched a lot more since then that I really wanted to follow up on. The challenge was in the massive throng of people that had descended upon the temple. It's quite an inefficient way of doing things, but the Nile River cruises tend to sail together in packs, massive flotillas that, in one sense, are kind of fun because it almost seems like the ships are racing each other up the river but then make exploring difficult at some locations because everyone is getting off at the same time. Edfu is one of those ports in which everyone gets off the boat for the same thing at the same time, and the place becomes packed. So, yeah, it was a bit of a mad house … but our time traveling couple from the flight to Luxor made another appearance. (This would be the third and final time. Quite appropriate.)

Not wifi, not a basket, not a rack of ribs. But is the object in his other hand possibly a blueberry muffin?

Mohamed had left us for emergency business he needed to tend to back in Giza, so Ahmed was our guide for the day and, smartly, took us through a side entrance. There's an interesting aspect of Edfu when it comes to the stargate symbolism in that it appears differently at this temple than in other locations. Instead of the hieroglyphs adorning either side of gateways, you'll find these glyphs within the story text of the temple. Edfu is an archive, a repository of information the ancient Egyptians wanted to retain, I believe, because they realized there was an eminent end to their culture, and they wanted some of that information to survive. Thus, Edfu isn't a stargate, but it contains information about stargates from which we can glean some understanding about how the ancient world worked. We find the hieroglyphs in text on the exterior walls, in passageways, on interior walls, and we passed many as we entered the open-air passage between the enclosure wall and temple. We even find a piece talking about a great many stargates, which is quite fascinating to comprehend. The group found many of these, but it almost became too much, and we needed to get to that "A" word.

It was there I launched into the story of Zep Tepi and the Primeval Ones, the story from which Plato's Atlantis originated, as told to Solon a couple hundred years before him. Instead of repeating the whole story in text here, I'll provide a video snippet of some of the basics.

From there, Ahmed showed the group the "WiFi" glyph within the temple itself — this really isn't WiFi, of course, it's an offering of some sort that we don't quite understand at this point. Some think it's a rack of ribs, but ribs aren't connected vertically in the middle like this representation does. To be honest, there are some hieroglyphs we simply don't understand yet because they're not used very often at all or only once in all the material that has been found to date. Sometimes we find only a single usage. In any case, it's not WiFi or a rack of ribs or Ahmed's suggestion of a basket. We need more context.

Important to us inside the temple were the scenes of levitation. This is represented as a "lasso" of energy surrounding the temple in one scene and levitating the temple in the next. This is depicted twice at Edfu, but unfortunately, the prettier version of this in a back room was inaccessible due to some restoration work. Instead, we dealt with the loud, overcrowded main hall, but it served our purposes.

We also find this scene of levitation at Kom Ombo, which is really our one primary tie-in to our stargates-based tour there. We tour this temple, however, because … well, to be honest, all the boats dock there, specifically, to tour the island. It's a smaller temple, and it's interesting that it is a dual temple, setup for both Horus and Sobek, so there are actually two entrances. It also has a secret passage that has been exposed over time and depictions of modern-looking surgical equipment on the back wall. It's a small temple even though it's a dual one, so it doesn't take long to walk

On the right: Levitation of the temple depiction at Kom Ombo. Less damaged versions can be found at Edfu and Esna temple.

through. Also worth exploring is the adjoining crocodile museum which houses the mummified crocodiles that were used to honor Sobek.

The rest of the evening involved the story of "murder pudding" over dinner and the Egyptian-themed party that night in which we dressed in traditional garb and danced. I can't dance worth a lick, but it was led by the crew on the cruise, and we all had fun. Ok, so what's murder pudding? I'm talking about Om Ali which is a dessert named after the first wife to the first of Egypt's Mamluk Sultans, Izz al-Din Aybak. Aybak had been killed in a plot by his second wife, Shajar al-Durr, who herself was killed in retribution of the murder. Om Ali created the dessert in celebration of al-Durr's death … and it is really freaking good. We haven't stopped talking about it.

Diving into a bowl of the "murder pudding."

Dressed for the occasion! On the sun deck after the dance.

Did We Find the Ark of the Covenant?

Egypt Tour Day 10: Philae, Unfinished Obelisk, and Elephantine Island

May 2, 2024

Article Notes: Due to certain restrictions when we gained access to a location that is off limits to the public, I was asked not to publish photos of the room that is believed once contained the Ark of the Covenant. This same restriction was applied last year when we visited the small pyramid on Elephantine Island. Since I don't want to get Mohamed in trouble, I've adhered to that restriction ... but I'll show you if you find me at an event and ask politely at my table.

How do you go out with a bang when it's your final day in Upper Egypt? You fill it with amazing locations like Philae, the Unfinished Obelisk, and Elephantine Island, the latter of which has always been a favorite of mine, especially with rumors of the Ark of the Covenant having been stored there. These are all in the area of Aswan where our Nile cruise ship has to stop because there's a dam in the way,

Temple on Philae flooded in 1908. (Brooklyn Museum Archives)

and we can't continue any further south, although there is not much further south as it is – Abu Simbel is the only prominent feature beyond, and by bus that is several hours. How would our final action-packed day of the tour play out?

We started the day by taking a motorboat to Philae – honestly, I thought we were visiting the quarry with the Unfinished Obelisk first, so I was surprised when we arrived at the wharf. We call it the Temple of Isis at Philae, but this isn't accurate. When the construction of the first of Aswan's dams was completed in 1902 a lake was formed behind the dam and flooded the temple on the island of Philae and continued to worsen as the height of the dam was raised over the years. With the construction of the second dam, Aswan High Dam, this flooding was going to be maintained year-

Temple of Isis in 2024.

round (there were a few months during the sluicing period of the first dam in which Philae was accessible), so an effort was made in the 1960s to save the temple, and it was moved to Agilkia Island. That is where we visit the temple today.

Some of my favorite water photos from Egypt are taken at Philae, and I always enjoy the boat ride there with the cool breeze off the water refreshing us. This is another temple that attracts quite a number of visitors, and why not? It's very picturesque resting in the middle of the lake. What's interesting to me about this temple is that it incorporates a lot of imagery of Hathor who plays an important healing role here, and there is a shrine dedicated to her here that emphasizes her connection to music. This is quite significant symbolism since it tells us that sound and music were used as part of the process of healing, and throughout the tour and our conversations that lasted deep into the night we kept coming back to the importance of energy, resonance, frequency, and vibration. Hathor embodies that. However, this is a Temple of Isis,

Hathor represented at Philae.

not Hathor, and it intrigues me that it's not at least a dual temple like Kom Ombo, but it's not.

We had a nice stroll about the island – there really isn't a lot regarding stargates here, but Philae is essential during a visit of Aswan – and we had a nice break with juices and other drinks at the café along the water when we finished. From there we motored back across the lake, bought a few items off the boat operator (they double as a vendor here), and we hopped back on the bus for the Unfinished Obelisk. Of note, while we passed it on our way from the wharf, we did not make a stop at the Nubian Museum this year. There just wasn't enough time in our day, but there are some important features there like the Napta Playa stones and several artifacts depicting portals that we have noted on other tours. Perhaps we'll revisit in November 2025 for the next tour.

The quarry of the Unfinished Obelisk is completely Aswan rose granite. This is where so many statues, sarcophagi, construction blocks, and, of course, obelisks come from. You can see plain as day where so many of these were carved from, but you can't fool us that these were carved out using basic diorite balls and copper tools. For one, copper can't cut into granite, and diorite balls would take painstaking years and would be nowhere near as precise. This is the primary purpose of coming to this location, to emphasize the fact that the ancient Egyptians had some sort of technology to create these things that we haven't yet found, something that has either been lost or deteriorated over time. The only drawback to visiting the quarry is that it gets blazing hot there, so much so that Lisa was actually feeling the heat through the soles of her shoes. A must during the visit to the Obelisk is also a visit to the bookshop on the way out of the complex. This is the best bookshop on the tour (second best would be at the Nubian Museum), and I've purchased several books there during my visits.

After a break for lunch back on the cruise ship, we hopped into another motorboat and jetted our way up the Nile to Elephantine Island. This has become a favorite of mine over the years since there's a lot going on here even though so much is in ruins, and we generally have the place to ourselves when we visit in the waning light of the afternoon. What all is present on Elephantine Island? How about stargates, imagery of Mayan headdresses, a small pyramid, and a possible resting place of the Ark of the Covenant. I covered some of this in a video I put together after my first visit three years ago.

This year on Elephantine Island, Ahmed brought us into the museum which I'd never been before on the island. What stood out to me there were the boomerangs, another connection we see from Egypt to Australia and we'd seen glimpses of previously at Hatshepsut's Temple and the visit to Punt Land. The notion the ancient Egyptians sailed the high seas has been met with scorn by traditionalists, but why? We know for a fact they got up to Ireland – ancient Egyptian beads have been found at Newgrange. So, why wouldn't they have also sailed in the other direction, eastward?

On our way up to the stargate area of the ruined temple at the top of the hill, we met a little black feline friend who followed us the rest of the way. She was quite vocal and quite happy to join us for the journey as we observed the gate and the decimated remains beyond, as if some sort of force had blown outward from the gate itself. If it had been a working stargate, had something violently

Destruction of the temple from the stargate beyond.

closed it from the other side? Did Thutmose III, to whom this temple had been dedicated and has long been associated with stargates, have a falling out with the factions on the other side?

The real treat for us today, however, was under the Temple of Khnum, the ram-headed god (neter, also nTr) of the Nile cataracts. After showing the group the Mayan headdress inside the temple – is this who they connected to with the stargate? – we ventured toward the temple exit when Kate asked, "Are we going to see where the Ark of the Covenant was?" Absolutely. We moved around the side of the building so I could show them where the small cave temple rests under the Temple of Khnum. It is within this small setting that, if you believe in the idea that the lost Ark of the Covenant made its way down to Ethiopia, it is here where it rested for some 400 years. Some people believe the Ark is still on Elephantine and is why excavations have been ongoing there for over 60 years even though it's a small island.

Temple of Khnum under which the Ark of the Covenant may have once rested.

As I stood pointing down the stairwell explaining these things, Ahmed spoke to the caretaker, and we were suddenly led down the stairs. Initially, I wasn't too surprised by this since I'd been down there before with Mohamed to take photos of the cave temple from outside a gated door but was happy this group would also get that opportunity. What shocked me, however, was when the caretaker actually opened the door and let us inside. This was rare, indeed. I didn't need to say a word to the group about how special this moment was; they were all cognizant of that fact and were extremely respectful and reverent of the moment. We could actually be standing where the Ark once stood – it could even be below our feet or behind the massive granite boulders in front of us. We paid our respects and took our photos; however, I can't share those photos since we agreed not to post them online publicly (but they'll be accessible in the member-only video blogs on the Connected Universe Portal). Doing so could get the caretaker in trouble (more

Gazing out across the Nile after our adventure on Elephantine Island.

on that when we get to the Great Pyramid), and that would hinder future groups from ever getting in again.

There's always something new for me when I return to Elephantine Island. Last year it was the ruined pyramid on the backside of the island. This year it was boomerangs and access to the temple that may have hidden the Ark. What a way to end our final day in the southern part of the country! This is one of the reasons why I keep going back to Egypt. There is so much to uncover and explore – it is almost endless. The mystery continues.

Our day ended with a jaunt over to a nearby beach where we all put our feet in the water, except Ellie who swam out to one of the bigger rocks and submerged herself in the Nile. This is always a magical way to end the Upper Egypt part of the tour.

How to Make the Great Pyramid Even More Mysterious

Egypt Tour Day 11: The Great Pyramid of Giza

May 5, 2024

Article Notes: I really can't explain the restriction on photography for us this time around. Within weeks of our visit, we all saw other groups posting photos from inside the Great Pyramid.

How does one go about making the Great Pyramid of Giza, one of the most enigmatic and mysterious structures on the planet, even more mysterious? Disallow photography. I was absolutely shocked. Each time I'd been inside the Great Pyramid prior to 2024, photography had been allowed, and I have some fantastic footage from inside. However, due to scores of people taking photos of themselves inside the coffer in the King's Chamber and posting them on social media, the Egyptian Antiquities Authority has been cracking down [at least that's what we were told]. As is so often the case, a few have ruined it for many, and I felt terrible for those in the group who had never been inside the Great Pyramid before. I have plenty of photos and footage from the other times I'd visited, so I wasn't upset for myself; I was upset for those who couldn't capture images of this once-in-a-lifetime opportunity.

Our day started in Aswan, however. We had a flight to catch from Upper Egypt back up north to Cairo – one last breakfast on our Nile Cruise. There was no murder pudding this time to send us off, however. Part of the drive takes us right over the Aswan dam, which provides for a nice distance photo of the Philae temple out in the lake where we had just been the previous morning. It was all going so fast now. The first few days of the tour had been a nice, slow ramp up to our deeper explorations, and now the days were flying by, the calendar pages tearing away at breakneck speed. Now, there were only two days left, and we were checking in to our final hotel and eating our farewell dinner at Mawlana BBQ.

Our private visit to the Great Pyramid of Giza began at 7:00 PM sharp and would conclude at 9:00 PM sharp. There's no messing around with time with these sorts of visits, and we took it right to the very end. Like I said, I was upset for the group to not get a chance to take photos inside the Great Pyramid, but when we were finished, they all said that wasn't a major issue for them. They all enjoyed their time in the pyramid and got to do the things they wanted to do, primarily, to meditate inside.

With Mohamed not rejoining us until the next day and Ahmed already dispatched to work with another tour, I was the sole guide for this venture. Since time was precious and I knew most members of the group wanted as much free time as possible inside the pyramid, my strategy was to give them a brief introduction to the chambers and then let them have at it. Since the subterranean chamber is a long trek and some didn't want to venture down the shaft, I took the group to the Queen's Chamber first even though the entrance to the subterranean chamber is first along the route. The Queen's Chamber, unfortunately, has become the storeroom for tools and equipment that are brought inside the Great Pyramid. This

From a previous visit: The niche in the Queen's Chamber with scorching and melted stone from something extremely hot.

room is off-limits to the public, so the authorities must consider the clutter irrelevant, but it's a real shame given that this is an ancient World Heritage monument.

Once inside, I first described the passage we used to enter the Great Pyramid, which is not the main entrance at all. What the public uses to enter the Great Pyramid of Giza is what's known as the "robber's entrance," purportedly created by Caliph al Ma'mun around 820 or 830 AD in order to steal the riches that were supposed to be inside. At this time, the white limestone casing stones were still intact on the pyramid, so the main entrance above was not visible. Thus, al-Ma'mun and his men blasted their way through. What's fascinating about this is, for one, of course, they didn't find any treasure, but they were also extremely precise in their penetration of the pyramid. Somehow, they curved their tunnel at the precise moment in order to intersect the small area where the main entrance shaft leads down to the subterranean chamber and the

Heading into the Great Pyramid of Giza for two hours with the Keeper of the Keys striking a pose on the right ... just before he performed a bag check for cell phones.

upper shaft that leads to the Grand Gallery and beyond. This causes some to speculate that al-Ma'mun may have had some sort of map, or there's an alternative theory that someone dug a way out from inside. The latter is a bit harder to believe because where inside the pyramid would a group digging themselves out have put the rubble they created? However, the precision of this intersection should cause us to question the details behind the al-Ma'mun story.

As for the Queen's Chamber, to me, this is the smoking gun behind the theories that the Great Pyramid of Giza was not a tomb but some sort of machine (some believe power plant). Here, in a corbeled niche on the left side of the room we find the black scorch marks of something extremely hot having burned here. In fact, it was so hot that it started to melt the limestone. The traditional idea is that this niche contained some sort of statue or idol, but that makes no sense given the physical evidence present. There is also a layer of salt on the walls of the chamber and a shaft that extends out from the niche and back into the pyramid about six meters in its original construction and seemingly lengthened in a rough manner by searchers in later years. Also present in this chamber are two very small shafts that were originally believed to be ventilation shafts but

The strange carved block of the Antechamber. This is not just for aesthetics.

are, apparently, more. One of the shafts is blocked by a limestone "door" with two copper "handles," the purpose for which we still don't know, but it should tell us there was a lot more going on with the Queen's Chamber than previously suspected. While this door was drilled into several years ago during a live broadcast, when a micro-snake camera was fished through the hole that was created the broadcast suddenly cut out. There is raw footage of what was recorded that can be found online and we have to trust what this very grainy, poor-quality video is showing us ... which isn't much other than looking at stone.

Yes, that's a lot to point out for just one chamber (and there's more), but I didn't want to tarry too long since we still had the Grand Gallery, Antechamber, King's Chamber, and Subterranean Chamber (for those willing) to explore, all of which I decided to describe once we were in the King's Chamber – there's just not a whole lot of room on the small platform in the Grand Gallery, and the Antechamber can really only hold about three people. In the video above you'll see me describe a number of interesting features about the King's Chamber, but the more and more I look at the Antechamber the more I believe it is a very important, often-overlooked piece of the whole functionality of the machine. The perfectly-carved vertical grooves here in the wall leading into the King's Chamber were already perplexing enough, but taking a better look at it this time, this block wraps around into the side walls of the Antechamber but only to a certain height. It's a very specially-carved piece for a specific function.

I could write about the Great Pyramid of Giza all day, and I will certainly be covering it in my forthcoming book. I do want to take a moment to address something I always say about touring Egypt – it is always life-changing. In my recent newsletter to subscribers of the Connected Universe Portal, I described the following:

> Let me first say that every time I've been to Egypt it has been a life-changing experience. I do not say that merely as a piece of marketing copy -- it seriously is life-changing. And this Stargates tour was no different, and in fact, was certainly even more so. We had an amazing group of like-

Farewell to another evening inside the Great Pyramid.

minded people who discussed -- deep into the night sometimes -- our soul connections to Egypt, to the universe, and beyond. This tour was a transformative upgrade on so many different dimensional levels, and I'm still trying to process it all. Once again, I received clarity on the direction of my next book, but I also received the inspiration of enlightenment and how to share that with the world through my work. Life was already changing this year, but now it will be on a whole other dimension. My time in Egypt was, seriously, a leveling up, and right now I'm figuring out the best way to present that to everyone.

As you can see above, one of the things I figured out – and it happened last time I was in Egypt – was the direction of my next book. If you've been following along then you know my next book was supposed to be on earth energy and a deeper dive into ancient sites of power and triangle areas of the world. It seemed like such a natural progression from *Travels Through Time* and my explorations into the fabric of the universe and what we call time. That meant my book on stargates, Atlantis, and ancient Egypt was to be put on the backburner to be the third installment in the series. After this adventure in Egypt, no … I must dive headlong into the stargates book and, instead, put the earth energy book on the backburner. I always find writing inspiration in Egypt, and this is the direction the universe has me pointed. There's still a lot of overlap between the two topics, so the direction of this blog won't change, but the focus will be shifted a bit. It's all part of the adventure!

Egyptian Goodbye, But Not Goodbye

Egypt Tour Day 12: The Civilization Museum and Tour Finale

May 8, 2024

Article Notes: There is definitely more to learn about this "Hanging Church" area since there are old maps which refer to the area as "Babylon." Is this, perhaps, where the real Hanging Gardens had been?

It's not really "goodbye" is it? The group that we had together on this second Stargates of Ancient Egypt Tour was absolutely amazing, very tight-knit, and we truly learned a lot from each other. That's not to take away from the other groups I've been involved with on my tours – all of them were also wonderful – but this one had a unique quality about it. I will never forget some of the immensely deep conversations we had about the nature of the universe, higher dimensions, the role of ancient Egypt, Atlantis, Lemuria, and other cultures in the distant past, and what that all means for us today. Thus, it was to be a bittersweet end to our fellowship when we set out that final morning. But it's not really the end, is it?

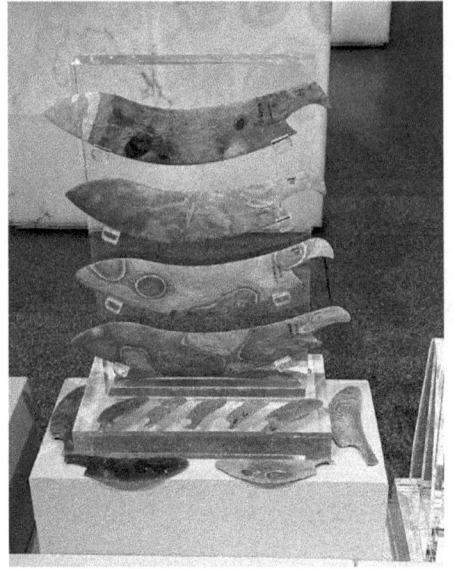
Finely crafted flint knives on display at the Civilization Museum.

Our last day together started with a trip to the Civilization Museum. It's not a particularly large museum, but it houses several interesting artifacts dating back to pre-diluvian times as well as the royal mummies. Mohamed was back with us and in fine form as he explained the discrepancies and unusual large gaps of time between eras and some of the advanced technology on display, particularly in the fine knives. We also saw examples of the spiral pattern in use on pottery and other items, something I'm also on the lookout for everywhere I go as I believe these spirals are depictions of portals or a memory of that ancient technology which connected worlds on multiple levels and dimensions – this was the Stargates of Ancient Egypt Tour, after all.

The royal mummies are always interesting to inspect, although this is another area in which no photos are allowed. This one I certainly understand – like historic paintings and vintage documents, flash photography would degrade the quality of these remains. (But don't even try to take a selfie down in that area against a blank wall. I've seen security pounce on people in the past for doing this even if there were no mummies in range.) The significant mummies to note are Hatshepsut and Thutmose III who do seem to have more elongated skulls. Now, these are not elongated like the Paracas skulls, but there is something unusual about the length of the back of their heads, and you can see it a bit in their descendants as well as you walk through the exhibit. The other really interesting mummy is that of the famous Ramsses II who carved his name into everything around Egypt, making it a bit more difficult to date some objects – and should be a lesson to us that other Egyptian rulers over the millennia had done the same. Ramsses had a very different look about him with his red hair and hooked nose. Now, he lived until he was 93, so the red in his hair at that age was dyed, but in his youth it was flaming red, and combined with his rather different nose ought to tell us he came from somewhere other than traditional Egypt. We do know his lineage, of course, as the son of Seti I, but there is certainly something peculiar about Ramsses II. After his death, there were power struggles in Egypt, which may be attributed to the fact he lived so long that he out-aged his heirs. A 93-year-old man at that time in history was rare, indeed … can we simply surmise there was definitely something different about Ramsses II without getting too speculative?

Following some time spent shopping in the newly opened lower-level mall area of the museum, Mohamed took us to a location in Cairo that was not on the original itinerary. While not "ancient Egyptian," we ventured to the cemetery of St. George's Church, a Greek Orthodox church that is absolutely beautiful. Here, we observed obelisks and other symbolism from ancient times that we now see in a more modern, albeit still historic, setting. Of course, we had to venture inside the church to take a few photos, but then we also trekked down the road a short distance to the Hanging Church, an old Coptic Christian church in which, again, we see a lot of that ancient symbolism, but it also has calls back to the story of the levitating mountain that we visited on my first tour of Egypt three years ago.

After that little surprise side trip, we had a farewell lunch – yes, we had just had a farewell dinner the night before – and headed back to the hotel, officially ending our tour. But that did not end our

Inside the beautiful Coptic Hanging Church.

fellowship. Between hanging out at the poolside bar, dinner, and sharing in drinks, we enjoyed each other's company late into the night, much as we had the entire tour. Again, this was a fantastic group to get to know and develop lifelong friendships with – and that is the part I really enjoy about these tours. Yes, there are some amazing ancient sites we get to see, there's definitely some fantastic information we get to learn, and new discoveries are made along the way, but it is the connection with the people on the adventure that's the most important. I can absolutely say that I met people from my soul family on this journey, and I can't wait until we meet again at some undetermined point in the future.

Evidence in Egypt of a Parallel Universe?

Discoveries and New Theories in Egypt Part 2

May 16, 2024

Article Notes: Here, more than two weeks after I returned from Egypt, we come to the end of our Stargates journey ... for now. During the tour, I tried to keep up daily like I had the first time I went to Egypt and made sure I had a video posted to the Connected Universe Portal every day. That has become more of a challenge to do so as a tour host. There were plenty of times I was writing blog articles while on bus rides to and from sites, but sometimes those bus rides weren't so long. At the hotels and on the cruise, I found some time, but I was also trying to be a good host and spend time with the tour guests. With this group, we really hit it off well, and to this day, we still drop messages in our WhatsApp chat. We all became fast friends.

It's hard to top the discoveries we made during the first week of the Stargates of Ancient Egypt Tour this year. How do you beat finding the ancient symbolism and structures we did in the catacombs of Alexandria or the construction methods used in the Room of Ships at Abydos? As much as the tour is about showing guests some of the more fascinating aspects of ancient Egyptian mysteries, we are always on the lookout for new discoveries – there is so much yet to still uncover! I've mentioned before this was my most impactful experience exploring Egypt. What did we find during the second week of this year's tour? Did we find evidence of a parallel universe?

Nut's Parallel Universe

The answer to the above question **is** an emphatic ... yes! While this was a "stargates" tour, any sort of evidence of parallel universes or dimensions wasn't necessarily something I was specifically looking for, although I'd certainly be happy if we encountered it. Like we did during the last tour, I figured our group would be on a scavenger hunt for the classic "saba" hieroglyphs – and we did find plenty of those along the way. But as I mentioned during the original Valley of the Kings blog article, there is much more to be gleaned from the roof of the sarcophagi chamber within the tomb of Ramses V and VI than just Nut of the Day and Nut of the Night. Yes, that is a part of it, but that's just scratching the surface.

Again, Nut (pronounced 'noot') is the goddess (neter, also nTr) of the sky, and she is typically depicted stretched out across the top of her murals, from horizon to horizon. In this particular chamber, she is depicted twice, back-to-back, mirror images, one with stars (the night) and one with the sun and stars (the day). The ancient Egyptians, however, weren't just so blatantly obvious and one-dimensional. Their work was loaded with symbolism, and I think it's quite evident that here we see the concept of duality, the hermetic principle of "as above, so below." And why wouldn't we? Elsewhere in the tomb, we find other mirror imagery as well as the

Nut on the ceiling in the Tomb of Ramses V / VI.

ouroboros, the snake eating its own tail, our oldest alchemical symbol which signifies a constant recycling and renewal of, not just the soul, but of the Earth and of the universe.

There is also the symbolism of duality contained within the ouroboros as well, and I cover this extensively in my book, *Travels Through Time*. Also, within that book, I link the concepts of the ouroboros to the scientific neutrino research conducted in Antarctica in which the scientists there concluded that the unusual results were indicative of a parallel universe running in reverse time. Is this what we're seeing on the roof of this chamber? Are the mirror images of Nut showing us two different parallel worlds? I believe so. I believe we're getting a glimpse of the principles of the universe, the dualistic nature of this world and the world beyond our own. How does this relate at all to stargates? Against the wall – and elsewhere throughout the tomb – you find the hieroglyphs for "star house." And how does one get to his or her star house? The connections are everywhere.

The other question we left unanswered was the question of who really built the tombs in the Valley of the Kings if not the ancient Egyptians. This one is certainly open for debate, but really any civilization before them. We see across the world a variety of civilizations having spent time underground and those underground systems being used multiple times throughout their history. So, was it some pre-diluvian culture? Probably. Which one? That, I can't quite answer. Civilization has risen and fallen many, many times over the millennia. Could it have been Atlanteans? Yes. Could it have been survivors of the last magnetic pole shift? Yes. We don't have enough information to say, specifically, who it was, but I believe the evidence that is present, like the unfinished wall I discussed in the Valley of the Kings article, is compelling.

Edfu Stargates

As previously mentioned, the temple of Edfu was quite packed with people but more inside around the Holy of Holies. The outer perimeter was generally bereft of the throngs, and we were able to explore more freely. This was great since most of the stargate symbolism can be found there, and we had the space to examine them, as well as cover the pieces of the story of Atlantis.

Amongst the plethora of stargate symbols we discovered on the walls at Edfu – again, they're found not on the doorways here but within the text – we found a different variation. In part, it was similar to ones we've seen before with the three vertical lines. The vertical lines added to this gives us a plural version of the term: stargates. This time, however, there was an additional curved symbol along with it. Ahmed wasn't sure exactly what it meant – did it give us a specific number of stargates, perhaps? I consulted with Mohamed after the fact and, according to him, this just gives us an additional letter: "w."

"Stargates" in the middle of the bottom line. Yes, there is "stargate" just above.

How did I not see that? I've been studying the hieroglyphic language off and on for three years. Ok, I'm no hieroglyphic scholar here, and my studies have been extremely sporadic. So, what this does for us is give us a way to pronounce the word for "stargates." Stargate is "saba" and now stargates is "sabaw."

(Addendum: Before publishing this article, I broke out my book on the hieroglyphic language and found that the hieroglyph inscribed, which seems to resemble an open quote mark, looks like a variation of the small spiral which depicts a 'w', but that is also pretty close to the one that depicts the number '100.' Which is it? Since we're talking multiple stargates, I'm guessing this is 103 stargates ... but maybe we also pronounce it sabaw.)

(Side note: You've seen me here use both the words hieroglyph and hieroglyphic. Here's the difference: one is a noun and one is an adjective. We generally use the adjective when talking about the language as a whole, i.e. the hieroglyphic language. We use the term hieroglyph when talking about the individual glyphs, in other words, the hieroglyphs on the walls.)

Archive Addendum: After additional conversations with Mohamed following the publication of this article, we now agree this variation of glyphs means "hundreds of stargates."

Hiding Evidence in the Great Pyramid Queen's Chamber

I wish I could have gotten a photo of this to compare, but damn that restriction on taking photos inside the Great Pyramid of Giza. Perhaps they knew that Ricksecker bastard was coming again to continue unveiling their secrets … well, probably not.

I had mentioned in the Great Pyramid article that the Queen's Chamber was filled with equipment and, essentially, being used as a storeroom. Well, some of that equipment was a collection of power tools strewn about in front of the niche I always point to as a "smoking gun." There was so much crap in the way that I could barely step up to the niche to show our guests the scorching and melting of the stone, but I should have rummaged through it before we left the room. What would I have been looking for? Well, I *did* notice a power saw amongst the items, but I should have looked around for a sander. Why?

Something immediately stood out to me when we entered the room. The scorch marks and melted stone didn't seem to go as far up the niche as I've seen the past. In fact, that whole back wall of the niche looked … lighter in color. I pointed this out to the group since I had just shown them a presentation a couple days beforehand with a photo of this strange feature which, to me, is indicative of something very hot having once stood there, a part of the machine. However, this time, it just really wasn't as prominent and noticeable as it has been in the past. It was, in part, there, but is the Egyptian

Image of the niche of the Queen's Chamber from my first visit in 2021.

Antiquities Authority actually sanding down this wall in the niche to hide the evidence? I seriously hope they're not, but if they are taking these kinds of measures to maintain their current narrative about ancient Egyptian history, then there is nothing whatsoever we can trust from them going forward. Of course, most of my colleagues already only trust them as far as they can throw the Great Sphinx.

So, there you have it! There were myriad new discoveries we made along the way during our epic adventure through Egypt, and I'm confident we'll find even more during the Stargates of Ancient Egypt Tour III in November 2025. And this doesn't even touch on the personal discoveries made along the way. There were plenty of those, too! I always say that visiting Egypt is a life-changing experience, and it certainly has been once again.

Archive of the Connected Universe: Volume 1

Part 4

Stargates and Portals

Notes on Part 4

Following the Stargates of Ancient Egypt tour, I dove headlong into writing *Portals to the Stars: Inside Stargates, Atlantis, and Secrets of Ancient Egypt*. The following articles certainly reflect my writing inspiration at the time as I dove into, not only stargates and portals in ancient Egypt, but also elsewhere throughout our world. This became an interesting time for the blog as I reduced output to once per week, sometimes even 10 or more days, while I concentrated on writing the book, and the articles I did write became a bit of a reflection of where my head was at. The content here isn't verbatim what you'll find in *Portals to the Stars*, but you'll definitely see where some of that material originated in raw form.

Are Portals Hiding in the Wilderness?

Be Careful Where You Step

May 24, 2024

Article Notes: Ok, we're really not done with stargates, just the Stargates of Ancient Egypt tour. Here, we start delving into portals of another nature, revisiting some of the material from Alaska's Mysterious Triangle *with more recent discoveries and insights from around the globe and, well ... in the wilderness. This eventually became the basis for my "Portals in the Wilderness" chapter in* Portals to the Stars *where I really expanded the scope to include a QHHT past life regression conducted by Katherine Swinn. I love it when small beginnings turn into something much bigger.*

In an interesting twist, when recently speaking at the MUFON International Symposium, my colleague, Jason Quitt, informed me the original X-points article on NASA's website in which they acknowledged these points in space are actually portals has since been removed. Sure enough, I took a look and the article is gone, *although you can find articles from other science-related outlets like phys.org discussing NASA's portals back in 2012 in their article "Hidden Portals in Earth's Magnetic Field." What is NASA trying to hide?*

Also to note, Ronny's response in the original article was a video snippet I provided within the blog which I have, instead, transcribed here for the reader.

It's become a concern for many in recent years, and the notion has been gaining traction. With so many disappearances occurring in bizarre fashion out in the wilderness we need to seriously consider some bizarre possibilities. Or *are* those possibilities really that bizarre? Perhaps they're more natural than previously perceived. I asked this question of my friend and colleague, researcher Ronny LeBlanc on a recent episode of *Connecting the Universe's Edge of the Rabbit Hole*:

"Do you think … you have a lot of these missing people cases, and sometimes these missing people are found, or they find their way back and they'll talk about … 'I was on the path, heard a noise off to the side, I took a step off the path, couldn't find what the noise was, turned around to get back on the path, and it was gone.' They're lost out in the woods. So, do you think that some of these missing people cases are maybe … they're stepping into – whether it's a portal or a vortex or whatever mode of transportation it is that the Sasquatch uses. Do you they're stepping into something like that?"

Ronny, who appeared on the first four seasons of *Expedition Bigfoot* on the Travel Channel, responded with the following:

"Yeah, I do. I think there's, you know, the Algonquian tribe talk about in Vermont that there is a specific boulder that if you step on

A portal in the wilderness most likely won't be an obvious gateway appearing in the middle of the path.

it, you're going somewhere. And so, they talk about it being this portal. And I think that's where some of these reports where people are going into areas and they're having rocks thrown at them or they're having these 'Bigfoot encounters' is they could be protecting people from going into these spots where you're walking in through a portal or something like this, because you just have these incredible stories where people are there one minute, and they're completely gone. David Paulides' work, *Missing 411*, terrifying stuff when you start realizing and reading about how people are just gone and no trace. What is taking them? Where are they going?"

I covered the phenomenon of these strange disappearances in my book *Alaska's Mysterious Triangle* since from 1988 up until the filming of the television show on which I was featured, *The Alaska Triangle*, it was estimated that 16,000 people had gone missing in Alaska during that timeframe. That's quite a large number since the entire state of Alaska only has a population that is about the same as the city of San Francisco. It's such a vast and large state as well, about two and a half times the state of Texas, so yes, some people probably really did get eaten by a bear or gored by a moose while venturing much too far out into the vast reaches of the frozen tundra. However, that 16,000 is still a massive number.

Some of these disappearances aren't even out in the middle of nowhere in which there are no witnesses or of a situation in which you have to trust the word of a seemingly-faithful hiking companion who is at a loss as to what happened to his or her friend. These things happen right in plain sight, too. In 2012, runner Michael LeMaitre disappeared right in the middle of the Mount Marathon race in Seward, Alaska. Along with all the other racers in the run, LeMaitre had ventured 1.5 miles up the mountain, but he never came back down. An extensive search of the area revealed nothing.

Discussions of portals usually tend to get tossed into the circle of metaphysical "woo," but portals do truly exist in nature. NASA has been so fully committed to the portals they found in space just outside of Earth that they sent satellites up there years ago to study the phenomenon. These particular portals occur at the convergence of the Earth's magnetic shield and the solar wind, are a variety of different sizes, and open and close at random intervals. Scientists still haven't been able to make much sense of these other than, when open, they allow the solar wind to penetrate the Earth much quicker. Likely to steer clear of using the term "portal," they called these "X-points," but they are portals, nonetheless.

Taking this even further, scientists have attempted to create operating wormholes in the lab – and have succeed! Since it was related to my examination of the nature of time and real time travel, I reported on this in my book *Travels Through Time*:

> "Published in the journal *Nature* in November 2022, scientists revealed they had created a baby "wormhole" on a quantum system in a laboratory environment. A rupture in space-time was not created in this experiment, and the technology is very, very far away from becoming something

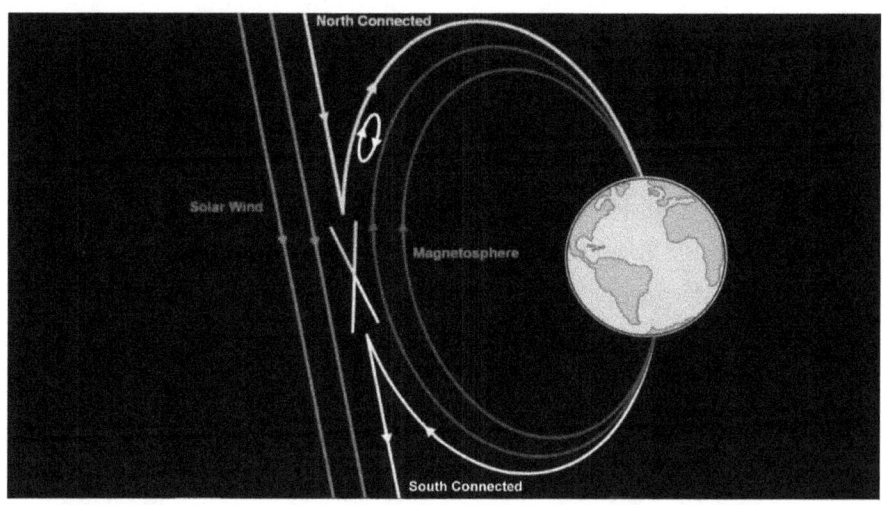

X-points spawn where the solar wind and Earth's magnetosphere meet. (NASA image)

we could send people through, but study co-author Joseph Lykken of Fermilab, America's particle physics and accelerator laboratory stated, "We have something that in terms of the properties we look at, it looks like a wormhole. We're in experimental science, and we've been struggling now for a very long time to find a way to explore these ideas in the laboratory. And that's what's really exciting about this. It's not just, 'Well, wormholes are cool.' This is a way to actually look at these very fundamental problems of our universe in a laboratory setting."

If people stepping off the path out in the wilderness are, in fact, stepping into some sort of portal or wormhole, where do they go? Sure, we've had a few return to tell their tale, as depicted at the very beginning of this article. What about the ones that don't? Could they be entering into some other dimension? Venturing off to some other location in the cosmos? What about another point in time? Let me grab another snippet, this time from *Alaska's Mysterious Triangle*:

"Let's revisit the missing Douglas Skymaster airplane

from Chapter 2 and we'll again ask, if this airplane did disappear into a portal, where did it go? If it did find itself in another place in time much more extensively than Bruce Gernon's experience in the Bermuda Triangle, where was that other point in time? Could it have jumped into the far past, say ... 500 years ago? If it possibly did, what would a massive Douglas Skymaster look like to the indigenous peoples of the far north at that time? They would have had no concept of what an airplane is. But something extremely large flying through the air with a wide wingspan and extremely loud sounds emanating from it ... how would they perceive that? Is it possible some of our missing airplanes lost through portals which took them back in time could have become some of the thunderbird legends of old? Were the indigenous peoples just describing modern technology they witnessed in the only context they knew at that time? It's certainly worth considering."

Did the Douglas Skymaster that disappeared in 1950 slip through a portal to another point in time and become a thunderbird legend?

We may never know definitively why these disappearances occur and where people truly disappear to, but I believe we need to keep an open mind about what may be happening throughout our world. As we've been exploring strange energetic hotspots around our world, these unfortunate incidents have been one of those head-scratching phenomena that occur in these areas. We'll dive deeper into the possibilities behind it all as we continue our journey.

Embracing Stargate and Portal Synchronicities

A Journey into the New Book

May 30, 2024

Article Notes: The reading referenced in the opening paragraph was the QHHT session Katherine Swinn performed that ended up included in Portals to the Stars *and an interview on Gaia TV.*

Signs are all around us. Trust the universe. These are a couple things I picked up while I was in Egypt last month. I've kept these things in mind, but when I posted the previous article, "Are Portals Hiding in the Wilderness," I wasn't expecting any immediate synchronicities. Yet, those synchronicities were, actually, almost immediate. A friend of mine reached out to me about some information she had gleaned from a reading which entailed portals and the Sasquatch's use of this method of transportation. I asked if she had just read my article thinking, perhaps, that reading the article had inspired her to share the information. She had not read the article. Later that morning, I recorded an interview with Blurry Creatures podcast (I'll link this when it becomes publicly available), and right off the bat they asked me about Bigfoot and its use of portals out in the wild. Again, I asked if they had just read the article I published that morning. Again, they had not. What else can I do but take this as a sign, the universe using synchronicity to guide me down this path of research?

I may have mentioned it in this blog somewhere, and I've certainly mentioned it on social media and in interviews lately that I have redirected the direction of the *Connecting the Universe* book series. It made logical sense that the second book in the series, following *Travels Through Time*, would be a piece on earth energy. It only made sense that after discussing the nature of time and the innerworkings of the universe that I would then tackle the energy of our planet, working from the ground up, so to speak (pun intended). However, Egypt once again affected the direction of my writings, and here I find myself diving headlong into a work on stargates, Atlantis, and ancient Egypt. I was always going to write this book anyway, but now I feel an overwhelming passion to just do it now. Trust the universe.

My goal is to have this book out by the holiday season, sequestering myself into a type of "hermit mode" over the summer to knock this out. Fortunately, I'd already written some pieces for it before I started, and I have plenty of work to draw from, having spoken on this topic for several years now. (For specifics, watch my interview with George Noory on Gaia TV, "Egypt's Area 51: Stargates and Wormholes," and several of my stargates videos on my YouTube channel.) Yet, it's still a lot to have to cover in a short amount of time, so if it seems I've gone a bit quieter than usual over the next few months, you now know why. Just to give you a bit of a sneak peek, here are the first couple rough lines from the "What is a Stargate?" chapter:

> "What is a stargate? First of all, stargates don't look like the giant massive circle devices found in the 1994 *Stargate* film and the several television show spinoffs that followed.

Capturing the light inside a stargate chamber in the Temple of Seti at Abydos.

When we begin to examine these structures more closely, we'll discover they come in all shapes and sizes and are found in more locations around the globe than just under the sands of ancient Egypt (although this book will certainly have a distinctive focus there)."

All right, that's not much at all. So, what's really going to be in this book? Well, it's not going to be exclusively about stargates. Yes, those are definitely going to be a major part of it, but I don't intend to duplicate the effort of my friend and colleague, Mohamed Ibrahim, who I found out just a couple months ago is in the midst of writing a *Stargates of Ancient Egypt* book, named for our tour. As previously mentioned, I will also be covering aspects of Atlantis (which I covered in some detail in the blog on Edfu temple) and other secrets and discoveries in ancient Egypt. How do all of these things tie in and relate to each other – and not only in Egypt, but around the world? And given the synchronicity with which I began this article, how will I incorporate portals out in the wilderness to such a project?

During the short time I've been writing this blog, I've been chronicling a journey, and sometimes that journey veers off in unexpected directions. This direction wasn't necessarily unexpected, but the turn down this road came a little earlier than originally anticipated. Thus, you can expect many of my upcoming blog articles to pertain to this subject, although you'll still see some one-offs on other topics that pique my interest or come to light along the way, such as opining about an article I might post for a Mike's Morning Mug. And besides, stargates are related to the energy of the Earth anyway, as we'll come to see, so a lot of that material will find its way into this book as well. While the direction of this journey may have changed a bit, just keep in mind it's all part of the adventure!

What is a Real Stargate?

The Truth Beyond Science Fiction

June 4, 2024

What exactly is a stargate? I teased you loyal readers in my last article "Embracing Stargate and Portal Synchronicities" when I gave you a very brief rough snippet from the new book I'm in the middle of writing:

> "What is a stargate? First of all, stargates don't look like the giant massive circle devices found in the 1994 Stargate film and the several television show spinoffs that followed. When we begin to examine these structures more closely, we'll discover they come in all shapes and sizes and are found in more locations around the globe than just under the sands of ancient Egypt (although this book will certainly have a distinctive focus there)."

Again, that doesn't touch on much at all, which is why I'm following up with this article. I can't tease like that and not follow through, although I can't give away all the goods here. That's what

What AI believes a stargate in Egypt looks like differs from reality. (Adobe Firefly AI).

the new book coming later this year is for. But let's delve into a few of the particulars here while I'm in the process of putting this new work together. Ok, what exactly is a stargate, and do we truly have them here on Earth?

A stargate is a doorway designed by an intelligent being that gives one access to other locations in the cosmos or on Earth, other dimensions, other levels of consciousness, or other points in time. These differ from portals in that portals are naturally occurring – although an intelligent being may have harnessed the power a portal and bent it to its will in order to create a stargate with it. Why am I saying "intelligent being" and not "human"? Simple. A stargate doesn't have to be of human design, it could have been designed by other beings within the universe *or even on this planet*, although, yes, a human could have designed a stargate as well.

In my article "Are Portals Hiding in the Wilderness?" I already talked about NASA's findings in space regarding "X-points," naturally occurring portals at the point in which the Earth's magnetosphere meets with the solar wind from the Sun, and the progress scientists have made in creating baby wormholes in the lab. So, I'm not going to dive into those topics in detail here, but it's

Alessandro Barsanti at the "Unfinished Pyramid" at Zayet El Aryan in 1904.

important to note that, through these examples, portals and stargates aren't just fanciful ideas created by our science fiction writers. These are real concepts acknowledged by science, backed up by Einstein's theory of general relativity, and scientists are busy trying to create these things with modern technology. Will they be able to do it?

While controversial in nature, I believe we already have – at least in the far distant past. There may actually be modern stargates and lab-created portals at work, but for now we can only view those possibilities as anecdotal stories. For example, in an interview I conducted with George Noory on *Beyond Belief* on Gaia TV, I discussed stargates and "Egypt's Area 51." Egypt's Area 51 is an Egyptian military installation at Dahshur right next to the Red and Bent Pyramids, and it contains the remains of several other pyramids within its complex. Unfortunately, these ruined pyramids in the area known as Zawyet El Aryan are completely off-limits, but their

Crew in the "Unfinished Pyramid" in 1904. Note the sheer size of the structure.

structures were massive. See how small Italian researcher Alessandro Barsanti looks in the photo below from 1904? However, the fact that these pyramids are in ruins haven't stopped a rumor that has come out of this military installation that modern Egyptians have an operating stargate on base which resembles something like an aurora on the ground, and you must step into it to pass through. It sounds almost like what may be happening to people out in the wilderness, although the portals out in the wild don't appear to have the aurora aspect. Again, this is an anecdotal story, and we have no photographic or written proof that this stargate truly exists, but it's still interesting to note, and we must keep our eyes and ears open for any new details that might emerge.

Now, I did mention I believe we have already had this technology in the distant past, and I've spent three tours in Egypt researching the ancient stargates there. The title image at the top of the article is what AI thinks a stargate in ancient Egypt looks like, but it's really far different, as we'll come to see. We'll explore ancient stargates in other parts of the world within the book, but for now in this article, let's examine stargates in ancient Egypt.

Where are they? Everywhere. Seriously. When you know what to look for, you start seeing the symbolism everywhere. It became like a scavenger hunt for us during the first Stargates of Ancient Egypt tour as we explored temples and spotted the inscriptions (for reference, see the video in the "Lord of the Pleiades" article). We see stargates at the temples of Abydos, Dendera, Luxor, Karnak, and more. My favorite stargate setup, however, is that of Hatshepsut's Mortuary Temple. Below is an excerpt from *Travels Through Time* describing how the stargate was laid out there.

> "At Hatshepsut's mortuary temple outside of Luxor, we find a massive staircase that stretches upward into the temple, which is built into the cliff face, and is the beginning of a direct path into the Holy of Holies. The sides of this staircase are flanked by sculptures of falcons, representing the god Horus, but on closer inspection, one can see that these falcons have snake tails that lead all the way up the staircase. It is believed by many that these falcons were once snake heads, possibly cobras, re-carved in ancient times when the temple was repurposed. Back in Chapter 1, we discussed how the serpent in the ancient world was a symbol of energy – life energy, healing energy, universal energy. To the southeast side of the temple are the remains of the base of a small pyramid – there is almost nothing left. Engaging in the debate on whether Egyptian pyramids were power plants or not is beyond the scope of this book, but whether you believe it was a power plant or that it was harnessing electrical energy from the telluric currents of the earth, it was there to power the temple. As one walks up the staircase, into the courtyard, and into the *barque* hall for Amun, each

entrance that is passed through is marked with the hieroglyphs for "stargate," or saba. The barque hall, literally means transportation for the gods, but there is more beyond, although the next chamber, the Holy of Holies, is blocked by a set of Egyptian guards. If one arrives early enough before the crowds and offers a large tip to these guards, entrance might be granted – but you didn't hear that from me. Inside the Holy of Holies is a cartouche full of stars, the ultimate symbol of passage to the cosmos. So, here we have an amazing setup: the symbolism of energy along the stairs, each entrance adorned with the stargate hieroglyphs, the cartouche full of stars within the most sacred room of the whole complex, and a pyramid powering it all. This lost esoteric symbolism and history is why I have joined forces with Egyptologist Mohamed Ibrahim to host an annual "Stargates of Ancient Egypt" tour."

Was there an activation for the stargate besides just walking into it? Was it the energy of the small pyramid there that was powering it? Perhaps in this case it was the pyramid, but only a few other temples, like on Elephantine Island, had these adjoining pyramids. However, we see depicted on the walls in several locations the offering of white cakes made with monatomic white gold powder that, when ingested, has a transformative effect on the body. A perfect example is the frieze below which is just outside two stargate chambers at Seti's Temple at Abydos.

What type of transformative effect does it have? From the studies David Hudson performed on the substance a couple decades ago, when heated to certain temperatures it becomes invisible but can't be manipulated. In other words, even if it's invisible to the eyes, stirring the powder should alter how the powder is distributed in the dish once it's cooled back down and you can see it again. The monatomic white gold powder in these experiments, when cooled,

Mohamed Ibrahim pointing out where in the Hall of Ptah-Soker the monatomic white gold cakes are offered before entering the stargate chambers.

looked as if it hadn't been touched at all. So, what happened to it? Did it not only become cloaked to the human eye but also disappear entirely, perhaps off to another dimension?

Sure, this bit becomes a bit speculative, but we're seeing all these pieces come into place as to how these stargates in Egypt worked. Apparently, there were a lot of moving parts to make it all work, but imagine stepping out of the stargate and walking down the stairs of Hatshepsut's temple to gaze upon the Nile beyond. It would have been majestic. Is this also why we see the depiction of a figure in a Mayan headdress in the Temple of Satet down the hill from the stargate on Elephantine Island? These are things we'll be exploring in the new book.

Last March of the Ents

What Have We Done to Our World?

June 8, 2024

A northern rātā tree in New Zealand which looks strikingly just like an Ent out of J.R.R. Tolkein's *Lord of the Rings* was just crowned "Tree of the Year" in that country in which most of the trilogy movies had been filmed. I made a Mike's Morning Mug post of the announcement on my social media, but seeing this tree standing sentinel, the last from a forest which has since disappeared, brings me to a question I have asked several times before: "What have we done?"

I travel a lot, and here I am sitting in a hotel lobby in Boulder, Colorado, waiting for my call time to film another interview with Gaia TV. I both fly and drive quite often – there's no way getting around that given what I do – and until a teleporter or Wonka Vision is invented, I'm going to have to continue to do so for quite a long time. However, there have been many times as I fly into various cities that I stare down from my window and gaze upon the urban sprawl and decay and ask that question above: "What have we done?"

The "Walking Tree" in New Zealand won Tree of the Year. (Gareth Andrews photo)

Tolkien's depiction of the Ents, the destruction of Fangorn Forest, and the Ents' invasion of Isengard, the medieval industrial complex created by Saruman and his orcs, was the author's way of voicing his displeasure for how much modern industry was (and still is) encroaching upon the peacefulness of the rural countryside. Yes, our global population keeps growing, and I'm all for advancing our technology – that's how this blog is coming to you today. But there is a connection with nature and the planet around us that we have definitely lost over the millennia.

I've been writing a book on stargates and portals, putting a pause on the earth energy book I'd been composing (although, there is a direct relationship between both), and there is no doubt in my mind that ancient peoples on our planet had a more symbiotic relationship with the natural world around them than we could ever imagine. They had a direct understanding of natural cycles, the balance between humans and other life on this planet, and the type of language the earth spoke to them. While several ancient cultures built magnificent structures and had advanced forms of technology, they were still reverent of the natural world around them, respected it, and listened to what it had to say.

When I travel, I try to make some sort of effort to get out into the wilderness to whatever degree I'm able (hopefully, I don't fall through a portal). It's important to breathe in the fresh air and listen to the rustle of the trees in the breeze, birds chirping, and the rushing of water down a creek. During this trip, I took a stroll down along Boulder Creek which maintains wonderful scenic walking and

The view along the Mount Sanitas Trailhead.

bicycle paths up into the mountains. I've hiked around the Boulder area before when I've been in town, taking in a 5 ½ hour jaunt along the Mount Sanitas Trailhead two years ago which was absolutely gorgeous. My body paid for it later, but it was completely worth it to enjoy the natural splendor.

Even locally back home, I try to take a handful of walks every day to stretch the legs and get some fresh air after sitting in front of the computer for far too long doing things like writing this blog, working on books, and editing video. Fortunately, my home city of Cleveland had the foresight to preserve the vast Metroparks area which is loaded with hiking trails, ponds, picnic areas, and a place I highlighted the other week in a reel on social media: Music Mound. This is a performance area for not only music but also plays and other live acts on a stage built of earth and stone. I conducted a little filming there for a project I'm involved with and paid homage to it while discussing how the supernatural is just as natural as the rest of

Stage left, Music Mound in the Cleveland Metroparks.

the world around us.

We need to take care of this magnificent blue marble we call home, however, and stop corrupting its beauty and the lifeblood it gives us. We can't live here without it, and while at some point in time we will need to figure out how to colonize some other planet in the universe before the Sun engulfs Earth billions of years from now, it is our home for the foreseeable future, and we need to appreciate and take care of her.

Not Your Grandfather's UFOs – Or Are They?

The "New" Claims by Harvard Researchers

June 14, 2024

Article Notes: When I published this article, one of the researchers on this project – ironically, the one from Montana, not Harvard – reached out to defend the research the team has been conducting. Michael Paul Masters commented, "In our June article, we were simply arguing for scientific openness to an idea that involved multiple explanations centering on an advanced civilization sequestering itself in Earth's environs, adding new information and a different perspective to an old idea."

My point wasn't to dismiss the research; my point was in the way it was being presented as some sort of "new" theory – which is really the fault of the media, not the researchers. It's good to see that there are scientists looking into the interdimensional hypothesis, but that hypothesis has been around since at least the days of Jaques Vallée and John Keel, and you can make a case it's been around far longer.

Are UFOs actually interdimensional?

I'm not even trying to uplift my own work. Zuni elder Clifford Mahooty who passed away a few years ago talked about this very topic for decades and should be recognized, amongst others.

I saw the headline this morning and immediately had to halt the writing I'd been doing on the blog article I was looking to publish today (more on Atlantis) and sound off on something that is almost becoming laughable to me but is still quite important to discuss. What am I talking about? I'm talking about the "startling" new claim by Harvard researchers that UFOs and ETs could be "living underground, on the moon, or even walking among humans." The idea that ETs are among us isn't the laughable part, it's the rest of it. While I appreciate the fact that academics are starting to take this field seriously again, this is absolutely nothing new and the ideas aren't all that startling.

Anyone who has been following the ufology community for, oh … the past 80 years knows that these ideas and concepts have been well-established for decades. When David Grusch told a Congressional hearing last year that the U.S. government had recovered crashed extraterrestrial spacecraft, he wasn't telling anyone things we didn't already know or, at least, seriously suspect. It's wonderful that Congress is starting to give credence to this field again and this information is being written into an official record, but I'm pretty sure most people these days have heard of Roswell. There have been several crashes before and after Roswell, but that's the one that lives in infamy. Through these new hearings, perhaps those who were sitting on the fence about the topic are starting to recognize there really is something to all of this UFO and UAP phenomena – after all, the government is now telling us so (don't get me started) – but let's not ignore the work that has come before the 2020s.

What's unfortunate is that those in ufology who have been researching this for decades should be the ones getting the headline articles for books they published long, long ago, not the Harvard academics who are seemingly riding their coattails and regurgitating old ideas into a "new" paper. Again, I appreciate that academia is coming into the fold on this, but there is a wealth of literature already published on these subjects, and anyone with a subscription to Gaia TV can watch hours and hours of television shows and interviews discussing these ideas. Heck, my conversation on that network with George Noory on his show *Beyond Belief* breaks down a number of these topics just in the region of Alaska, alone, in the episode "Portals & Disappearances in Alaska."

It doesn't just stop there, however, with the information that's been proliferated since the 1940s. We can look back into our ancient past and find these stories as well, accounts handed down through the ages that are now simply regarded as legend and myth. For example, there's a story that's been passed down from indigenous tribes of the American Southwest regarding peoples who lived underground that helped save humans during the last great cataclysm.

Another fascinating aspect of our modern perspective on this is calling these beings that might live underground "extraterrestrial."

Just by their very nature of living inside the ground, they are certainly more terrestrial than humans, but even if they did come from some other world, how long must they live on this planet before they are deemed Earthlings? For example, I'm an American, but the Ricksecker's came here from Switzerland over 300 years ago, long before the Revolution (actually, it was the Ruegsegger's and the name was Anglicized to Ricksecker in Philadelphia, but that's a story for another time). I don't call myself Swiss unless strictly speaking about my heritage, and I certainly don't call myself an immigrant or a foreigner. The same can be said for those German, Scottish, Polish, and Hungarian parts of my lineage even though those ancestors came to America a little more recently. And who knows where those ancestors may have been living 1,000 years ago and more. The same can be said for those beings that may being living underground, under our oceans, or among us, and I would call them Earthlings at this point, especially if they've been here longer than us. I wonder if those Harvard scholars have an opinion on this.

I'll return to my piece on Atlantis for the next blog article, but I felt compelled to opine on this since this whole scenario, to me, is reminiscent of when big corporations or networks decide to jump into something popular. For example, when a new social media platform suddenly takes off corporations jump on it to post and advertise all over, or how every major television network now has to have a streaming service; they act like they invented the wheel when it's actually been there all along.

Portals and Star People of the Southwest

What Secrets Have Been Lost to Time?

June 21, 2024

What did the ancient peoples of this planet know that we didn't? Much. Too much. They were far more connected with the earth than we are today, the modern technology that makes things like this blog possible and the ability to interact with others across the world simultaneously creating a wide chasm between us and the globe upon which we live. Vast quantities of ancient knowledge have been lost to time, but we still see remnants of it scattered across the face of the Earth. We need to pay attention to what those remnants are, what they're telling us, and that includes the legends of portals, star people, and more. What are those secrets that have been lost to time?

Back in February, on the way to the Conscious Life Expo in Los Angeles, [we] spent a night in Albuquerque, New Mexico, where "the towels are oh so fluffy" (if you're familiar with the Weird Al song, you get it). The afternoon we arrived we ventured to Boca Negra Canyon, to the Petroglyph National Monument, where I knew

The indigenous peoples of the area provided a map at the bottom of the mesa.

somewhere among the stones were depictions of portals and star people. What I didn't expect was a twisting, winding path up a small mesa where, on top, rested a stone circle – and, oh yes – we did find petroglyphs of portals and star people on our hike upward. You can watch the video I posted about it [on YouTube] (the longer version is accessible to Travelers of the Connected Universe Portal).

There's a lot to learn from this area, and our time was limited, but as we traversed up through the boulders, I thought we made pretty good use of our time. At the introduction of the video, we're at the bottom of the hill, and there's a fascinating rock adorned with carvings that I didn't immediately understand. Later on, after having trekked up the mesa, it became clearer as to what it was, and that was a map of the area. Given the layout of this map, however, it did make us wonder as to if the orientation of the map was actually a traditional horizontal map or if it was, possibly, vertical up the mesa. That might not seem relevant for our quest to discover portals and

The first of the spirals discovered along the eastern part of the mesa.

star people, but it does give us some glimpses into the mindset of these ancient peoples.

It didn't take long to find our first portal. Along the east face of the mesa, perhaps about a third of the way up, we discovered that familiar spiral pattern we've been accustomed to finding all over the world. Again, I have to emphasize here that it is not my idea that this symbol is representative of a portal, and it's not the idea of my colleagues in this field or what some might call "pseudoscientists" – it has been the indigenous peoples that have stated these spirals are representative of portals. It is their tradition that the star people used these portals to come to Earth to visit and impart their knowledge upon the tribes. So, when an academic tries to tell us his or her interpretation is that the spiral is a calendar or a migration pattern or is representative of water, I have to shake my head. Why is that person's interpretation supposed to be better than the descendants of those who actually created the symbols?

Just about a dozen feet further up the path, cutting back to the south, we find rock carvings of our star people. That these are in close proximity to the portal symbol, I believe, is important, as we'll see a bit later. Now, that doesn't mean every single petroglyph of a person on these rocks are depictions of star people. We do find some that appear to be a type of tribesman or chieftain, but when you have images of beings with stars around them or appearing as if they are actually coming out of a portal, well, those are clearly the star people.

When we got to the top of the mesa a chill ran up my spine. There in the very center was a stone circle, just rubble, but the rubble of stone was arranged in a circle with an opening to the east. Again, our portal symbol on this mesa was on the east side, and of course, the sun rises from the east. And again, we see all over the world a connection with stone circles, earth energy, astronomical alignments, and portal technology. Also, just off the beaten path north of us in Utah, I couldn't help but think of the stone circle on top of the mesa at Skinwalker Ranch which, during a Native American drum circle below the mesa, caused the stone circle at the top to glow hot on infrared.

We investigated the top of the mesa for a while, but time was running short since the park was closing, and we headed back down. It was on the way down that [we] noticed a petroglyph that resembled a snake, a component from other depictions of portals and star people we've seen at other locations like Chaco Canyon. This was the first one we'd seen at Boca Negra, but it was definitely important since the snake was representative of energy in the ancient world. However, we would find a much better depiction of this the next day since, as we drove out, [we] noticed a spiral petroglyph along one of the canyon walls.

The next morning, we returned to Boca Negra Canyon to have a look at this spiral before we continued westward to Los Angeles for the Expo. The spiral was nestled at the top of a slight incline off the

All in a perfect line along the canyon wall from the bottom to the top: star people using energy to enter the portal.

short climb upward, however, there was also a set of petroglyphs depicting the star people – literally one of them carved inside a star – a set of glyphs I had seen photos of before and was hoping to find. I was not expecting the perfect setup of all of these glyphs, but there it was. At the bottom were the star people, at the top was the spiral, and in between was a petroglyph of a snake. The whole story was right there: the star people using energy to enter the portal.

This is just a quick rundown of what we discovered there at Boca Negra, and I will be providing a much more detailed account in my upcoming book, *Portals to the Stars*. And, of course, there's the big question: Does this mean the star people are aliens or extraterrestrials? Perhaps. Or, perhaps, they are from some other dimension. And there's the possibility that they could be both, travelling here interdimensionally from some other planet across the universe. They could even be from our own planet but on another plane of existence. But these are stories for another time.

On the Trail of Atlantis in Egypt

Edfu, Sais, Plato, and ... Eve

June 27, 2024

Article Notes: This piece here is another glimpse at some of the text that became Portals to the Stars. *I love drawing these connections, and once I had a copy of Eve Reymond's book in hand, those connections became even clearer.*

What was the lost continent of Atlantis? Truly? This is a hotly debated topic within many circles with a wide variety of answers about what it actually was, when it actually existed, and where on the planet it rested while others completely disregard the whole thing as just a fanciful myth spun by the ancient Greek philosopher Plato. It's a topic that, while we may be searching for stargates in Egypt on our tours, we always find those Atlantean connections along the way. What was ancient Egypt's role in all of this? For that, we need to look at Edfu Temple.

We covered this in part during the Edfu travel blog back in April, "Exploring the Origins of Atlantis ... and Murder Pudding," and this is definitely going to be a topic we explore in my upcoming book. Let's first take a look again below at the account I provided to the tour group while standing near the records of the "Primaeval Ones" on the walls of the temple, and then we'll explore.

What we actually have of the Atlantis account as told by Plato is very small. There are a handful of paragraphs concerning it in his work *Timaeus*, and the full account he began telling in *Critias* is cut off mid-sentence as Zeus is about to speak about "the wretched state of this admirable stock." We do discover throughout these two texts that the story did originate in Egypt and was brought to Greece by the philosopher Solon who was an ancestor of Plato. Solon, however, never fully told the story as related to him in Egypt because, as we learn in Timaeus, he was more concerned with "the uprisings and other evils he found here on his return."

Still, there is plenty of information in these works that we can start to formulate some sort of picture as to what Atlantis was and where we might find more of these stories from the culture where it originated: Egypt. The text from Plato does specifically point us in the direction of the temple at Sais in the Nile delta region. Unfortunately, the temple there has long been in ruins, and there is almost nothing left of it. One other small fragment that we know of from the Atlantis story comes from Plutarch who was a Middle Platonist philosopher born about 400 years after the death of Plato, and he tells us that the priest Solon spoke to in Sais was named Sonchis. That's not a whole lot of extra content.

This is, in part, why in addition to the research I've been doing in Egypt on stargates I've also been keeping my nose to the ground about Atlantis. Keep in mind, however, that just like the name "Egypt" is not actually an Egyptian word but is Greek, the same can be said for the name "Atlantis." You will not find the name "Atlantis" among the Egyptian texts because that is not what the ancient Egyptians would have called this civilization. What we find in the video above when we visit Edfu is an origin story about the

Neith, the tutelary goddess (or, neter) of the lost Temple of Sais.

"Homeland of the Primaeval Ones" during Zep Tepi, or "The First Time," and it was destroyed by water and fire in similar fashion to what Plato passes down to us about Atlantis. So, why Edfu?

In the Connected Universe we look for, well, connections. The massive amount of text recorded on the walls are, primarily, creation texts. Just for a taste of what we're talking about, here's a very brief segment out of *The Mythical Origin of the Egyptian Temple* by Egyptologist Eve Reymond (writing as E.A.E Reymond) published in 1969 which is an entire breakdown of the Edfu texts:

> "The time-span of this *Home of the Primaeval Ones*, we may anticipate, appears to be limited, and ended in darkness. The first event that was believed to have occurred in this *Home* seems to have been the bringing into existence of the form. We suspect that this statement alludes to the origin of the subsequent generation of gods, who are in our sources described as the *Kas* of the Primaeval Ones of the *Generation of the Great Shining One*."

I'm going to skip the inclusion of a "great shining one" for now, but keep that inclusion in the back of your mind for a later discussion. We find stories of these "shining ones" all over the world, after all, and I don't want to get sidetracked. The point here, however, is in creation, and when we look back to that destroyed temple of Sais, one of the things that we know about it is that the temple's tutelary goddess – a protector or guardian goddess – was Neith who is said to be the first and prime creator, the one who created the universe and everything within it. See the connection here? This is one of the primary reasons why I believe much of the information that was housed at Sais was written on the walls of Edfu, preserving it for us to remember today what had once been.

As far the destruction of that ancient world from which the Primaeval Ones came, there is much, and we will do a deeper dive in the greater work, but in another quick glimpse from Reymond's work:

> "The first era known by our principal sources was a period which started from what existed in the past. The general tone of the beginning of the first record seems to convey the view that an ancient world, having seen constituted, was destroyed, and as a dead world it came to be the basis of a new period of creation, which at first was the re-creation and resurrection of what once had existed in the past."

Eve Reymond may have titled her book *The Mythical Origin of the Egyptian Temple*, but it's far from a myth. It's a memory.

Part 5

Earth Energy, Atlantis, and Antarctica

Notes on Part 5

While I had, essentially, abandoned the *Energized Earth* book concept by this point – at least for now – it still became an integral part of *Portals to the Stars*. During this stretch of blog writing, I was clearly in the depths of writing that particular chapter of the book and exploring drafts between the blog and the primary text of *Portals*. Out-of-print texts I dug up for the research regarding earth energy and stone circles included *Circles of Silence* by Don Robins and the findings of the Dragon Project back in the late 1970s and early 1980s, a group of scientists who studied the electromagnetism of these sacred sites and were astonished at what they discovered. It also included *Needles of Stone Revisited* by Tom Graves, a professional dowser who worked with Robins on the Dragon Project. As a scientist, Robins couldn't explain precisely how dowsing rods worked, but he bore witness to the fact they truly do. Another recommended work from this research is *Seed of Knowledge Stone of Plenty* by John Burke and Kaj Helberg which Helberg has made freely accessible online since the passing of John

Burke some years ago.

While I was diving into this extensive earth energy research, I was approached to film an Alaska Triangle episode of *Hunting History with Steven Rinella* for the History Channel and found myself, once again, exploring the wilderness of the Great White North. Well, it was the middle of July in the greater Anchorage area, so it was green and rainy, but you can see where I was inspired, once again, to delve into the mysteries of triangle areas and vortices. Apologies for some of the redundancy in that topic.

Ultimately, to alleviate some of that redundancy, I eliminated one of the articles from this text, July 27's "Getting Lost in Triangle Vortices: Bermuda Triangle, Alaska Triangle, and more!" There really wasn't much new ground broken there, and I wanted to save the reader from too much repeat information.

Unlocking Mysteries at Drombeg Stone Circle

Discoveries During an Ireland Adventure

July 5, 2024

Article Notes: I still contend, imagine thousands of years ago when these stones were in their full glory, all of them were there, and you had loud chanting and musical instruments. The effect would have been incredible.

Have you ever had a place really resonate with you? I talk about personal resonance and vibration all the time, and there are some locations around the world in which the moment you walk into it you seem to immediately connect with it. Two years ago this week, I was in Ireland hosting the Ancient Mysteries of Ireland tour with a fantastic group of people through Mysterious Adventures Tours and creating so many amazing life-long memories. (You can relive the experience and make your own discoveries from this tour in the Secret Library of the Connected Universe.) I can absolutely say that several of the locations we visited around Ireland I connected with, and one in particular resonated with me on multiple levels, because, well, it was actually built for the purposes of resonance.

Drombeg Stone Circle in County Cork may be small in comparison to other famous stone circle structures around the world, but it is big on energy. I was looking forward to this particular visit as it was the first of the significantly more ancient sites were visiting on this tour at about 3,000 years old (we also visited Grange Stone Circle later which is much bigger and is closer to 4,000 years old). It was an adventure getting up the hill on a single lane road in our massive tour bus, but our driver, Eddie, worked his craft impeccably even with cars coming down the hill at us in the opposite direction. How he managed to never get the bus stuck in some of the extremely tight corridors we needed to maneuver, I'll never know – it's all part of the adventure – but we eventually crested the hill, and he dropped us off. To this day, our group still has no idea how Eddie got the bus turned back around for our return journey down the hill later.

The stone circle at Drombeg is an axial stone circle which means it's a type of megalithic structure with one of its stones lying down on its side horizontally, marking the axis, this particular one in a northeast-southwest direction. Like other stone circles, the remining stones are standing tall and vertical, but only 13 of the original 17 that are presumed to have been there still exist. Two "portal stones" mark the entrance – these are taller than the rest – and they align with the axial stone with the setting sun on the winter solstice. According to an old Celtic myth, on the solstices of each year the Oak King, representing the light, and the Holly King, representing the dark, would fight, with the Oak King emerging victorious at the winter solstice, enabling the return of the light. It is a celebration of the shortest day and longest night of the year, but since the days begin to lengthen once more following this, it is seen as an occasion of rebirth and renewal.

Of course, we weren't there to witness the winter solstice at Drombeg, we were there in the middle of summer, but that didn't make the site any less energetic — or majestic (the view overlooking

The majestic view at Drombeg.

the countryside out to the sea is absolutely beautiful). You could absolutely feel that energy when you walked into the middle of the circle, and I don't mean that as any sort of metaphysical woo-woo hyperbole. If you stand right in the middle of the circle and just simply talk, your voice resonates off the stones right back at you and you can feel it within your body. It has the effect of being in a sort of bubble, separated from the rest of the world. As I shared this phenomenon with others, I remarked, "Imagine being here when this site was in its full glory thousands of years ago when all the stones were still here and not weathered down by the elements over time. Imagine how your voice would sound in the middle of the circle then while in the middle of a ceremonial chant."

That absolutely would have been the idea, using a type of sound technology for a variety of purposes. There's clear evidence that ceremony was performed at the circle, although we don't know specifically what they did and what the purpose was for, but this type of use of sound could have been used for healing, meditation, entering into altered states of consciousness, even to open portals to other dimensions and realms. They would have known the right frequencies, the correct harmonies, and pitched their voices

Looking through the "Portal Stones" of Drombeg Stone Circle.

correctly to activate the circle. Or, perhaps, they may have even used instruments. We don't know all of those specific details, and that is what always makes this work so intriguing. There are always pieces of the mystery still to solve. And like the bus ride up to the top of that hill, those mysteries are all part of the adventure.

Ancient Hermetic Secrets at Charleville Castle

Discovering Duality in Ireland's Architecture

July 12, 2024

Did you know Ireland has a Triangle? Yes, I mean a triangle area like the Bermuda Triangle or the Alaska Triangle. That was news to me, too, when we toured Ireland two years ago this month as part of the "Ancient Mysteries of Ireland with Mike Ricksecker" tour through Mysterious Adventures Tours, and triangle areas are a subject matter I'm known for. Thus, I was immediately intrigued when we were standing in the gorgeous entrance hall of Charleville Castle marveling at its architecture and were informed that such an area existed there in Ireland and Charleville was a part of it. "Please, do tell me more," I thought.

First of all, Charleville Castle is actually a "newer" castle in the Midlands of Ireland with construction beginning about 1798 by Charles William Bury, Earl of Charleville, and built on top of the site of an older manor house. It took about 14 years to complete the Gothic revival castle, and was greatly inspired by the Earl's partner, Lady Catherine Maria Bury who was an artist and includes elements

The looming towers of Charleville Castle.

of Masonic symbolism. The castle includes epic staircases, massive ornate rooms, and even secret passageways and doorways. I highly recommend visiting it if you're ever in Ireland.

The triangle area consists of three haunted castles – Charleville Castle, Kinnity Castle, and Leap Castle, the latter of which many people consider to be the most haunted castle in Ireland. We visited two of the three on this particular tour, also exploring Leap Castle and its famous "Bloody Chapel." Would we experience any effects of the triangle during our visits? Does some sort of earthly energy enhance the hauntings at these historic castles? This notion cued me in to exploring the energy at Charleville, but we didn't have a whole lot of time to spend there. Fortunately, I had some quick old school tools with me in the dowsing rods I'd brought along.

I'm not going to get into the debate here as to whether or not dowsing rods are legitimate tools to use on paranormal investigations – that's beyond the scope of this blog article, and I wasn't conducting a paranormal investigation anyway. I don't use dowsing rods as communication devices to speak with ghosts and spirits; I use them for their original purpose: to find energy. On *The Alaska Triangle* television show, I used dowsing rods on Flattop Mountain outside of Anchorage to find a current of energy running toward the city, modern surveyors still use dowsing rods to find old,

The gorgeous entrance hall of Charleville Castle with duality embedded in the floor tiles.

uncharted pipes in the ground, and a project undertaken at Vaughn Hill Cemetery in Wood River, Illinois, used dowsing rods to find several unmarked graves throughout the grounds. There are many uses.

I was drawn to "The Red Room" in one of the towers of the castle and was quite intrigued with the results with the rods. During this shot-in-the-dark test, I discovered the rods pointing in two very different directions: one pointed north while the other pointed west toward the other tower. But that wasn't the half of it. The intrigue was heighted when I took the rods into the library in the other tower and found the rods pointed in the complete opposite directions: one pointed south while the other pointed east back toward the other tower. While discussing this fascinating observation, our hostess at the castle took out a pendulum and showed how it spun in the library. We didn't have time to verify the result in the other tower because we had a bus to catch, but according to her, it spins in the

The author using dowsing rods in the library at Charleville Castle.

opposite direction in the Red Room.

Given the results of the rods and the pendulum, these two towers are energetic opposites, a mirroring of each other that would have had to have been a part of the building's design. This symbolism of duality is far deeper than the black and white checkered floors of the entrance hall that also tease us with hidden wisdom. This is the Hermetic principle of "As Above, So Below" embedded into the very core of the architecture of the castle.

How did the architects of Charleville Castle make that possible? Were there specific stones they used within the construction of the two towers arranged in such a way for them to be magnetic opposites and connect them energetically? Did they tap into the power of the triangle emanating from the earth to make that happen? Well, we had that bus to catch, but it's definitely something I wish to explore further the next time we tour Ireland.

I Could Have Used a Stargate

Adventures in (Not Time) Travel

July 19, 2024

Article Notes: Originally, I was going to write this as a moment-by-moment journal, sort of a "day in the life" type of read. However, as I got busy and the days got away from me, it ended up turning into a regular blog article recapping the travel adventure. The filming in Alaska turned into an episode of Hunting History with Steven Rinella, *while the filming in New York, unfortunately, was for a pilot episode of a proposed television show for the History Channel which has never aired. I assume they scrapped it.*

    6:00 AM: Alarm goes off.
    6:09 AM: Alarm goes off again because, you know, Snooz. I'm not a morning person, and on a regular day I would probably hit the Snooz again.
    6:49 AM: Rushed to get showered and ready to go. I was able to sneak in a quick meditation.
    6:57 AM: Mom sends a text message that she and my dad are here to pick me up for the airport.

7:23 AM: Through TSA Pre-Check and now sitting at the bar of The Pub. Just ordered a coffee and an omelet and am checking social media for the first time today.

7:40 AM: Decided to unschedule my blog post from 8:00 AM so I could publish immediately and get social media posts out before I take off.

8:37 AM: All settled in on the plane. First leg is to Denver, about a three-and-a-half-hour flight.

In flight: Flying gives me a rare opportunity to write without much distraction. Sure, it's a little more cramped and uncomfortable, and at the time I'm jotting this note I really need to get off my aching rear, but I generally don't purchase wi-fi service, so there aren't a bunch of notifications blowing up at me to grab my attention. The only downside is if I need to look up something for research purposes.

On this flight, I've been working on the new book, starting with some additional detail I added to the initial "What is a Stargate?" chapter. I got into a small zone, and I liken this to a form of channeling. Given what I ended up writing … yeah, I channeled some bit of information from the universe to share, an idea that should give us more to consider when it comes to … well, I can't say. You'll have to wait for the book.

From there, I also worked on a couple stories for "Portals in the Wilderness." I do bounce around quite a bit when I write. It keeps me fresh and prevents writer's block.

This is how a typical travel day starts for me …

I've spent the past several days bouncing around the country on airplanes – from Cleveland to Denver to Anchorage to Seattle (practically lived in Seattle, it feels) back to Cleveland to New York to Detroit and finally returned home to Cleveland. I'm usually pretty lucky with flying and generally don't experience very many delays,

On the trail of a spot to film near McHugh Creek at Chugach State Park.

but that's pretty much all I experienced. It started in Anchorage on my return trip. We were delayed leaving from Alaska due to a maintenance issue that caused me to miss my Cleveland connection in Seattle. The delay was a whopping 12 hours, so I spent my day at a wine bar working on my writing, and when I'd had enough wine that I could no longer write, I partook in the bar's banter regarding the Colombia – Argentina game that was on television. This is humorous because I know little-to-nothing about soccer/football. I played two seasons as a kid and watched the film *Victory* with Sylvester Stallone. That's about it. Yet, I was having a good time chatting it up with the Scotsman who sat to my right until finally, mercifully, it was time to stagger to my flight. I was supposed to have originally touched down at 5:30 PM, but it wasn't until 5:30 AM the next morning – and then we still got stuck waiting on the tarmac in Cleveland an extra 30 minutes waiting for another plane to clear out of our gate while it dealt with maintenance issues.

Before moving on to the New York – Detroit – Cleveland fiasco, you may be wondering what in the world I was doing in Alaska. Well, I can't specifically say, but yes, I was filming for a television show, and yes, the topic did cover the Alaska Triangle. It rained on us the whole time, but it was quite the adventure trying to find the right spot to film while the weather remained uncooperative. The rain and mist also created a wonderful atmospheric condition as we discussed the mysteries of the triangle, and I expect it's going to come off really well. The production team was extremely happy about it, as was I. I'll have more information to come about this particular show whenever it airs.

I crashed for a couple hours in my own bed, but I got right back up to record a podcast with my friend Dr. Heather Lynn for her Midnight Academy show. Following that I started preparing to leave for New York the next day as well prepping the house for a couple of my kids who were coming in later in the week to help celebrate my 50th birthday on the 21st. The New York interview was to cover more than just the Alaska Triangle, but other triangle areas around the world as well. This was a studio shoot indoors rather than out in the rain on the side of a mountain, but still just as fascinating.

So, my travel that day ... let me just say this. This past week, it seems I've been channeling the airport luck of my good friend, Dustin Pari. He is always traveling, and it seems half of the social media posts I see from him are of him being stuck in some terminal at an airport. Comparatively, the Cleveland-to-New York jaunt wasn't too bad. We only sat on the tarmac in Cleveland waiting for some weather to clear up in New York before taking off. It was the return trip that turned out to be a bit insane.

So, you may have heard that lightning and airplanes don't mix too well. Following my film shoot in New York, I headed directly to LaGuardia Airport. Perhaps I should have just stayed in town for an extra day (I couldn't, though, with the kids coming in on Thursday, and it was Wednesday), because what transpired over the

Blueberry cheesecake at Junior's is always a must whenever I visit New York.

next several hours was just bizarre. Due to thunderstorms all throughout the east, flights kept getting delayed. I received numerous notifications of my flight to Cleveland getting pushed back until, finally, they just outright cancelled it. Naturally, I wasn't very happy about it, but I found I could rebook for New York to Detroit and then Detroit to Cleveland that evening. I would get in really late at night, but it was available. Here's where it starts to get crazy. While trying to peacefully enjoy a dinner and some wine, my phone started blowing up with all kinds of new notifications. My New York to Detroit flight took several more delays and was pushed back past the departure of the Detroit to Cleveland flight. When I looked at the airline app on my phone to try to make sense of the notifications I'd just received, the airline had completely dropped the Detroit to Cleveland flight and suddenly only had me booked to Detroit. Well, getting stuck in Detroit certainly wouldn't do. I quickly finished the remainder of my meal and went to seek some help from customer service. After quite a wait in line – some poor guy couldn't find an available flight to his destination for two whole days – they worked with me to reestablish my Detroit to Cleveland connection ... the next day at noon. There was nothing for it, of course.

At that point, the Detroit flight was leaving at 11:28 PM. Throughout the night they changed it to 12:28 AM, 1:14 AM, and then a gate change to the ass end of LaGuardia Airport. (Actually, they've done a really nice job with the remodeling work at LaGuardia, so the ass end wasn't too bad). Finally, a plane came in at our new gate that we could, technically, board, and we had pilots. What we didn't have at that point were flight attendants, so we sat around even longer waiting for a flight to come in that would have the personnel we needed. They pushed us back to a 1:30 AM takeoff ... and then, I think, they just stopped updating the departure time. I actually, finally, boarded the plane at 1:25 AM, and then, if it hadn't been enough, there was a bit more weirdness.

Nearing 2:00 AM, one of the attendants called a series of passenger names off a list whom they wanted to talk to in order to confirm they'd had the right people on board. That took several minutes, of course, and I actually started to fall asleep a little bit. I don't usually fall asleep on planes, but my eyes were getting heavy. At some point after 2:00 AM we finally started pulling away from the gate. Oh, but wait. We weren't done! We mysteriously pulled back into the gate and sat for some more time. This was perplexing, but we eventually got an answer that they had misfiled some information about the flight plan regarding the weight of the plane and the number of people on board and had to pull back in to redo it. I was a little fuzzy on the matter. Finally, at incoherent o'clock, we took off. I seriously don't know what time it was; I had stopped looking by then. But it's about an hour and a half flight, and we landed in Detroit at 4:15 AM. Couldn't they have just let me parachute out the plane as we passed by Cleveland?

I had an amazing view of this city that did not want me to leave its airport.

After all of that, if you'd asked me how I was doing I would tell you that, "I'm ready to rock-n-roll," and all of this craziness ... well, "It's just all part of the adventure." And yet, I still wasn't quite done. I still had a flight to Cleveland awaiting me seven hours later. Fortunately, that one went off without a hitch – finally! Of course, the flight time on that one is only 20 minutes, and as soon as you're in the air you begin your descent. They may as well just shoot us out of a cannon across Lake Erie to get from one city to the other. I was finally, mercifully, home, totally wiped out and exhausted, but I am now absolutely looking forward to the birthday festivities this weekend with my family. That thought alone is enough to keep my energy up at a premium.

Yeah, I could have really used a stargate for these journeys, some sort of teleporter to get across the country. But now I have more travel stories to share.

The Age of Atlantis

It's Just Simple Math, Right?

August 5, 2024

Article Notes: I always enjoy diving into the ancient texts, finding connections, and discovering what's truth and what's myth. I've been researching Atlantis for years, and here I gave blog readers a taste of where that research had gone and what to expect on the topic in Portals to the Stars.

How old is Atlantis? When did it actually exist? This past week I shared an article on my social media about the sunken Greek city of Pavlopetri and how the writer of the article related this city to the lost civilization of Atlantis. Could this have been Plato's "inspiration"? The problem with that is simple math: Pavlopetri only dates back to 3000 BC while the Atlantis destruction, according to Plato, dates back to 9,000 years before Solon brought the story back with him from Egypt, which would put it at about 9600 BC. To find Atlantis – or what the Egyptians originally called it, "The Homeland of the Primaeval Ones," since they certainly didn't call it "Atlantis" – we would need to look at ancient sites that date back some 11,700 years ago. So, why the confusion?

Here I go talking about Atlantis again, and as irony would have it, I've recently been asked to become a brand ambassador for Atlantis Nutrition. Check them out and use the discount code RICKSECKER10 at: https://www.atlantisnutrition.com

Plato lived approximately 427 – 348 BC and was the middle character in the infamous Greek philosopher triumvirate with Socrates as his teacher and Aristotle as his pupil. Nearly everything he wrote was in the form of a dialogue between philosophers. The *Timaeus* and *Critias* are a part of the Socratic dialogues and included the participants Socrates, Timaeus, Critias, and Hermocrates. These two dialogues were written about 425 BC toward the end of Plato's life and could very well be why the *Critias* is incomplete. Plato may have just simply passed away before getting a chance to finish writing it, although it does seem odd the text cuts off mid-stream, so there could still very well be some lost extracts of continuing dialogue we haven't yet found.

Still, there is plenty of information in these works that we can start to formulate some sort of picture as to what Atlantis was and where we might find more of these stories from the culture where it originated: Egypt. The text from Plato does, specifically, point us in the direction of the temple at Sais in the Nile delta region. Unfortunately, the temple there has long been in ruins, and there is almost nothing left of it. One other small fragment that we know of from the Atlantis story comes from Plutarch who was a Middle Platonist philosopher born about 400 years after the death of Plato, and he briefly tells us who Solon spoke to in Egypt: "He also spent some time in studies with Psenophis of Heliopolis and Sonchis of Sais, who were very learned priests. From these, as Plato says, he heard the story of the lost Atlantis, and tried to introduce it in a poetical form to the Greeks. Next he sailed to Cyprus, and was greatly beloved of Philocyprus, one of the kings of the island."

We have, generally, focused on Sonchis of Sais when discussing the tale of Atlantis because in Plato's work he only mentions Sais as

You know the research is getting real when you have to break out the Egyptian Book of the Dead (front left). Also pictured is E.A.E. Reymond's The Mythical Origin of the Egyptian Temple (front right), Plato's Timaeus and Critias (back left), and underneath it all, Magicians of the Gods and America Before by Graham Hancock.

a source and not Heliopolis:

"There is in Egypt," said Critias, "At the head of the delta, where the Nile divides, a district called the Saitic. The chief city of the district, from which King Amasis came, is called Sais. The chief goddess of the inhabitants is called in Egyptian Neith, in Greek (according to them) Athena; and they are very friendly to the Athenians and claim some relationship to them. Solon said that he came there on his travels and was highly honoured by them, and in the course of making inquiries about antiquity from those priests who were most experienced in these things found that both he and all his countrymen were almost entirely ignorant about such matters. And wishing to lead them on about to talk about early times, he embarked on an account of the earliest events known here, telling them the myths about Phoroneus, said to be the first man, and Niobe, and how Deucalion and Pyrrha survived the flood and who were their descendants, and he reckoned up the generations after them, and tried to calculate how long ago the events in question had taken place. And a very old priest said to him, 'Solon, Solon, you Greeks are ever children; there is no such thing as an old Greek.' 'What do you mean by that?' inquired Solon. 'You are all young in mind,' came the reply: 'you have in your minds no belief rooted in old tradition and no knowledge hoary with age. And the reason is this. There have been many different calamities to destroy mankind, the greatest of them fire and water ...'"

And thus begins the brief Atlantis account in the *Timaeus* with the more detailed narrative to continue in the *Critias*. In a previous blog article, "On the Trail of Atlantis in Egypt," I quote Egyptologist Eve Reymond's fantastic work on the Egyptian Edfu Temple texts, *The Mythical Origin of the Egyptian Temple*, several times, and in another area of her work she tells us:

"At this point we see a link between the fate of the island as it is known from the Edfu sources and a thought expressed in the *Book of the Dead*, Spell 175; according to the latter, the Earth, after it was created, disappeared beneath the primeval waters. The Edfu account, therefore, adds many details to this view and, moreover, gives it dramatic context."

What is this reference in *The Egyptian Book of the Dead* (more precise title is *The Book of Going Forth by Day*)? Ironically, it's a scene I referenced in my book *Travels Through Time* when I was showing an example of how the ancient Egyptians viewed time and how, to them, there was a constant recycling and renewal of the universe as depicted in the symbol of the ouroboros, the snake eating its own tail. Here, the creation god Atum is talking to Ani, an Egyptian scribe:

"I will dispatch the Elders and destroy all that I have made; the

Much of Heliopolis has been lost, including the "Inventory Building."

earth shall return to the Primordial Water, to the surging flood, as in its original state. But I will remain with Osiris, I will transform myself into something else, namely a serpent, without men knowing or the gods seeing."

This is a vague reference to the destruction of Atlantis or the Homeland of the Primaeval Ones, and Solon may not have been aware of this specific reference, although he almost certainly was aware of the imagery of the snake since we find its use throughout the Edfu texts.

Given Plutarch's reference and the significance of the city, Solon very well could have received some of this information from the priests in Heliopolis as well since Heliopolis was the capital of Egypt at the time and a center of learning. There are even some today who believe Heliopolis was the capital of Atlantis, and while I don't subscribe to that idea, I do believe it could have been an important city or a colony of the lost civilization as a whole.

English Egyptologist I.E.S.Edwards pointed out that Heliopolis was the site of the "Inventory Building" and had been a center of astronomical science closely connected to Giza. Sir Alan H. Gardiner whose dictionary is the backbone of our understanding of hieroglyphs believed that the Inventory Building was some sort of archive in which King Khufu was searching for information about "the secret chambers of the primeval sanctuary of Thoth." Thoth was the Egyptian god of knowledge. To support that theory, the Westcar Papyrus, which dates to the Middle Kingdom, about 1650 BC, but was a copy from older source material, talked about a "chest of flint" hidden in Heliopolis which contained a document describing the "secret chamber of the sanctuary of Thoth" which Khufu wanted "to copy for his temple." Did the Inventory Building, which sounds like a library, perhaps even the inspiration for the Great Library in Alexandria, also contain documents concerning this earlier Atlantean civilization?

So, I come back to my original question ... why such the confusion over the date of the demise of Atlantis when the math provide above is so seemingly simple? I believe the confusion is equally as simple: a vast number of people believe that Plato's writings on the lost civilization of Atlantis is a complete fabrication, and he used elements from his own time – or at least "close" to his time – to create a myth. But is that really logical? For instance, many have thought that the island of Santorini was the inspiration for the Atlantis story, if not Atlantis itself, if it truly existed. However, the eruption of the volcano on Santorini occurred in 1600 BC, predating Plato by 1,200 years and coming 8,000 years after the setting of the Atlantis story. So, this really seems unlikely.

With such a rich history behind Plato and Solon's Atlantis dating far back into the annals of ancient Egypt as well as so many other cultures that speak of a great cataclysm, it's obvious that *something* happened long, long ago. It's pretty simple.

Atlanteans in Antarctica?

How Far Did Their Civilization Spread?

August 12, 2024

Article Notes: I first proposed the Atlantean connection to Antarctica in Alaska's Mysterious Triangle, *but this idea was inspired by a hypnotic regression I had years ago in which part of the information gleaned was that the lost technology of the ancients was hidden under the ice in Antarctica.*

Since we've been covering the topic of Atlantis lately, I wanted to take a moment to discuss a topic I introduced in my book *Alaska's Mysterious Triangle*: Atlanteans in Antarctica. Wait, what? Antarctica is cold, to be sure, but it's on the exact opposite side of the globe from Alaska. And the idea of the lost civilization of Atlantis reaching as far as Antarctica? What kind of sorcery is this?

First, let's recognize that the ancient world knew of Antarctica's existence long before European explorers discovered the land in 1820, and we find its depiction in historic maps like the 1513 Piri Reis map. This work is only a portion of a greater whole that has been lost to time, and it includes the coastline of Antarctica which modern explorers didn't discover until 1820. What has survived is only about a third of the original map, and it includes a large island off the coast of Florida that includes a depiction many people believe is the Bimini Road – but that's a story for another day. Piri Reis was an Ottoman admiral and cartographer, and he based this map off many others he had access to, including eight Ptolemaic maps, in other words, maps from the reign of the Ptolemy line of kings during Greek rule in ancient Egypt. So, when we look at the Piri Reis map we could very well be looking at knowledge that was passed down from the Great Library of Alexandria.

As for location and proximity to the north, the Antarctica island wasn't once where it currently rests. The land was once further north in a warmer climate, and ice core samples taken by scientific teams in Antarctica have discovered an ancient jungle hidden under the ice. Land masses, naturally, move about via continental drift and, perhaps, via Earth crust displacement, as theorized by Charles Hapgood. Antarctica, it seems, may have drifted or been displaced to where it now sits more recently than other areas of the world, which is not unheard of as different tectonic plates around the globe move at varying speeds. (In 2016, for example, National Geographic published an article boasting "Australia Is Drifting So Fast GPS Can't Keep Up.")

So, if this is true, and Antarctica was much more accessible to the world population than it is now, what maritime civilization of old would have settled this continent that now rests at the South Pole? Enter our Atlanteans.

Through Plato's work – and I'll refer the reader to some of my more recent articles "On the Trail of Atlantis in Egypt" and "The Age of Atlantis" rather than repeat myself here – we find in the *Critias* that the civilization stretched far and wide. It wasn't just an island with a concentric ringed city:

"They and their descendants for many generations governed their own territories and many other islands in the ocean and, as has already been said, also controlled the populations this side of the straits as far as Egypt and Tyrrhenia."

Many believe that remnants of Atlantis can still be found in several parts of the world, survivors who forged new civilizations following the great cataclysm. Many of those surviving civilizations, such as Egypt, still mystify us as to how they built the amazing structures we see today, structures we can't currently build or have just now developed the technology to do so. How did they perform these miraculous feats? How did they machine their works during a time in history that traditional archaeology tells us these peoples were only using copper and stone, something that could never have built and carved the pyramids or so many of the magnificent granite sculptures that have stood the test of time?

If the Egyptians are the descendants of the Atlanteans and there are Atlantean remains under the ice in Antarctica, then is the technology the Egyptians used to build their structures buried under the ice at the South Pole as well? What if that technology includes some sort of anti-gravity device these ancient peoples employed to build their magnificent wonders, passed down by their Atlantean forbearers? Wouldn't discovering that be worth the substantial and costly effort that's been launched in Antarctica? Is that what the Nazis were searching for in the frozen wasteland during World War II?

Ok, that's a lot of ideas and concepts to throw out there all at once, and that last paragraph is nearly verbatim what I included in *Alaska's Mysterious Triangle*. I wanted to get readers thinking outside the box, but Antarctica is a bit outside the scope of Alaska, so I hit them with a bunch of quick shots. Dare I say some of this came up in a hypnosis session some years back (it did), but there's some real history we can put behind this.

Starting out in 1938 and arriving in January 1939, Adolf Hitler sent a secret Nazi research expedition to Antarctica, established a presence there, and called it *Neuschwabenland* (New Swabia). One of the goals was to establish their own whaling industry in order to harvest oil themselves rather than to have to buy it off the Norwegians. But there are many who believe that they were secretly hiding weapons there as well as searching for ancient technologies lost to time. Hitler spent considerable resources during his reign on hunting down historic items and artifacts that he considered would give the Third Reich more power. And he did his homework. He was likely familiar with these ancient maps that showed Antarctica as a thriving island and was aware there may be lost technologies there for him to acquire.

Of course, there's the famous Admiral Byrd expeditions – five of them – including the famous flight he described in his personal diary near the South Pole at the end of Operation Highjump in which he entered a massive cavern in the earth that housed some sort of lost civilization. Sounds too good to be true in such a remote and starkly cold area of the planet? We know there's subterranean geothermal heating in Antarctica. It's why Lake Vostok, which resides under nearly 2.5 miles of ice, is actually a liquid water lake about the size of Lake Ontario and far deeper. Of course, there have been scores of UFO and UAP sightings in Antarctica, and don't get me started on the neutrino research there in which the scientists published a paper in *Annals of Physics* a couple years ago which stated this phenomenon was indicative of an anti-universe, a parallel universe running in reverse time. I cover that in detail in *Travels Through Time*.

What's really hiding under the ice in Antarctica we can only guess, and when it's discovered it may not be shared publicly. But what's there may actually be lost remnants of our human past, possibly the Atlanteans, or possibly an even older civilization we've also forgotten over the millennia.

Secret Stargates in Antarctica?

What Lies Hidden Under the Ice

August 19, 2024

Article Notes: This article was inspired, in part, by filming an episode of The UnXplained *titled "Tales From Antarctica." Once again, the universe dropped something in my lap that coincided perfectly with topics I was already covering in* Portals to the Stars, *specifically the vile vortices, and gave me more topics to fully flesh out and add to the case I was building, such as the intriguing Admiral Byrd story.*

Antarctica is really one of the most inhospitable places on Earth. It's covered in ice and glaciers that are miles thick, the winds are absolutely brutal with windstorms sometimes lasting for days, and Antarctica is actually a desert. It's the driest continent on the planet. So why have so many countries around the world maintained such a fascination in a locale that is so stark and bleak? Last week we explored the possibilities that ancient Atlanteans may have, at one time, colonized Antarctica. This week let's jump down a deeper rabbit hole … are there stargates in Antarctica?

Is this yet another preview of the upcoming book? Mayhaps.

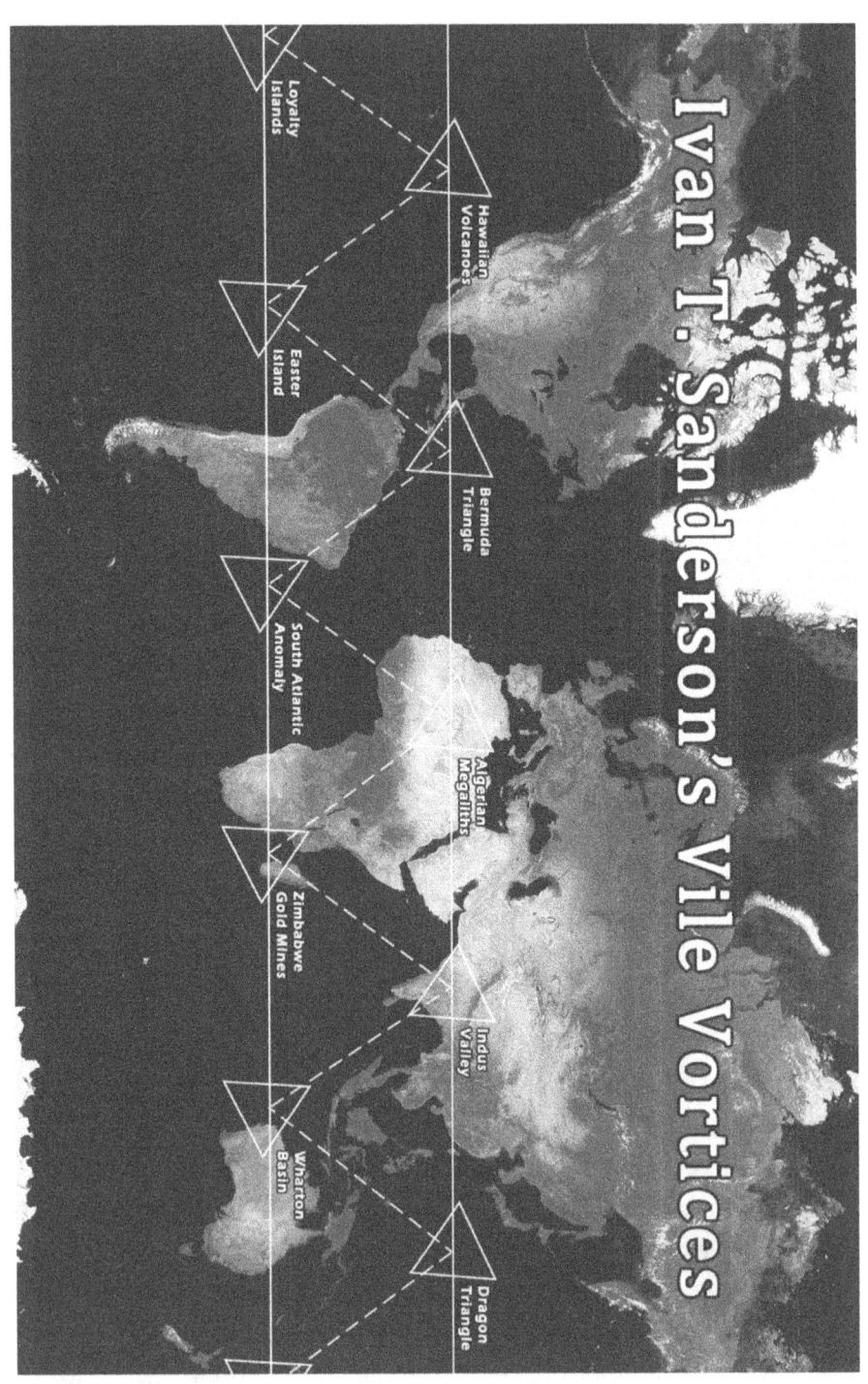

I've had an extremely busy summer filming for a variety of television shows and have found myself in Boulder, Anchorage, Los Angeles, and New York (multiple times). In between all of that I've been writing as much as I can on the new book for which I've given myself a very strict deadline – and that is fast approaching. The Antarctica angle, while I covered it in *Alaska's Mysterious Triangle*, has now found its way into this new book as well, but since it was one of Ivan T. Sanderson's "vile vortices," it makes sense we should cover it, at least in brief, with this work, too.

Ivan T. Sanderson was a British biologist and writer who had a profound interest in the paranormal and supernatural, was an early follower of Charles Fort (where we get the term "Fortean"), and wrote about several of these topics in the mid-Twentieth Century. He founded the Society for the Investigation of the Unexplained, but he's probably most known for his 1972 article in *Saga* magazine, "The Twelve Devil's Graveyards Around the World." In this work, he postulated that there were geographic areas around the globe that contain hotspots of energy in which strange and mysterious things tend to occur. Ten of Sanderson's Vile Vortices are situated in the world's tropical atmospheres: five of them fall inside the Tropic of Cancer and the other five inside the Tropic of Capricorn. You'll recognize some of the names associated with these locations, such as the Bermuda Triangle, the Dragon Triangle near Japan, and Easter Island. The other two hotspots are situated at the North and South Poles. Together, the Vile Vortices structure the vertices of an icosagon, a perfect twenty-sided polygon, creating a sacred geometric shape out of the globe.

Now, there are plenty of other hotspot areas around the planet that fall outside the purview of Sanderson's vortices, such as the Alaska Triangle, Sedona, and the Giza Plateau in Egypt, but he certainly had a deep understanding of how the Earth's energy grid works. So, if Antarctica is resting on top of one of these Vile Vortices, what sort of strange activity occurs there? For such a

Unloading supplies during Operation Highjump, 1946 - 1947.

sparsely populated island – only about 1,000 – 5,000 people live there at any given time – the location is rife with UFO sightings, tales of ghosts, and survival stories that absolutely defy the odds.

One of the most fascinating and controversial legends of Antarctica includes one of its most famous explorers: Admiral Richard E. Byrd. Admiral Richard Byrd was a famed aviator who became known as the first to fly over the North Pole in 1926 but became even more well-known after he conducted multiple expeditions to Antarctica, including the largest ever in Operation Highjump. These expeditions greatly helped in mapping Antarctica, he was the first to fly over the South Pole, and he set up meteorological stations so we could learn more about the harsh environment there. It was following his death in 1957 that his son stumbled upon his personal diary, and what he discovered was truly surprising. Admiral Byrd had been a highly respected explorer and had received the Medal of Honor for a lifetime of amazing

What did Admiral Byrd truly witness at the South Pole?

achievements, so when it became public that he'd written an account of flying into an underground world in Antarctica, most people couldn't believe it. Skeptics have totally dismissed it.

According to the account, while Admiral Byrd was flying near the South Pole he discovered a deep entrance into the Earth, large enough that he could fly his plane into it. The cavern turned lush and green and led to a shimmering rainbow city that looked like it was made of crystal. Flying disc-shaped objects surrounded him and they took remote control of his plane. His plane was lowered to the ground, and, after landing, he was led to a large, cavernous area and introduced to a being called "the master." This being said their civilization was highly disappointed with the humans on the surface and what they were doing with nuclear weapons. Again, while this story sounds fantastic, we have to remember that Admiral Byrd was a Medal of Honor recipient, and this was his private diary. This was never supposed to be made public. In a later entry within the diary, in a staff meeting at the Pentagon, Admiral Byrd was ordered to remain silent about everything he had seen in this underground world in the interest of national security and for the sake of humanity.

Some have run with this story and have argued that this account proves that our planet is actually hollow. I'll be quite clear in my view that I don't believe in the "Hollow Earth" theory in the traditional sense that there are huge gaping holes at the poles which lead to a massive inner planet with its own sun. I do, however, believe there are very large areas within the Earth's crust, old magma chambers and lava tubes, that very well could be supporting some sort of underground civilization. How could one possibly survive in Antarctica with how cold it is? Isn't the idea of lush vegetation far too fanciful in a part of the world where nothing grows?

Well, things did once grow in Antarctica. Ice core samples have shown that the island's surface did once reside in a much warmer climate on the globe and was home to an ancient jungle. As for the heat that would need to be required today, we know from Antarctica's Lake Vostok that there are subterranean geothermal heat sources below the island. Lake Vostok is a sub-glacial lake that is about the same size as Lake Ontario, but far deeper with about four times the volume, and has been isolated for anywhere from 13,000 to 14 million years, depending on who you talk to. The water is still liquid, not solid, warmed by that subterranean heat source I mentioned. Trapped under nearly 2.5 miles of ice, this is an isolated ecosystem totally developing on its own. Heat sources like this could very well help explain the green vegetation Admiral Byrd claimed to have seen in his diary … if this journey truly took him into a physical location within the planet. What do I mean by that?

Remember, we're supposed to be talking about stargates here. It's very possible that what Admiral Byrd passed through in order to access this civilization with its flying discs and crystalline city was some sort of portal, taking him almost anywhere. If this potential portal, powered by the earth energy there, is controlled by the intelligent beings living within this city (or by its "master"), then that makes it a stargate. While this idea requires a certain degree of

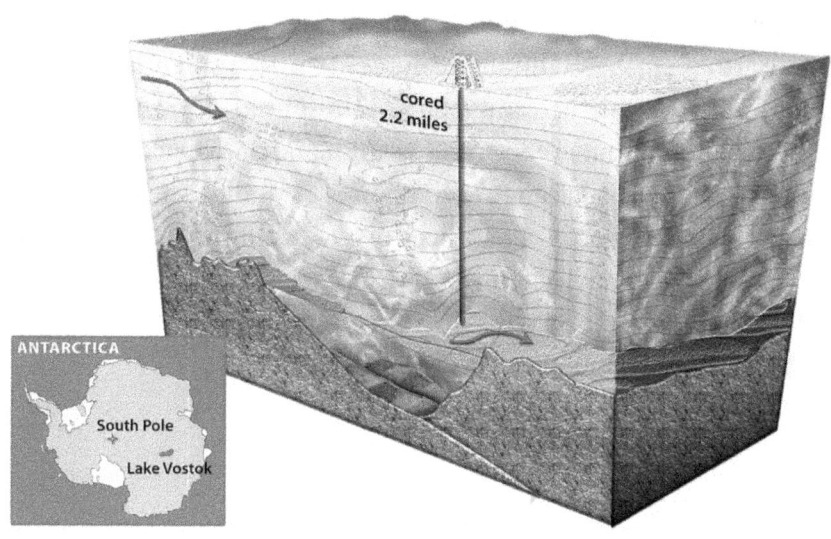

Lake Vostok drilling. (Wikimedia Commons)

speculation, here we can entertain the notion that these beings saw Admiral Byrd en route to their location and opened the stargate for him to venture into. After he left, they very well could have closed it behind him, leaving it invisible to us today. Why Admiral Byrd? Very simple. He was a highly respected member of the U.S. armed forces, one who had been to Antarctica several times, someone who would be the ideal candidate to bring a message to the U.S. government about their concerns regarding nuclear warfare. Although they live beneath the surface, or perhaps, within another dimension on our planet, these beings have a symbiotic relationship with us. What affects us will also affect them. That's simple Gungan – Naboo wisdom there for you, folks.

While these past two blog articles might be a little difficult for readers to fully accept – after all, we're talking Atlanteans and stargates in Antarctica – there's enough story circulating out there to at least understand that something unusual is going on down at the South Pole. Remember, this is a part of the globe in which scientific research there detected evidence of high-energy neutrinos that were supposed to be arriving from space actually coming up out of the Earth's surface without a source. In 2022, scientists working on this project published a paper in the journal *Annals of Physics* which expanded on the neutrino research and supported a universal symmetry, that this strange behavior was indicative of an anti-universe, in other words, a parallel universe running in reverse time. Thus, Antarctica may actually hold the secrets to accessing other dimensions and time travel. So, why might it not also hold the secrets to Atlantis and stargates as well?

Everything is Connected

It's Not Just Some Mystical Notion

August 26, 2024

This past weekend was bittersweet, and thousands of people descended on the uppermost point of Michigan, Sault Ste. Marie, to celebrate and honor the fourteenth and final Michigan Paranormal Conference. I've been speaking at this conference for the past five years, so I came a little late into the game on this one, but the friendships and connections I've made there since 2019 have been absolutely amazing, and I'm sorry to see it go. This had become one of my favorite events of the year, and it was always so well-organized by Brad, Tim, Tara and crew. My final appearance on stage for this one was a fantastic panel with my friends and colleagues Shane Pittman and Heather Taddy with Tim Dennis moderating, and it couldn't have been a more appropriate topic: the connection of strange phenomena.

Yes, everything is connected. We mostly talked about different types of unusual activity, whether that was ghosts, extraterrestrials, Sasquatch, and more, and we'll get to all of that in a moment. But first, as I've done with my first book in the *Connecting the Universe* series, *Travels Through Time*, let's start at the root. When I say

From left to right: Tim Dennis, Heather Taddy, Shane Pittman, and Mike Ricksecker.

"everything is connected" I don't just mean that in the sense of some sort of cryptic spiritual mysticism (although I believe in that, too), there is actually a physical connection between all beings throughout the known universe. Years ago, the Chandra X-Ray Observatory, a telescope specially designed to detect X-ray emission from very hot regions of the universe such as exploded stars, clusters of galaxies, and matter around black holes, in trying to determine where the universe has been hiding most of its mass since the Big Bang, took a wide image of the cosmos, and the results were striking. The bright balls of light (image below) are galaxies, quasars, and other large celestial objects, and they're all shown being linked together by interstellar gas filaments. We literally are all connected.

Let's bring this back to Earth. We've discussed here before the connection between the Sun and our planet, the X-points or portals in space that open and close at random intervals to allow more powerful streams of the solar wind to access Earth at faster speeds than it normally would take to pass through our magnetic shield. However, we also have that energy throughout the globe that is also connecting us, that magnetism that protects us also energizes

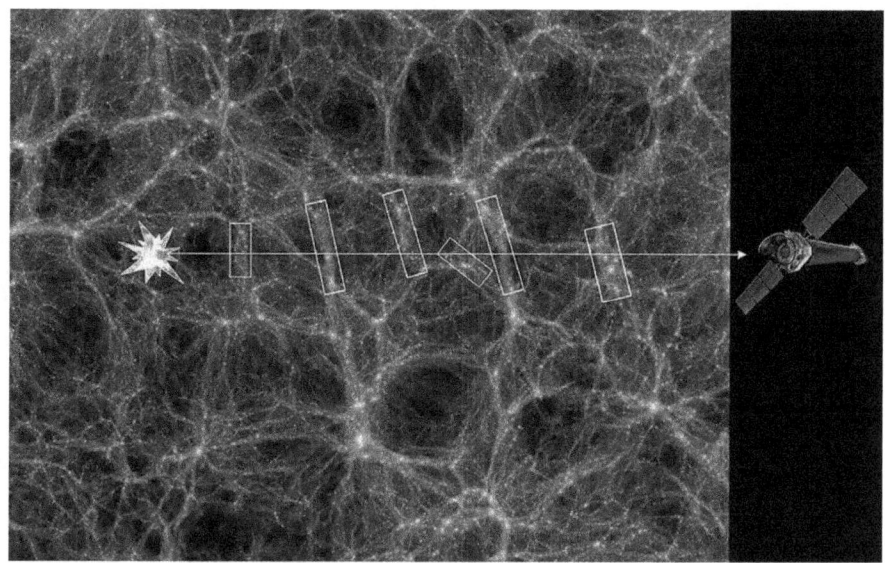
We are physically connected to the rest of the universe. (Chandra X-Ray image)

specific areas around the world in such a fashion that some seemingly strange and bizarre things occur. The reason for this isn't overly complicated. As that magnetism rises up from the core of the Earth, which is a spinning molten ball of iron, it passes through various mineral and metal deposits, and depending on what it passes through and how large the deposit is, it creates various localized magnetic fields that encourage these phenomena.

One of the questions that a member of the audience asked during the Q&A session was about if there was something specific to the location that might attract a wide variety of activity such as UFO sightings, paranormal activity, and more, and the short answer is, "Yes." The medium answer is above, and the more detailed answer can be found in books I and others have written, but the land and environment around it absolutely plays a significant role in why we might experience more of these encounters there than at other locations. I've done a lot of work with what's known as the Alaska Triangle (yes, think Bermuda Triangle in Alaska) which is known for an exorbitant amount of missing people and airplanes, UFO and UAP sightings, supernatural activity, ghost ships, scores of cryptid encounters, and more, and we can trace some of the science behind this to a 1965 magnetic survey by the U.S. Department of the Interior which detected "negative anomalies" throughout the 100,000 square miles they covered (Alaska is 663,300 square miles):

"The magnetic profiles show numerous anomalies caused by variations in magnetization of the rocks, principally the mafic and ultramafic varieties, but also some granitic and metamorphic rocks. This magnetization is a combination of that induced by the present earth's field and the remanent magnetization – the latter tending to be largest in the mafic volcanic rocks. In some cases the direction of the remanent magnetization is reversed to give a negative anomaly."

Whenever I'm asked about my opinions on Skinwalker Ranch which, similarly, experiences UFO and UAP sightings, shadow people in the old homesteads, and, of course, sightings of the legendary skinwalker creatures, I always point to the ground. I believe there's some sort of massive mineral deposit under the Uintah Basin region that is the cause of all of this strange activity. Some think it's an ancient UFO buried within the mesa on Skinwalker Ranch, and while they have uncovered some interesting metals from a bit of drilling performed there, I'm still a bit skeptical of that notion. What's there could still have cosmic origins, and I am more open to the idea that there may be an ancient meteorite buried there with a high concentration of metals and minerals that when the magnetism from the core of the Earth passes through it causes some really strange and bizarre things to occur. Does the interaction of these things create wormholes or portals, almost like the ones we see in space, to allow things to come through from other dimensions, points in time, or even other locations in the universe? All of these options are on the table, and the intrigue of trying to solve the mystery is one of the things I absolutely love about this field.

Everything is connected.

Nikola Tesla's Earth Energy Quest

What Did He Rediscover from the Ancients?

September 2, 2024

Article Notes: I don't get into it here, but I believe one of the reasons Tesla was so ahead of his time was because he was tapping into what I call "Eternal Knowledge," what Carl Jung called the collective unconscious, and others call the Akashic Records. However, because what he was tapping into was from the distant future, his peers and potential investors were restricted by their era from seeing the full vision which came to fruition in a 100 years time. I dive into the concepts of Eternal Knowledge in Travels Through Time.

There was a bit of a chill in the air one evening in mid-October 1899 just outside Colorado Springs when a tall, lanky Serbian inventor, Nikola Tesla, strode out from his laboratory to conduct yet another one of his experiments to harness wireless energy. At this point, there had already been claims that he'd lit up 200 light bulbs wirelessly from a distance of 26 miles, and he'd been extremely vocal in the press regarding the real possibilities humans could generate free wireless energy on demand in mass quantities. On this particular day, Tesla had plugged several cold lamps into the soil and backed off about a mile away where he had instructed his assistant, Koleman Czito, to watch for his signal.

As the Sun sank behind the horizon and Colorado Springs began illuminating their streetlights, the inventor waved at Czito to fire up the equipment they were testing that evening. What happened next has become the stuff of legend.

Tesla biographer Mark J. Seifer describes the event in his 1998 book *Wizard: The Life and Times of Nikola Tesla*:

> "The sound began as a low rumble and built to a "roar [that] was so strong it could be plainly heard ten miles away." The ground trembled with the noise as the inventor gazed over to a nearby corral to watch a half-dozen horses rear on their hind legs and gallop frantically away. "Butterflies were carried around in … circle[s] as in a [whirlpool] and could not get out, no matter how hard they tried," as the flume of streamers stormed up the shaft of the lab high above the roof of the lab and blustered out from the apex, splitting lightning bolts fully 135 feet in length. Kaboom! Zip! Zap! Kaboom! Looking to the sky, the wizard held his wireless torches up in triumph as they flickered in his thunder."
>
> The end came abruptly, the Springs plunged into darkness. He had shorted out the town."

Nikola Tesla was a visionary far ahead of his time, discussing concepts of wireless technology, artificial intelligence, drones, and more 100 years before they became a part of our daily lives. For these types of concepts, he was largely laughed at, although he was

Nikola Tesla's famous electricity photo from his Colorado Springs workshop.

still well-respected for his "more practical" accomplishments of the era in the development of alternating current (AC), early fluorescent lighting, harnessing Niagara Falls, and the 300 patents he held.

Tesla's famous Wardenclyffe Tower in New York, built in 1901, was designed to be a prototype of a global, wireless communication system that could broadcast music, news, stock market reports, secured military communications, even facsimile images around the world, using the Earth itself as a conductor. Tesla's dream was to not only revolutionize telecommunications by creating a system for relaying information wirelessly, but also to create a viable method for transferring power currents around the globe by capturing the Earth's natural energy. He believed the Earth's own resonant frequency could be used as a massive carrier wave to distribute vast quantities of electric power. In an article on *Collier's Weekly* published when he began work on Wardenclyffe, Tesla stated he could use:

Tesla's Wardenclyffe tower in the height of its glory (1901 - 1903).

"... the Earth itself as the medium for conducting the currents, thus dispensing with wires and all other artificial conductors ... a machine which, to explain its operation in plain language, resembled a pump in its action, drawing electricity from the Earth and driving it back into the same at an enormous rate, thus creating ripples or disturbances which, spreading through the Earth as through a wire, could be detected at great distances by carefully attuned receiving circuits. In this manner I was able to transmit to a distance, not only feeble effects for the purposes of signaling, but considerable amounts of energy ..."

Unfortunately, because Guglielmo Marconi was making great strides with radio devices (using Tesla's technology – Nikola Tesla would eventually be recognized as the inventor of radio after he died following a lifetime of arguing that Marconi was wrongfully credited with his work) and investors began flocking to him, Tesla kept increasing the scope of his project. At one point, he wanted to construct a 600-foot tower but pulled back to 300 feet after a meeting with his primary investor, J.P. Morgan in August 1901. As fate would have it, Morgan decided to discontinue his financial backing of Wardenclyffe, leaving Tesla to scramble for other investors which were scarce. The famous inventor entered into many legal battles over the property after its last operation in 1903, the facility turned to ruin, and the tower was torn down in 1917.

While Nikola Tesla's grandiose plans to harness to power of the Earth were scuttled and he never saw many of his more eccentric concepts come to fruition, he was definitely an advocate for our modern-day philosophy of "go big or go home." Perhaps turning Earth into one gigantic dynamo wouldn't have been the best idea (I expect cases of cancer would have gone through the roof), but the idea of controlled harnessing of the planet's energy for human consumption is not without merit, and it is certainly not unprecedented. On a much larger scale, Tesla was trying to tap into something the ancients had known about for thousands of years, and we see the evidence of that lost knowledge all over the world.

Stone circles and other megalithic structures were built by the ancient to harness the earth's energy in order to ... well, that's the big question. Why exactly did they build these structures and for what exactly did they use the energy? Was it for healing purposes? Was it to enter into altered states of consciousness? Was it to access portals and other dimensions? Perhaps it was for all of these reasons and more, but they used the same general principles Tesla was trying to apply, they just used stone rather than steel.

Back in the late 1970s and early 1980s, a group of researchers and scientists formed The Dragon Project whose goal was, specifically, to examine energy anomalies produced by stone circles. Why was it called The Dragon Project? This harkens back to the representation in the ancient world of earth energy being represented by a serpent, in this instance a dragon, since in Chinese geomancy the concept of earth currents is represented by the greatest serpent of all – the dragon. The electromagnetism they discovered emanating from the stones wasn't a steady stream, but it pulsated and seemed to change with the time of day and the time of year. In his 1985 book *Circles of Silence*, Don Robins, one of the scientists from The Dragon Project, tells us about the Rollright stones in the UK:

> "Shortly before dawn, positioned at the Kingstone, I watched the fluctuations in the dreary grey light, and suddenly the fluctuation patterns changed slowly into the regular, rhythmic pulsing! As they did so the intensity gradually increased until there was a full-scale deflection, from 0 to 10. The length and character of the pulsing was just like the previous visits – whatever had waned at the solstice was back with a vengeance. … The most surprising observation was to find that the circle and the dolmen also had the same level of activity, and this was true for a considerable distance all around the site. Backwards and forwards we went, the full-scale pulsing evident at all the points, and this went on for over two hours after sunrise."

There are many more examples of the types and amounts of energy that have been detected at stone structures around the world, including massive sites like the Great Pyramid of Giza. Many of Nikola Tesla's concepts for harnessing the earth's energy were derived from the pyramids, but he was trying to bring that energy to us in a much more modern context and on a much larger scale. When my new book, *Portals to the Stars*, comes out later this year we'll be taking a hard look at a lot of these different kinds of concepts. You just got a small taste of it here.

Part 6

The Writing Path

Notes on Part 6

Writing, at least for me, is a journey. I know where I'm starting and I have a general idea of where I want to get to, but everything else in between is an adventure with many twists and turns and can certainly change over time. Since I also own and operate my own publishing company, Haunted Road Media, this certainly provides even more adventurous aspects, not only for my own books, but also for the other books I publish for a number of authors. At this point in 2024, I was in the midst of the final stage of publishing *Portals to the Stars* while also remaining busy in other areas. Like I've said before, the juggle is real.

The Big Cover Reveal

Portals to the Stars Coming Soon!

September 9, 2024

I wasn't expecting it to be ready this past Friday, but there it was sitting in front of me, and I smiled. I liked what I saw, and it was pretty close to the way I imagined it. Those that I sent it to before I made the post also agreed it looked good, and thus, very unexpectedly, I made a post on social media revealing the cover to my upcoming book, *Portals to the Stars: Inside Stargates, Atlantis, and Secrets of Ancient Egypt*.

In recent years, as the publisher of Haunted Road Media, I have outsourced a number of the more recent book covers to some very talented graphic artists, but I have continued to create the artwork for my own works (the only exception being the second edition of *A Walk in the Shadows*). So, when I look at one of my books, they really are one of my "babies," a personal accomplishment of which I can forever be proud. The cover of this new book, *Portals to the Stars*, really speaks to me, especially having hosted multiple tours now exploring the stargates of ancient Egypt (we'll be returning in November 2025). However, there's a lot more in this book than just stargates. As the second entry to the *Connecting the Universe* series, you'll discover that I've connected a lot of my previous work like the Alaska Triangle and our explorations there with earth energy to this new book. There are even connections back to *Travels Through Time*, my journeys into the nature of time and the possibilities of real time travel.

When is the book due out? I'm currently looking at the end of October, either the 22nd or 29th. Ideally, I would already know this date, but this particular project has taken many twists and turns, starting as *Energized Earth* before morphing into *Portals to the Stars* following this past April's Egypt tour (Egypt has done this to me before). "Energized Earth" is still a chapter within the new book, so you'll still get plenty of that content, and I may still write a full book on the subject at a later time. Again, by operating my own publishing company, I have a lot of flexibility here and can really take a project down to the wire like this. It's not ideal, but I absolutely want this book available for a special event I'm presenting in Rahway, New Jersey, on November 9.

Hosted by the Merchants and Drovers Tavern Museum, not only will guests be the first to get their hands on a copy of the new book, but they'll also enjoy a special four-part presentation exploring many of the topics covered in the new work, including:

- Stargates, Portals, and Ancient Symbolism
- The Egypt – Atlantis Connection
- Triangle Areas of the World
- Consciousness and Time Travel

These special presentations will explore some of the most fascinating connections within our world and universe, seeking out where lost ancient wisdom is still present in our world today and revealed in a variety of phenomena. Make your own personal discoveries and become part of the story!

Archive of the Connected Universe: Volume 1

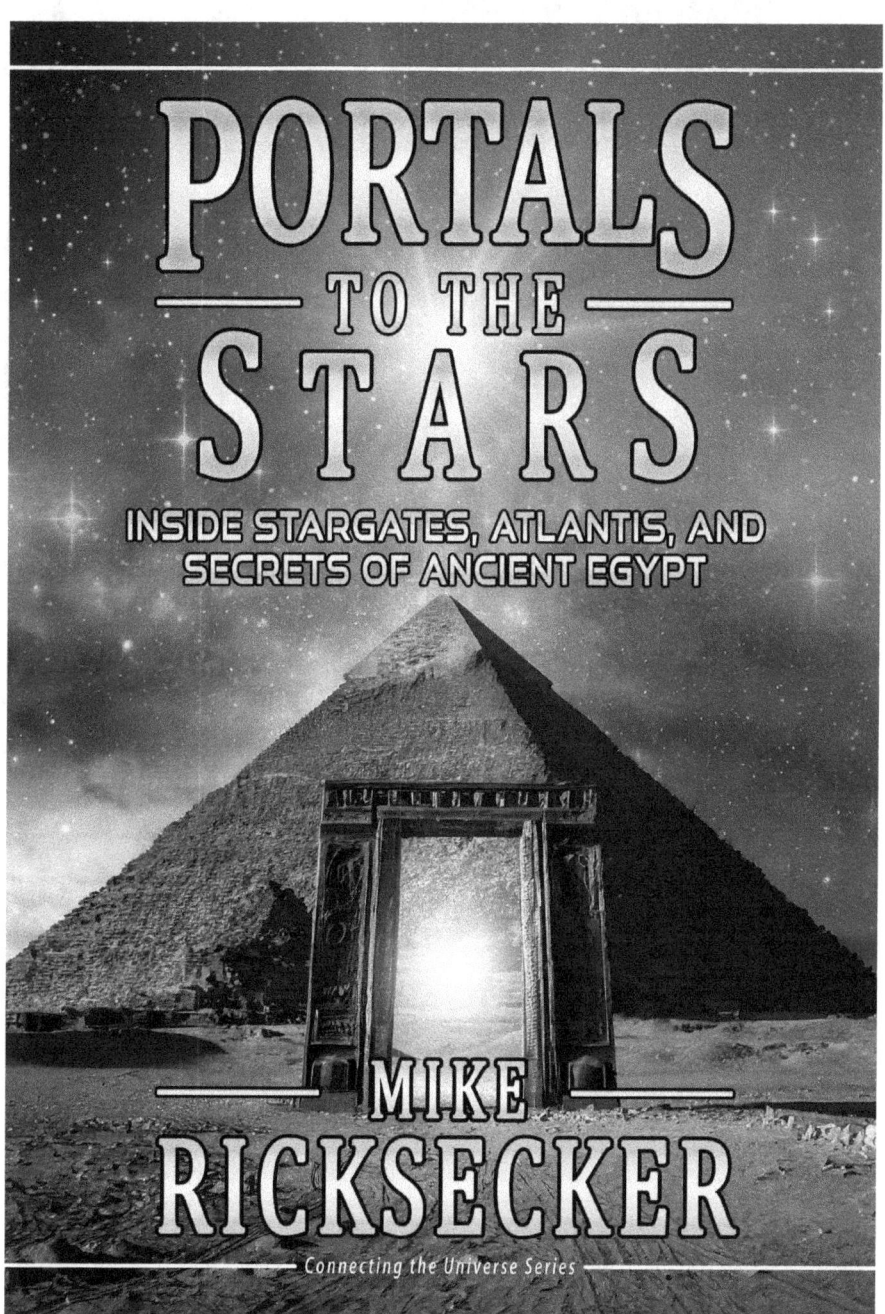

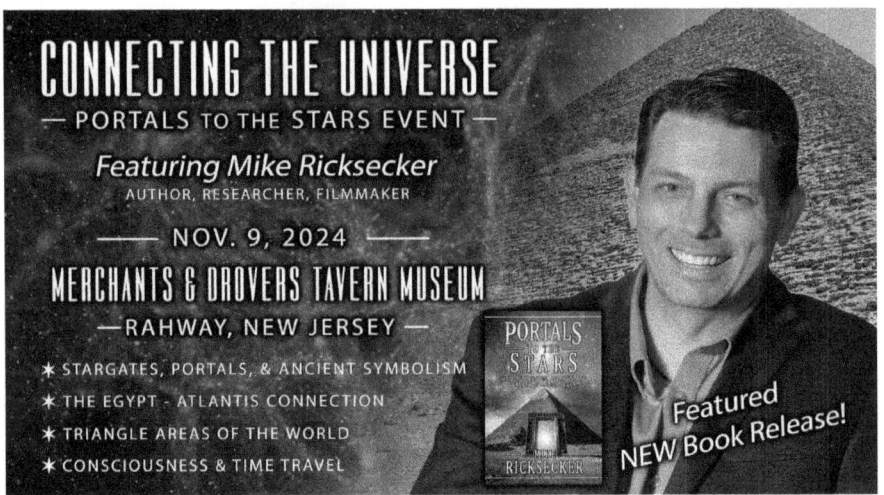

Ok, that's my brief pitch for the event, but it really is going to be an absolutely fantastic time, and I always enjoy the discussions I have with guests during these events. We typically find ourselves engrossed in deep discussions about the nature of the universe, experiences we've had, and unexplained phenomena we're still trying to make sense of (and the ancients likely had the answers for). And that is largely what the book is going to be about! I can't wait to share it with everyone!

Journey of a Lifetime

My Unconventional Writing Path

September 16, 2024

It's been a hell of a journey. Twenty-one years ago this month I signed my first book contract for a mystery novel, *Deadly Heirs*, which celebrated its 20th anniversary back in April. I didn't really celebrate it because that anniversary fell on the first day of my most recent Egypt tour, and well, I may have been a little preoccupied with pyramids and ancient temples. It's something I'm quite proud of even if it wasn't a massive best seller. It was the first of thirteen that I've published so far (the fourteenth is on the way next month), and it's certainly been a rollercoaster ride to get where I'm at now.

Writing has been a passion my entire life. Before portals and stargates, before shadow beings and historic haunted houses, before theories on real time travel, I knew exactly what I wanted to do as a seven-year-old in second grade. From the moment I started cobbling together whole sentences the year beforehand in Miss Steele's classroom at Juniper Park Elementary, I knew I could tell stories with these words, but it was that second grade year when it all clicked and I knew I wanted to be a writer. I absolutely loved the

A young writer being creative at our Uncle Paul's house in Rhode Island, June 1982.

Encyclopedia Brown detective series by Donald J. Sobol in which a young boy solved neighborhood crimes using his keen intellect for just 25 cents per day – plus expenses, of course. I wanted to create my own little detective stories, so I set out to writing and ended up with quite an assortment, many of which, thankfully, still exist today because my mother. I also wrote some small little ghost stories, and – if you can believe this from a seven-year-old – historic fiction. Now, at seven and growing up for ten years in Massachusetts, this amounted to American Revolution tales of George Washington and his lieutenant with stick figure battles for illustrations.

It was a start. My stories were shown to the school administration, and I was asked to read some of the tales to my class. When the reading concluded, I signed my first autograph for a girl named Marybeth right in the middle of Mrs. Ahearn's classroom. Fun!

My writing evolved as a kid depending on what I was into at the time. Before the film came out, I wrote a version of *Rocky III* in which Rocky became friends with Apollo Creed, and he ended up

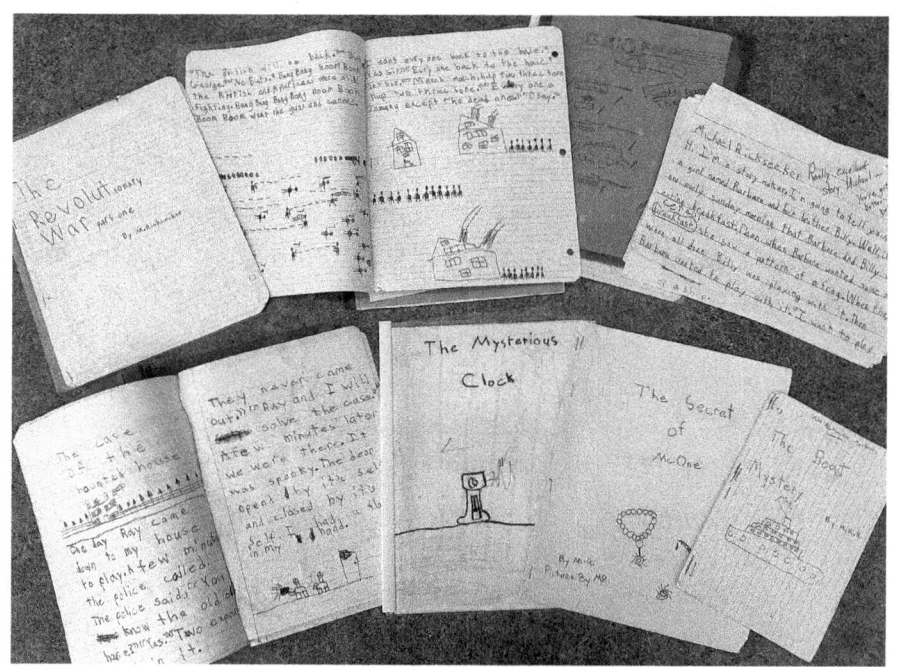

A collection of early writings.

fighting a Russian boxer (I recount this tale in full in *Travels Through Time*). I created my own versions of *Choose Your Own Adventure* books. I wrote scores of *Dungeons and Dragons* modules and campaigns and was shocked at the beginning of the first episode of *Stranger Things* – here was a kid named Mike with the same moppy black hair I had at the time playing the Dungeon Master for a group of friends in the early 1980s around the same age we would have been at that time in the 80s. It was literally like watching a moment pulled out of my own life.

I wrote adventure stories, *G.I. Joe* comics, time travel stories, and even dabbled in a little romance as I got older. In junior high and high school, I started working extensively on another kind of writing: song lyrics. Oh, I wrote tons and tons of songs that were never recorded musically and still run around in my head today. These glorified poems were an outlet for my emotions and teen angst, and I wish I still had those today. Unfortunately, the box I kept them in was lost during my move out of Alaska in 1995 when the Air Force was transferring me to Maryland. Most of my old *Dungeons and Dragons* writings and material had tragically been in that box, too. I have a couple rough recordings on an old cassette of a couple of those songs that actually made it to music, but that's it. I did play in a band during my senior year of high school, but most of that material from Pandora's Box was written by my friend, Ron.

After reading all of this, naturally, you think I was geared up for a career in writing, right? Perhaps I was going to go to college and major in English or journalism, correct? Nope. I won an award as Wooster High School's "Outstanding Senior" in the business department in 1992. Say what? Yeah, here was my flawed logic ...

First of all, aside from writing, I loved baseball. I absolutely wanted to become a Major League baseball player and had been pretty darned good when I was younger. In fact, while I may have given my first autograph in second grade, I actually started developing the signature I have today when I was 12 years old because I thought I was going to be signing my autograph on a lot of baseball cards (I still have a massive collection of cards today, by the way). As a backup, if baseball didn't work out, I felt like I still wanted to be comfortable, financially. Well, there's money in business. So, I took every business course my high school had to offer and geared myself up for getting a degree in business administration in college. I'd play baseball for the school, hopefully move on to play professionally, earn my degree, and writing ... well, that would always be there, I thought. So, naturally, I enlisted in the Air Force and found myself in boot camp two weeks after graduating high school. Say what, again? I said at the beginning of this it's been a hell of a journey. (See the Acknowledgments in *Alaska's Mysterious Triangle* for a few more details on that particular story.)

To make a long story short (too late), I spent six years in the Air Force and ended up with a 30-year career in IT. The career in computers wasn't completely out of left field. I'd always had an

Summer 1992. What the hell was I doing here?

interest, and my father had the foresight to bring a Commodore computer into the house in the mid-eighties so my sister and I could get familiar with it. At his job, he'd seen how industry was going more and more towards computers and knew it was going to be a part of our future. So, I learned to program on the computer and took some of my stories into those programs as well. In fact, that's where I decided I wanted to take my detective stories in the mid-nineties as computer adventure games became popular. Inspired by the Tex Murphy line of futuristic detective games like *Under a Killing Moon* (James Earl Jones who passed away last week did voice work for this) and *The Pandora Directive*, I took a private investigator character I created in high school, Chase Michael DeBarlo, and began developing a game script around him. In the meantime, while my Air Force career centered around computers, I also became the editor for the squadron's newsletter. This included writing most of the articles, artwork, formatting, and more. It was a nice change of pace.

I imagine back issues of the The Monitor *are pretty rare.*

In 1998, I exited the Air Force right in the midst of the big tech boom and found ample opportunities for my budding IT career. The game script idea, however, took a different turn. Somewhere along the way, I realized that as a busy father with three children (number four would come along in 2002) I didn't have the time to develop an entire game on my own, and I certainly didn't have the capital to hire a team. Thus, the game script was transfigured into a book and eventually became the novel *Deadly Heirs*.

I set to work immediately on a sequel, but then the universe decided to push me in another direction. Trust the universe, right? An editor for Schiffer Publishing, Dinah, reached out to me over MySpace (that tells you how long ago this was) where I had been marketing my book, and asked if I would be interested in writing for them. While I was a fiction writer, she saw that I had an interest in the paranormal and Schiffer was looking to expand their line of paranormal offerings (most likely because paranormal television had really started to take off in the early-to-mid-2000s). "We need someone to write a nonfiction book about true hauntings in the state

The last remnant of the detective computer game concept can be found on the back cover of Deadly Heirs.

of Maryland. Would you be interested?"

This decision had quite its own little adventure in a premonition I had while sleeping that evening and can be found in the introduction of *Ghosts of Maryland*. I accepted the offer, of course, and my career in writing about the paranormal and supernatural began. Yes, in some ways it kind of fell into my lap, but I'd already been a writer, and yes, I did have an interest in the paranormal, had supernatural experiences throughout my life, and had written some spooky short stories. I even had a brief scene with a psychic medium named Mystical Marina in *Deadly Heirs*. So, the idea wasn't too far-fetched. It was just a bit of a course correction by the universe.

What I really enjoyed about writing that book was giving a voice to those people forgotten to history, forgotten to time. Many of the stories I'd been encountering in my research were just fragments of information. I loved diving into the history and uncovering stories from the original sources that had been forgotten for decades, sometimes centuries. That's something I still do today. While I might find a reference in an article or book that is helpful to my research, I want to find where that bit initially came from and get the full context of that original piece.

I would say the rest is history, but there are always curveballs along the way. After *Ghosts of Maryland* and the subsequent *Ghosts and Legends of Oklahoma*, I was still trying to find a taker for mystery novel's sequel. I wasn't happy with my first publisher and got the rights back to *Deadly Heirs*, so it was almost like starting over for the follow-up and, in many ways, made more difficult because I was trying to pitch a book that was a sequel in a series to a low-selling book that was no longer in print. (I eventually published a 10th Anniversary Edition of *Deadly Heirs*). Frustrated, I decided to self-publish *System of the Dead* through Amazon. While still not a best seller, that experience led to something else: *Haunted Road Media*.

I was computer savvy, decent at digital art, and a good writer who had learned the process of publishing in two different arenas: traditionally through my two publishers and digitally through Amazon. I also had people constantly asking me for advice on how to get published. I would give them some tips and throw them to the wolves. But now ... I could become a publisher and, instead of throwing them to the wolves, I could take them through the process. So, that's what I did. I could use Amazon for printing and do everything else myself. (I now also use Ingram.)

My first attempt was with a small anthology, *Encounters with the Paranormal*. I asked people for contributions of personal encounters they'd had and gave them a copy of the book when it was published. This was mildly successful, but I was developing a process and started taking on other writers. I also asked for more contributions to *Encounters* and developed a set of four, the last three of which include a featured location: the Goldenrod Showboat, Mineral Springs Hotel, and Ferry Plantation. (The first volume featured the Stone Lion Inn on the cover, but only my single story

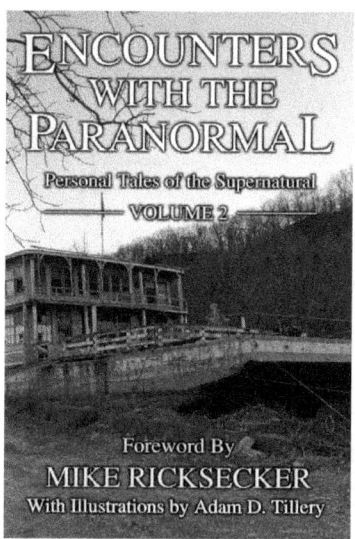
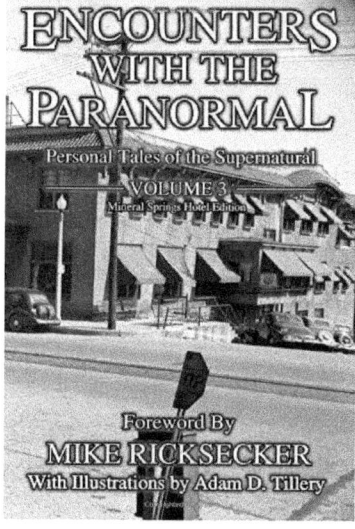
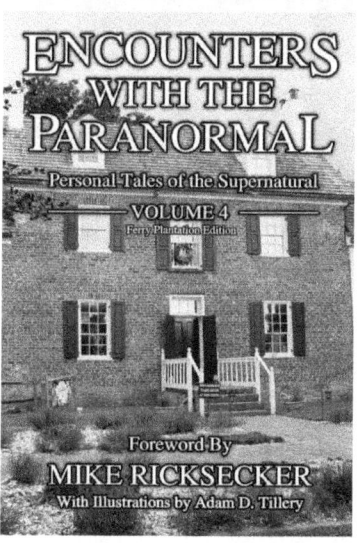

The four volumes of Encounters with the Paranormal.

discussed it.)

My own writing had stalled out a bit, however. Yes, I had a few of my own stories in each anthology, but it had been a while since my last Schiffer book, *Campfire Tales: Midwest*, and my own *Ghostorian Case Files* which one of those *Campfire* stories

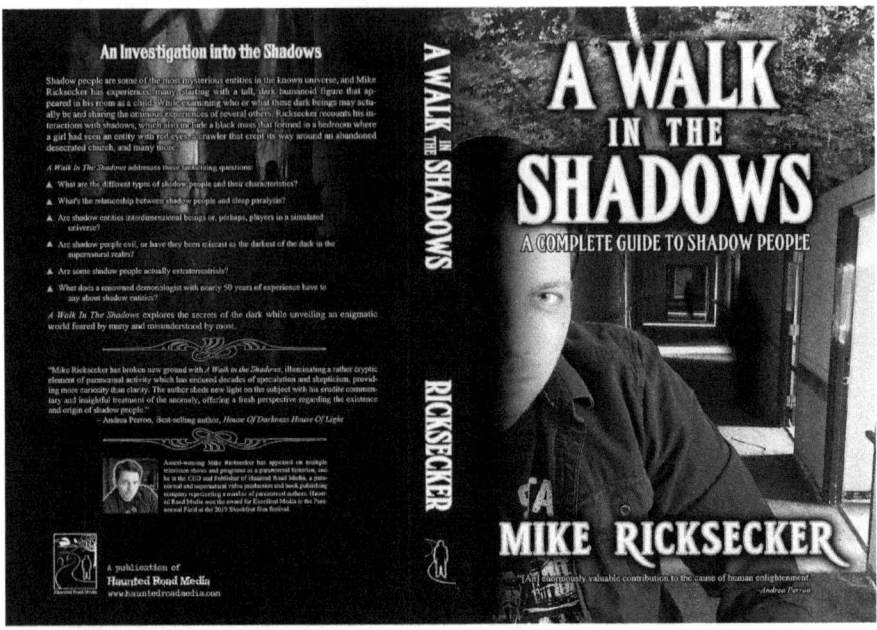

First Edition cover of A Walk in the Shadows. The book dropped and then COVID hit. I released a second edition with the better book cover and more content in 2021.

influenced and was really another trial run for Haunted Road Media. The research I'd been conducting for years was far more than just ghost stories and tales of hauntings. The paranormal is just the tip of the iceberg to something much larger, something much more expansive across the universe – and across dimensions. I'd had piles of notes, several videos I'd put together, presentations I'd given, and my own personal experiences I'd had dating back to when I was eight years old. It was finally time to put it all together and write my book on shadow phenomena, *A Walk in the Shadows: A Complete Guide to Shadow People*.

For me, this was the big one that really started a new wave of writing for me. I consider now my first 10 books to be the training ground, places where I honed my craft over the years. I always tell aspiring writers, "Read, read, read; write, write, write." You're not going to get better if you don't practice, and now *A Walk in the Shadows* (with its blatant Queensrÿche reference) was like making

Back in Alaska for The Alaska Triangle, May 2019.

my Major League debut.

The universe then had another curveball for me: Alaska. I'd spent three years there as a young airman, and I'd been called back to film up north for *The Alaska Triangle* television show. Wild Dream Entertainment had contacted me about a little-viewed video I'd posted on my YouTube channel about the relationship between hot spot areas of earth energy, portals, and supernatural activity, and when they discovered I'd also spent time in Alaska, it was a natural fit.

Of course, I had to write about it (*Alaska's Mysterious Triangle*), revisit my time there, and learn deeper details about some of the stories and legends I'd heard about during my time in service. However, it also caused me to dive deeper into the relationship between electromagnetic activity and strange phenomena throughout the world. I'd already made that connection, of course, given that they found me through a video talking about it, but this inspired me to make it a greater area of my research. And this led me back to Egypt.

I had been fascinated with Egypt since – well, I grew up in the 80s, so there was Indiana Jones, of course. But it really started in 1993 with the *Mysteries of the Sphinx* special hosted by Charleton Heston and featuring the work of John Anthony West and Robert Schoch redating the age of the Sphinx. I was completely fascinated. The following year, the movie *Stargate* hit the box office, and I can't tell you how many times I watched that film when I first rented it from Blockbuster. So, it had always been with me. In the early 2010s, I started work on a YouTube series titled *Ancient and Historic Supernatural Secrets* which only amounted to a trailer and one vlog-type preview of me talking about knowledge lost to time and asking the question, "How old is antiquity?" (Seeing me on camera back then, good God, I've come a long way.) But now, I was inspired to dig deeper and expand my horizons yet again. Thank you, Universe.

Thus, I'm now co-hosting trips to Egypt with Mohamed Ibrahim and writing books about stargates and portals. I even included a bit about stargates in my last book *Travels Through Time* even though it's a book on the nature of time and the possibilities of real time travel (again, channeling early interests of mine like *Somewhere in Time* and drawing upon ruminations I'd had 20 years beforehand on how the universe works).

If you've stuck with me this far, wow! I sincerely appreciate that. What started off as what I thought was going to be a playful reminiscence of my writing journey turned out to be almost like a mini autobiography. There's much more on the way, however. The journey doesn't end here. The upcoming *Portals to the Stars* is only the second in the *Connecting the Universe* series, and – dare I say it – there may be some of my fiction work returning to print. I haven't presented any of that since my brief foray into the *Time Channeler Chronicles* webisodes with artist Adam D. Tillery about six years

Still writing, still climbing. (Working on Alaska's Mysterious Triangle in 2021)

ago, but I've been jotting down ideas, notes, and little story pieces for a long, long time, and I think it's due they got some love. Soon. First, on to *Portals* ...

September 2025 Addendum: Those little story pieces have come a long way since I wrote this blog article, and I've now written several chapters of a sci-fi fantasy novel which I've really enjoyed creating.

Stargates and Time Travel

The Next Tour and the Latest Interview

September 27, 2024

Article Notes: Sometimes you just end up with a simple piece that promotes the latest interview on Gaia TV and a corresponding tour. Here, the third Stargates of Ancient Egypt tour was announced more than a year ahead of time to be available for those who watched my interview with George Noory when it dropped. Yes, it's pretty blatant, but it's also pretty smart.

The timing has been impeccable. I've been busily pushing forward with the new *Portals to the Stars* book, which includes the subtitle *Inside Stargates, Atlantis, and Secrets of Ancient Egypt*, and my Egyptian partner in crime, Mohamed Ibrahim, published the registration page for the next Stargates of Ancient Egypt tour in 2025. While it's more than a year away at this point, time flies, and suddenly we'll be exploring pyramids, temples, and the secrets of the ancient stargates in no time.

This next Stargates tour we'll be visiting an entirely new location I haven't yet been before: Faiyum. There's a lot for us to explore here, including Hawara Pyramid, Lahun Pyramid, Mastaba 17, and the Egyptian Labyrinth. All of these are quite interesting, but one that really stands out to me is Lahun Pyramid, also known as the Pyramid of Senusret II whose son, Senusret III, is one of the five kings of Egypt who bore the "Stargate" title. It's no wonder then that this pyramid has been home to several UFO sightings over the years. Usually, we start delving more into the stargates when we head south for our Nile cruise where there are several temples which housed stargates. At Faiyum, we'll be able to start taking a deeper dive into stargates quite early in our adventures.

Of course, the big question about stargates is what did the ancients actually use them for? Did they travel across the universe, across the world, into other dimensions? Did they enter into altered states of consciousness? Were they actually able to use a stargate to travel through time? Perhaps it was for all of these purposes – or for reasons we haven't even yet considered.

This past week, my latest interview with George Noory on *Beyond Belief* dropped on Gaia's streaming service, and we discussed at length the nature of time and the possibilities of real time travel. Titled "Time Slips and Ghosts from the Future," we did briefly discuss the idea of using a stargate to travel through time, harkening back to my interview with George on Gaia last year which specifically covered stargates. I really enjoyed this last interview (well, I've enjoyed them all) since it spotlighted a number of different topics I cover in my book *Travels Through Time: Inside the Fourth Dimension, Time Travel, and Stacked Time Theory*.

In many ways, what we find throughout ancient Egypt seems out of time. They possessed some sort of engineering skill, some sort of knowledge, that we don't possess today to be able to build these massive structures that we would be hard-pressed to construct with our modern technology. Some of these insanely heavy stone blocks they were able to move back then we lack the equipment to be able to lift them in the 21st century. Did they use their stargates to acquire

The date of the third Stargates tour is just after publication of the book in your hand.

that knowledge, whether that was actually traveling to a distant future or communicating with a more sophisticated civilization in the cosmos, or perhaps, tapping into the eternal knowledge of the universe and downloading the information?

We've seen evidence of advanced machining that our traditional archaeology says the ancient Egyptians shouldn't have possessed, that everything we see was built with stone and copper tools. But then we look at something like a half-cut granite sarcophagus in the Egyptian Museum in Cairo and find the very distinct markings of the use of circular saws, one on top of the other, to cut the lid of the sarcophagus off the underside. What kind of circular saw (which, again, they weren't supposed to have) can cut through granite? Today, we would use diamond-tipped saw blades for that. What did *they* actually use, and how did they have that sort of technology at their disposal? These are all things we'll explore on the next Stargates of Ancient Egypt tour in November 2025!

Mysterious Lights in the Woods

Interdimensional Beings or Something Else?

October 7, 2024

Article Notes: At the time of this book's publication, post-production for The Shadow Dimension: Beyond the Shadows *will have been completed with a potential release date for early 2026. Also of note ... I had a skeptic journalist remark on this account that it's "typical" of paranormal investigators to not go chasing after these things they see and just provide these cryptic observations from a distance. Again, the large ball of light was on someone else's property who Dan, the owner of Hinsdale has had challenges with. I respected that boundary. Otherwise, yes, I would have, as I usually do, gone chasing right after it. But as you'll see ... the phenomenon came to us later in the evening.*

It's been just over five years since the mysterious blue lights floated down out of the woods behind the Hinsdale House in New York, mesmerizing both myself and my friend, Meghan Talbert, but it's still one of the most amazing things I've seen on a paranormal investigation, and it's an event I got to revisit in my upcoming book

The stairs which lead into the woods behind Hinsdale House from which the small blue lights descended upon us in the backyard.

Portals to the Stars: Inside Stargates, Atlantis, and Secrets of Ancient Egypt. We're also revisiting it in the upcoming second part to *The Shadow Dimension* docuseries (I know it's been a long time coming, but at least it hasn't been as long of a wait as it has been for George R.R. Martin's *The Winds of Winter*). Still, to this day, we don't know for sure what exactly these little blue lights were, and no, they were not fireflies.

This particular incident occurred at the end of September 2019, not the middle of summer when fireflies are prevalent. Also, these were blue, and while blue fireflies do exist in the United States, they are rare and are generally confined to the Carolinas — in June. Again, we were in New York. So, what were these and what exactly happened?

Full details, of course, are in the upcoming book, but essentially, it all started when we spotted a large blue ball of light in the woods back behind the house that evening. Where this thing was sort of gliding through the trees we couldn't explore since it was on someone else's property, and we eventually had to abandon our attempts at interaction and return to investigating the house. As the night wore on, we eventually went out to the backyard to take a

The historic Goldenrod Showboat in 2016 just a couple years before it was lost in a tragic fire. It used to host prominent entertainment on the Mississippi.

break and enjoy the fire. That's when little blue lights started trickling down from the woods. They were really quite amazing ... the ones floating in the air twinkled while the ones on the ground slowly morphed in and out of existence.

We were absolutely amazed, and we tried to debunk these things as bugs, getting down on our hands and knees with flashlights, but there were no bugs we could see. The most difficult thing was to try to get these things on camera. Try as we might with IR and full spectrum since it was nighttime, the only bit of luck we had was about a two second clip with a video camera in its regular mode in which I just barely picked up a slight blue glow. The strength of the blue just wasn't strong enough for the camera to really pick it up, but we could plainly see them with our eyes.

This wasn't the first time I had seen something that I've, essentially, chalked up to as "fairies." Back in 2016, following an event we ran on the historic Goldenrod Showboat, there were three of us who witnessed a yellow ball of light bouncing around the boat's showroom for nearly five minutes before it finally zoomed into the lobby and out the front door. The most interesting aspect of this event was how transformative it was, at one point becoming a bar of light on the ground before "fluttering" (it's the best term I can use to describe it) and taking to the air again.

This, of course, was quite different than the blue lights we saw at the Hinsdale House, but I believe they're related to a degree. Both of these were some sort of small being or entity that emanated a light, one a tiny soft blue glow, the other a small bright light when it was on the ground and then becoming a translucent yellow in the air. The one from the Goldenrod I might even call a "water sprite," if such things truly exist, just because we were docked on the edge of the *Illinois River* at the time. As for the Hinsdale House ... your classic woodland fairies?

It's really hard to say what they were and give a definitive answer, and trying to dive into fairy lore is almost impossible. There's been so much legend and lore built up over the centuries that it's near impossible to determine what's really true and what's not. I do believe there are grains of truth within all of that lore, and people have been witness to these types of tiny beings for as far back as recorded history. But what exactly are they? Are they something interdimensional? We do find a number of tales of humans being taken into the "fairy realm" where time works very differently, and these experiences sound reminiscent of our modern UFO abduction stories.

Fortunately, Meghan and I were not abducted, nor were the two ladies and I on the Goldenrod Showboat. However, we did get to experience something rather unique that has remained a mystery and could very well be evidence of travel between our world and other planes of existence. We'll explore more in *Portals to the Stars* soon!

Writing Portals to the Stars

A 2024 Publishing Odyssey

October 28, 2024

Article Notes: Anticipation was high for the release of Portals to the Stars *with my first interview late this very night on October 28 with Jimmy Church on* Fade to Black *and then the following evening with George Noory on* Coast to Coast AM. *Every book release becomes a very busy time and always toasted with wine.*

Each book I've written has its own story, its own metamorphosis and it grows and matures into the work that eventually ends up in the hands of curious readers. My latest book which will drop on Tuesday, *Portals to the Stars: Inside Stargates, Atlantis, and Secrets of Ancient Egypt* is no different. The topics of this particular book were supposed to be part of the third installment of the *Connecting the Universe* series, yet, it became the second. What happened?

In many ways, it's like what happened with *Travels Through Time*. I was in Egypt. (It seems like I say that a lot.) I had been in the process of writing a book called *Energized Earth*, and it was going to focus on the magnetic energy our planet has provided our

ancient sites of power and what ancient peoples may have used that energy for. That information is still a part of this new book, but it is a chapter (titled "Energized Earth," of course) rather than its own entire volume. Basically, I became inspired while on tour to go ahead and write the "stargates" book now.

As with other tours in Egypt, we had a very special group, really in tune and in sync with each other. While in 2023 we had a special group that was finding stargate symbolism left and right, this particular group in 2024 would sit around together for hours after our day was done discussing the deep meaning of the stargates and other aspects of the universe – and, yes, how everything is connected. We shared stories of adventures, not only in Egypt, but around the world, our explorations of sacred sites, the power they hold, and what it all means in the grand scheme of, not only the universe, but also of humanity. Those discussions motivated me to expedite the process in writing *Portals to the Stars*, although it did put me behind schedule of publishing the second entry to the *Connecting the Universe* series by the autumn.

I tried to sequester myself this past summer, tried to put myself into what I called "hermit mode," spending my days and nights writing and researching to get this book done in time. Of course, the universe had other ideas and threw amazing challenges my way.

Even when we were having fun on our last night on tour in Egypt in 2024, we always wound up in immensely deep conversations about the universe – the launchpad for Portals to the Stars.

"Yes, Mike. Write the book," it said. "But you're going to do so while on an airplane to Alaska." And Los Angeles. And New York (twice). Challenge accepted. And those challenges to simultaneously film those television shows while writing the book were truly fantastic because those topics flowed right into what I was writing about. At this point in time, I can't share with you what those television shows and episodes are going to be, but once you read the book and watch the shows when they eventually air, you'll see where these things all tie in together. The universe works in amazing ways like that sometimes.

The publication schedule became a bit hectic, but since I also operate my own independent publishing house (Haunted Road Media, representing several other authors) I've had some flexibility – although I would not say the process for this particular book has been ideal. With my last book, *Travels Through Time*, I had everything I needed done about a month and a half ahead of time. With *Portals to the Stars* ... well, let's just say there was some kind of mix up in which the paperback pre-order is not available on Amazon while the Kindle pre-order *is* (and already became a #1 New Release in UFOs), but Barnes and Noble actually has the paperback available for pre-order. Strange times, indeed. The audiobook also won't be available until at least late November since it's still in post-production as I write this. That said, it's always rewarding to have accomplished writing another book. The publishing aspect of it is just the formality of making it available, and within a month or two no one will remember the bit of a jumble it was to get it out the door.

With that in mind, as I post this particular blog article the day before the book's release, I will provide those pre-order links here for now. Once the book goes live tomorrow, I will update those links as need be.

Overall, I'm extremely happy with this new work. There are stories within it I've been wanting to tell for a long time, adventures that I've been wanting to pen for years, and connections I've absolutely been looking forward to revealing. As with other books, I've also asked for other experts in their respective fields to add their perspective to parts of this work, including Ronny LeBlanc, Dr. Heather Lynn, QHHT Practitioner Katherine Swinn, and Amy Waine from Amy's Crypt. Other voices are shared throughout this book as well, either through interview segments, shared stories, or their own written works. And the chapters on Egypt could not have been possible, of course, without the vast insight and knowledge my friend and colleague, Mohamed Ibrahim, has provided while we've been on tour together.

My wish is that *Portals to the Stars: Inside Stargates, Atlantis, and Secrets of Ancient Egypt* will open minds, souls, and the human consciousness to the myriad possibilities this universe provides. Or, as I say in the final paragraph of the introduction to this book:

My hope with this work is multi-faceted. For one, I hope you find the information here intriguing and will continue to pass on the knowledge to the next generation, so these ideas are not lost to time like so much else has been. Secondly, I hope some of what I present here will impact you on a much more personal level, providing a launching pad for transformation, a place to get you started on this interdimensional journey through the cosmos and consciousness. We're all in this together. Scores of people across the globe feel alone with their thoughts and ideas about how the universe really works, afraid that others will consider them nutjobs for saying something that flies in the face of convention and challenges the current narrative. I'm here to say, you're not alone. Speak your truth. Your drop in the ocean may be the one that changes the world – or even the universe.

Proving the Legends True

Relinquishing Stubbornness and Embracing Reality

November 4, 2024

Are legends and lore just only that, fantastic stories that have been passed down over time to recount over campfires? I've always contended there are always grains of truth to many of these tales that have been passed down over the years, but in many cases, they may actually be true in their entirety.

Just a few days ago, I posted an article on my social media (one of my daily "Mike's Morning Mug" posts) which detailed a recent discovery in Norway. For centuries, the "well man" legend was passed off as a piece of folklore regarding King Sverre Sigurdsson's reign during the 12th Century, and in 1197 he attacked Sverreborg Castle in a bloody raid in which he burned down the stronghold. In the midst of this attack he decided to poison the water supply of his adversaries by throwing a dead body into the well. Since Norse sagas are well-known for their flair for the dramatic, it was believed this part of the story was an embellishment. However, a recent excavation of the site revealed the remains of a male body within in the well which is about 900 years old, putting it right in the timeframe of the story. The legend of the "well man" is actually true.

Last night, I was interviewed by Dave Schrader on his Paranormal 360 radio show, and we got into a great discussion about what LiDAR technology has been revealing to us out in the jungles of the Amazon. For centuries, the stories Friar Gaspar de Carvajal wrote of the river expedition of explorer Francisco de Orellana, with whom he traveled, were considered tall tales and propaganda of vast cities throughout what became known as the Amazon. He described dense populations, extensive road systems, and massive construction, including one part of the river in which, "There was one town that stretched without any space from house to house, which was a marvelous thing to behold." The problem was, when later explorers ventured into the area, these cities were nowhere to be found. It must have all been Carvajal's vivid imagination, right? Perhaps he took ill or ate one of those "funky" plants.

Modern Light Detection and Ranging (LiDAR) technology, however, has been able to pull back the jungle landscape and reveal to us that, yes, in fact there were once large civilizations that occupied the jungle, their structures now lost beneath the canopy of the trees. Just showing up in my feed this morning was the report of a lost Mayan city near Compeche, Mexico, which contained over 6,000 structures, found using LiDAR. This technology is helping to confirm that many of the stories that have been passed down over time are not mere legend, but are actually true, and we need to reevaluate our previous prejudices and keep an open mind. Looking back at the Carvajal story, it's likely that the disease Europeans introduced into South America wiped out millions of indigenous people since the natives of the land would not have built up the necessary immunities in their bodies.

We see this type of obstinate stubbornness all over the world. For centuries (starting to sound familiar?), it was believed the city of Troy never existed, and it was just part of a myth written by Homer 3,000 years ago. However, self-taught German archaeologist

The discovery of Troy in 1871 proved the city wasn't just stuff of legend. It was real.

and businessman Heinrich Schliemann believed the story of the Trojan War as told in the *Iliad* was based on fact. Eventually teaming up with another amateur archaeologist, Frank Calvert, Schliemann proved his belief to be true when they discovered the ruins of the fabled city in 1871.

It's discoveries like this that keep me hopeful we'll eventually discover more concrete evidence of the civilization of Atlantis, a topic I wrote about at length in my latest book *Portals to the Stars: Inside Stargates, Atlantis, and Secrets of Ancient Egypt*. Perhaps we'll learn greater detail about what happened during the "Great Flood" or the "Great Cataclysm" stories that permeate throughout nearly every culture on Earth. And in other scientific realms we may uncover the secrets behind stories such as Rhys and Llewelyn, a fascinating account of one man's "five-minute" trip into the fairy realm which got his friend accused of murder when he continued to be missing nearly 24 hours later. We need to keep an open mind and understand that so many of these presumed legends are truly based on real events.

It's Unbelievable

Finally, the Blog About Filming the Unbelievable with Dan Aykroyd

November 15, 2024

Remember earlier this year when it seemed I was jetting around the country multiple times per week, but I never really explained what it was I was doing? Some of that secrecy is finally coming to an end. I was quite happy earlier this week when I was finally able to announce that I will be featured on the Season 2 premiere of *The Unbelievable with Dan Aykroyd*, "It Came From Above." So, what sort of unbelievable adventures transpired during my travels … besides cashing in on my traditional cheesecake at Junior's?

Really, the trick for me this year has been the tightness in which my schedule has operated. I've been to New York twice so far to film *The Unbelievable*, and the first excursion in May ran right up against the annual ParaPsyCon event in Mansfield, Ohio. The second time around in August took some maneuvering since I was filming for another show in Los Angeles on the 14th while I needed to be in the studio in New York on the 15th. And in between, I had the red-eye flight from L.A. dropping me off back home in Cleveland for a handful of hours. I don't sleep very well on planes,

In the studio discussing the Betty and Barney Hill story.

so, since I only live about 15 – 20 minutes from the airport, I decided to go home and sleep for a couple hours and freshen up before heading back to hop on the flight to New York. It was pretty crazy, especially, considering I was prepping for four episodes, the one in L.A. and three episodes of *The Unbelievable*. (There was also the Alaska trip in July which coincided with another New York trip, but that's a story for another day.)

One of the things that caught me by surprise was when I first got to A+E Studios in New York. The other shows I've worked on to date have, generally, been on location somewhere like a historic building, whereas this was the actual A+E building in New York with security turnstiles, two guys working reception, and a publicly viewable studio behind a glass wall off to the left. Something was going on there that day as I checked in with the front desk. The studio had an audience, and a woman with a microphone was addressing them. I paid it no mind at first, and I sat down to wait for someone from the filming crew to come and get me. As I was checking messages on my phone, I suddenly heard the woman introduce Sean Bean to the audience. Thunderous applause. *What? Sean Bean? Seriously?* My head swiveled to the left, and I thought

Hanging out with Brian Cano at Junior's after filming in August.

for a moment I saw the top of his head (if I'd heard correctly and it really was Sean Bean), but from my right came a different voice. "Mike?"

"Yeah, Abe Frohman. That's me." Er, well, Mike Ricksecker … and I was suddenly whisked away up the elevator. I have to say that most every crew I've worked with so far has been very professional, and those from Six West Media Group at A+E are no exception. They are absolutely top notch. I hung out in the green room for a short while, went over the material once more, and then was ushered into the studio. I was a bit surprised to find we were totally going to be green screen (although, after watching the first season I should have realized that), so that was a first for me. But really, whether it's green screen or sitting in "Mike's Office" in Pasadena, all I'm really doing is having a conversation with a producer. The producer driving the questions for this first episode was my friend, Laura Marini, who I have the thank immensely for the opportunity to work on this show. It's been amazing! Oh, and it must be noted that, no, Dan Aykroyd was not there. They film him elsewhere on a different set.

I'm not going to divulge what all we discussed during the filming – you'll have to watch the episode for that – but these were truly some fascinating topics, and I must admit, that some topics that I end up discussing on these types of shows will find their way into a few of my books. We make connections. And, of course, once it was all said and done after three hours with three different producers, I found myself sitting in Junior's with some wonderful blueberry cheesecake. It's become my tradition, something I treat myself with while I'm there … and then I walk Times Square and find some exploratory route back to my hotel. On occasion, I might meet up with a friend, like that time in August when Brian Cano joined me for some of that cheesecake. I'm not really a big city guy, but I have found something that works quite well for me while I'm there.

As more of these shows start to air, I will be happy to divulge some more details. For now, this is the first in a string of episodes we'll start to see – and there will be more from other shows as well. Remember, it was quite the busy travel summer, after all.

What Lies Beyond the Holidays?

Audiobook Updates, Black Friday, and New Projects

November 26, 2024

Article Notes: There are a couple paragraphs I've deleted here from this article since they were simply sales copy for Black Friday. For those looking for discounts on signed copies of my books that's usually the best time or through one of the other periodic sales I run. The Time Channeler Chronicles *mentioned here has, indeed, in part, found some of its elements integrated into the new sci-fi fantasy work I've been writing. I can't say much more about it at this point.*

Finally! Post-production of the audiobook for *Portals to the Stars* has concluded and my 2025 odyssey of publishing this latest work is done. Audio books have become more and more popular in recent years, and I've had several people asking me about when this format will be available for the new book – give it a few weeks while it processes. I'm also happy I was able to record the voice over myself, which is a ton of work, but listeners tend to prefer when an author voices his or her own work. So, now that *Portals to the Stars* is truly complete, what's next on the horizon?

Speaking of 2025, I have quite a few projects I'll be working on in the coming months. Will there be a follow up to *Portals to the Stars* in the *Connecting the Universe* series? Of course! Deciding what that will be is always precarious, however. After all, this last time I was working on a manuscript called *Energized Earth* which became a chapter within *Portals to the Stars*, but there was so much more to cover that I could expand that work. The partnerships I've made overseas this past year have really helped with this line of research that really brings us back to the origins of what the ancients were trying to channel.

I also put a feeler out there on social media the other week gauging what everyone's reaction would be to me diving back into some of my fiction writing. My first published book was a mystery novel, and while the work I have in mind wouldn't be a mystery, it's been gnawing at me to get written for quite a while. I have notes, ideas, and partially written chapters going back some years, and I started writing down more notes and ideas as I was about to board the plane for Egypt back in April. (There's always something about Egypt, isn't there?). This is something that wouldn't get seen by the public until at least 2026, but it will allow me to explore many of the concepts I've been discussing in my other books and apply them to a world where these things were readily accessible. If you're thinking that ideas from *Travels Through Time* and *Portals to the Stars* would probably fit some sort of sci-fi fantasy setting you would be correct.

That doesn't mean we've seen the last of my detective character, Chase Michael DeBarlo, whose adventures we last read during the abbreviated *Time Channeler Chronicles* a good seven years ago. It just means we might see him in different ways. (The *Time Channeler Chronicles* only lasted a few episodes, and I didn't edit it very well, but I really appreciated the amazing artwork Adam D. Tillery created for it. The last full DeBarlo novel was *System of the*

Cornelius Bones (who I always called Benjamin), Elise, and Chase Michael DeBarlo may find their various paths into the new fiction work. (Artwork: Adam D. Tillery, 2017)

Dead back in 2012.)

Additionally, *The Shadow Dimension: Beyond the Shadows* maintains its slow crawl through post-production, but I'm expecting that to be finished in early 2025. Yes, finally! I know, it's been three years of waiting for a follow up, but I mentioned this production several times in *Portals to the Stars*, so it absolutely needs to be completed soon. For those who may have missed the announcement about it earlier this year, instead of a follow-up season, this is going to be a 90-minute film meant to complement the original six-part series.

These are just a handful of items that are on my docket heading into this holiday season and on into the New Year. In the Mike's Morning Mug video I posted on the Connected Universe Portal, I also broke down a number of events I'll be speaking at during the first half of next year, starting with the annual Conscious Life Expo in Los Angeles. It's going to be quite a busy start to 2025, and I look forward to seeing many of you out there on the road – so, be sure to check my event calendar!

Adventures in Audiobooks

What Caused Such the Delay for Portals to the Stars?

December 23, 2024

Article Notes: This article was actually published a month later in December, but I decided to move it up to this particular section since the topic was more appropriate for this part of the archive.

For a couple weeks I've been meaning to post an article about the *Portals to the Stars* audiobook, which was just recently released, and I would have done it, too, if it wasn't for those meddling drones. More on those below. However, with Christmas night and much family time scheduled for this week, I thought I would finally get around to writing about my audiobook adventure, drones be damned. What happened that caused the delay of the audio version of *Portals to the Stars* to be released about a month and a half after the print version?

To understand that, first of all, one has to understand I run a small independent publishing house, Haunted Road Media. Over the years, I've published about 15 different authors of varying related works in the metaphysical realm, which is quite a lot of work along with everything else that occupies my time on a daily basis. This means I take care of editing, formatting, and everything else that goes into publishing a book, including creating the cover art on most occasions (although, there have been a few times in which I've hired that out). If that already sounds like it takes a great deal of time, it does, but it pales in comparison to audio.

When it comes to audiobooks, it's almost a whole other world. The amount of time it takes to record, edit, and produce is breathtaking, especially for longer works. There are specific requirements that must be met by the audio publishing platform (ACX), so post-production can get a little finicky sometimes. Due to the arduous process, thus far, I've only produced audiobooks for my own works, although I'm open to my other authors producing audio if they want to put in the recording legwork. It's just so time consuming working as an independent.

Simply reading one's own work isn't as easy as it might seem. There can be no mistakes. Sure, you can fix mistakes in editing, but that's just transferring time from one part of the process to another. *Portals to the Stars* is just over eight hours in length in audio. It's about double the time to actually record it. That probably sounds like I'm exaggerating, but I'm really not. As I read through, I might trip over my own tongue, say a word incorrectly, or discover I want to inflect my voice differently on a particular line, and have to record that line once again. I also use reading the audiobook as another means of editing the text of the book since slowing down my mind to read aloud allows me to find small mistakes I may have otherwise missed, which I'll correct on the spot.

That's all well and good, but why so long to get *this one* done? That should only take 16 hours of recording time, right? Sure, but that's also not getting recorded in one day. Technically, one could knock that out in a single day, but a couple hours in, the voice starts to get pretty dry, and the quality dissipates, so the recording needs to get spread out over several days. So, I planned for that, right? I

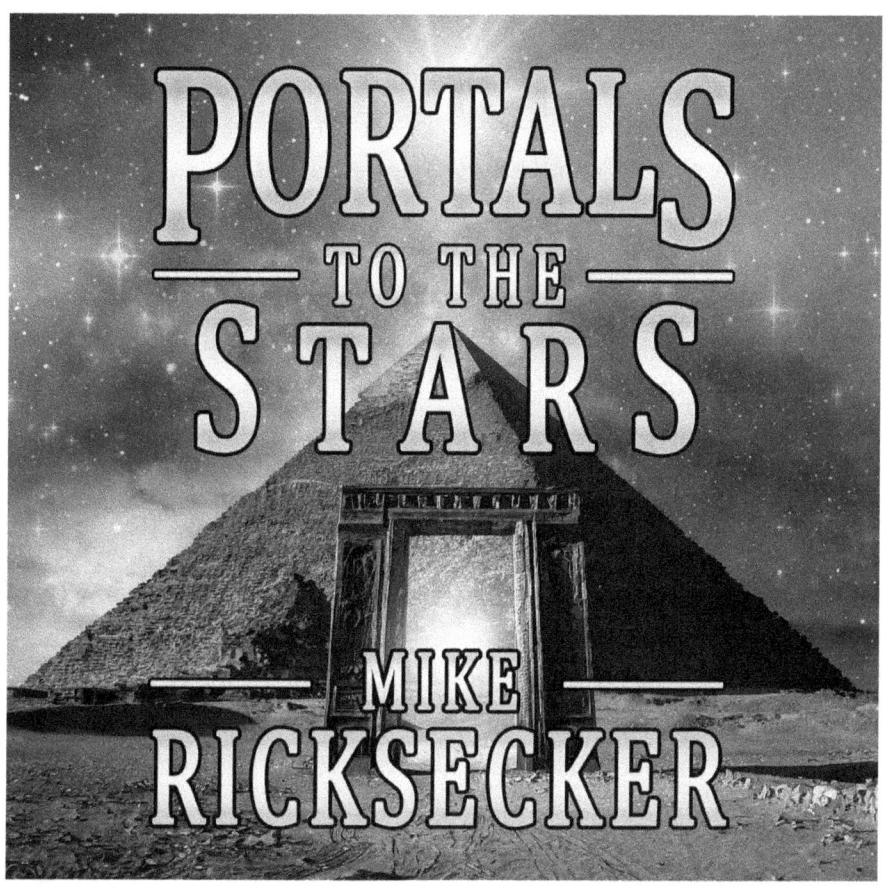

Audiobook cover for Portals to the Stars.

sure did, and even though I was rushed to meet the deadline, I had it all planned out to record over a few days. But … I tried getting a bit too cute about it.

While recording my previous books, I was always a bit annoyed that even though I have nice studio equipment, the production software I use always picked up my voice rather low making post-production a challenge to meet the publishing requirements without sounding off. Now, I've been podcasting for years, and my voice always gets picked up on the livestream quite well for *Connecting the Universe*. So, what's the difference? The biggest difference is the environment. I don't record the audiobooks in the room I broadcast *Connecting the Universe* since it's actually rather large without any sort of sound proofing, so you can distinctly hear a bit of an echo and my voice sounds a touch hollow. Thus, I record in my bedroom closet. Yep, I sure do. I drag all of my equipment into my closet, set up a recording station, and with my changing clothes providing the sound proofing, I spend hours tucked away in there recording my books. So, I actually have a better environment for sound when I record. What else is different than my podcast? The software. I go live over Streamyard, and most of the time it sounds really good. My voice usually has good body to it when I'm live. So ... yeah, I decided to record an audiobook with Streamyard.

In principle, this probably sounds ok. Except for when you're on the road a few days later and discover while editing the second chapter that the internet connection must have glitched out for a moment because there were suddenly some small gaps in the audio midsentence. Now, editing can take double the time of recording – see how the process grows exponentially in time? – so, I was a couple days into editing when I discovered this was a problem. I checked a few other files, and it did happen occasionally in a couple of those as well. I had to throw it all out. I also had to wait until I got back home to record it all again.

I went back to using the audio software on my computer (Adobe Audition), played around with my soundboard and computer settings for a while, and spent days recording the book all over again. Success! Mostly. I didn't have any broken audio this time, but I did discover that I must have been sitting a bit too close to the microphone. Even though I have a nice Lewitt condenser microphone, there were far too many mouth clicks and breaths it picked up. Well, I wasn't recording that all over again, especially since my voice was about shot by that point, and I was a bit tired of being trapped in the closet during a beautiful autumn season, so I probably quadrupled my time in editing. The editing slipped past the release date for the paperback version of *Portals*, so my calendar was filled to the brim with interviews and promotion for the new book along with everything else I usually do throughout my week (blogs, videos, podcast, etc.). While I tried editing the audio as much as I could, it's easy to see how doing so was suddenly made more difficult and dragged out far longer than I wanted it to.

So, there you go! Finally released during the second week of December, the *Portals to the Stars* audiobook is now available. And I've barely been able to talk about it because of all those pesky drones! Our last livestream of the year, an *Edge of the Rabbit Hole* episode on *Connecting the Universe*, featured researcher Ronny LeBlanc and remote viewer Scott Davis discussing what's really behind these drones, who might be launching them, and if there might be an interdimensional UFO / UAP aspect to them. Scott lives in New Jersey and has seen the drones fly over his house while Ronny has been using his years of research to investigate the strange phenomenon. You'll find Scott's footage and insights from both in the episode below.

That's also it for this blog for 2024! I hope everyone has an amazing holiday season and a wonderful New Year! There's a lot on deck for 2025 – many events, another Stargates of Ancient Egypt tour, exclusive projects, and much more – so stay tuned!

Part 7

Portals and Dimensions

Notes on Part 7

Here, at portals and dimensions, we come to the end of our journey ... at least for now. It was pretty interesting timing that as I started talking about underground civilizations and whether or not they're physically on this plane of existence or reside in another dimension alongside us, all of a sudden, the "Drone Flap of 2024 – 2025" took off and became quite prominent. That phenomena became quite a focus of my December, but since it carried over into January, I decided to include one of the articles from the following year in this archive even though it was supposed to end with the conclusion of 2025.

Personally, I do believe most of the drones were some sort of government testing even though they were extremely slow to finally admit it; however, I don't believe 100% of the drones witnessed were this testing. There's still too much unknown about the glowing balls of light in the sky and the drones seen entering and exiting them by, not only civilians, but also government officials. Plus, this activity is still happening.

What Lies Beneath

Are There Underground Civilizations Within the Earth?

December 2, 2024

Article Notes: My Edge of the Rabbit Hole *co-hostess, Victoria Mundae, and I debate the topic of "Hollow Earth" often on our show. She's more of the belief of the traditional Hollow Earth Theory while I believe there are places throughout the Earth's crust which are large and cavernous in size, old lava tubes and magna chambers which would make for a "Hollow-ed Earth" where civilizations could thrive. But I don't believe in an interior sun at the center of the planet.*

Remember back in June this year when the internet suddenly became quite abuzz after Harvard researchers published a paper featuring a "startling new" claim that UFOs and extraterrestrials could be "living underground, on the moon, or even walking among humans?" I rolled my eyes and chuckled – no, actually, I rolled my eyes and wrote a blog article and stated, "The idea that ETs are among us isn't the laughable part, it's the rest of it. While I appreciate the fact that academics are starting to take this field

Who or what lies in secret underground?

seriously again, this is absolutely nothing new and the ideas aren't all that startling." What did I mean?

First of all, anyone who has been following the ufology community for, oh ... the past 80 years knows that these ideas and concepts have been well-established for decades. Again, this isn't anything new. In my latest book, *Portals to the Stars*, I covered this topic in a couple different ways, first discussing the possibility of interdimensional travel through stargates and portals, and then I explored some of our indigenous legends here in America about underground beings who saved humanity during the Great Cataclysm. I even broke down some of the stories that have come out of Antarctica describing underground civilizations living in deep cavernous areas kept warm by geothermal heating but kept hidden by the harsh bleakness of the Antarctic landscape. What secrets lie under the earth?

Let's get one small point out of the way up front. If extraterrestrials are living underground on this planet and have been for a long time, then should we still be calling them extraterrestrials? If these beings have always been on our planet living alongside us, then they aren't extraterrestrials at all; they would actually *be*

Montezuma's Well in Arizona may hold many secrets to underground civilizations.

Earthlings. Back in the 1960s, investigative journalist John Keel and other researchers came up with an adequate term in *ultraterrestrials* which seems to have almost become forgotten over time in favor of the more wordy "interdimensional beings."

    There is, of course, the possibility that actual extraterrestrials, beings from other planets in the universe, have journeyed to Earth and established underground dwellings out of sight to most of us. But at what point do we stop calling them extraterrestrials and start calling them Earthlings? After all, with all my ancestors coming over from Europe, including Germany, Switzerland, Scotland, Hungary, and Poland, I am an *American*. How many generations did that take? Two? Three? If extraterrestrials have been living among us for several decades – or even several hundred years, for that matter – they likely would have had offspring born here on Earth and native to the planet. I harken back to some of my other works in which I've cited the arrogance of humanity in these areas.

Where do we see evidence of these potential civilizations? For one, we could be experiencing evidence of these on a daily basis in what has become known as "The Hum," a mysterious low droning noise scores of people from across the world have reported hearing and has made headline news. I hear it here as well in the western outskirts of the Greater Cleveland, Ohio, area in North Ridgeville. Are we hearing the sound of some civilization thriving beneath the Earth's surface? Even archaeologists working on megaliths and stone circles in Scotland have at times captured on their equipment an ultrasonic hum emitted by the stones just before sunrise when the Earth's magnetic field is at its most potent.

Our primary source, aside from modern UFO and UAP sightings that speculate on an interdimensional source, we find it in our legends and lore across the ages. For instance, Montezuma's Well in the Verde Valley in Arizona carries a fantastic indigenous origin story centered on the Great Cataclysm in which humans had no place to run and were facing total annihilation. The "ant people," underground beings who lived in the Verde Valley, escorted the surviving humans through the entrance of the well before it was filled with water and gave them refuge until the world stabilized again. Once the waters from the cataclysm subsided, humanity returned to the surface, and in that area of the country, they began building their cliff dwellings. That's just one of many tales of this nature from across the world.

However, we also find evidence of these civilizations hidden in plain sight. A location like the underground city of Derinkuyu in Turkey which burrowed some 18 levels under the Earth, more than 275 feet, we know at least housed humans, perhaps as many as 20,000 at one time, at several different points in history. It's unknown who, specifically, constructed the expansive metropolis, and when that would have occurred since we can't carbon date rock and stone, but many believe the work goes at least as far back as the Hittites around 1200 BC. But the construction could go back even

The underground city of Derinkuyu in Turkey. (Ahmet Kaynarpunar photo)

further, and the Hittites could have repurposed it. After all, their use was believed to be for protection from attack by the Phrygians. Who has time to excavate that much rock when facing attack? And if **you**'re trying to hide in secret, where do you put that much rubble so as to not be noticeable? The Hittites weren't going to slip it in their trousers and spread it out across a courtyard above ground like Andy Dufresne in *The Shawshank Redemption*. Derinkuyu could certainly be far, far older than originally believed. How far?

In *Alaska's Mysterious Triangle*, I discussed the shifting of the Earth's magnetic pole and how when it last occurred some 42,000 years ago, the Earth's protective magnetic shield would have been in flux, down to as much as 6% of its current state, causing dramatic climate change. The solar wind from the sun would have pounded the Earth with radiation and likely causing the extinction of many species. The air would have been more ionized creating far more electrical storms and aurora sightings all over the Earth. According to evolutionary biologist Alan Cooper with Blue Sky Genetics and the South Australian Museum, "Early humans around the world would have seen amazing auroras, shimmering veils, and sheets across the sky. It must have seemed like the end of days."

Is this, perhaps, why we're discovering so many cave drawings around the world from that timeframe in history? Had humans taken shelter there to protect themselves from the scorching sun and wild electrical storms? Is that what a place like Derinkuyu would have truly been about? After all, that last pole shift lasted about 400 years, plenty of time to excavate a massive underground city like that. There may even be some evidence of this in the Valley of the Kings in Egypt, [a story I discussed earlier in this blog].

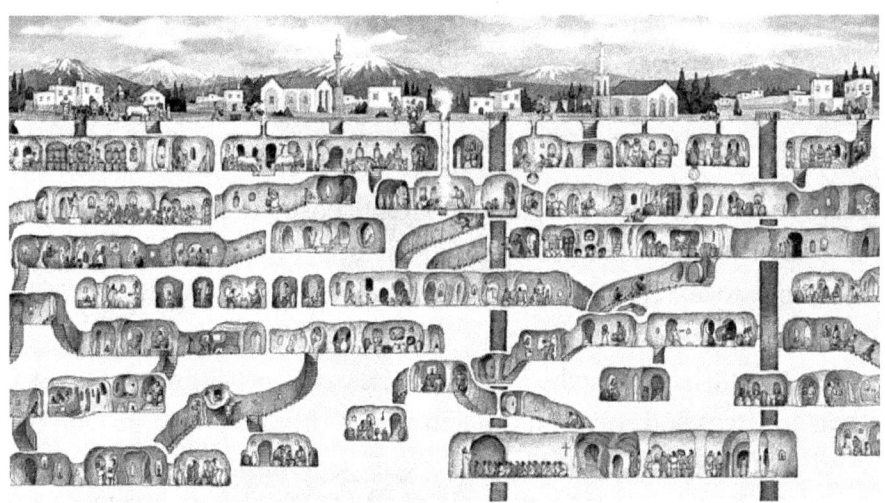

The underground labyrinth of Derinkuyu. (Yasir999 illustration)

What Are the New Jersey Drones?

All Possibilities on the Table as Officials Remain Tight-Lipped

December 12, 2024

Article Notes: I need to thank Scott Davis for providing eyewitness accounts and images of the drones during this time since he was right there in the New Jersey epicenter of the Drone Flap. Many of the images that have been proliferated across the internet I couldn't use for this publication due to copyright restrictions, so Scott's imagery from that time is much appreciated. You can watch an interview I had with him and researcher Ronny LeBlanc from that time discussing the drones and related activity across the world on my YouTube channel in the video "Drones Over New Jersey with Ronny LeBlanc and Scott Davis." This is one of a series of videos, and you can find an entire playlist there on YouTube.

    What in the world are these mysterious drones that have been flying over New Jersey the past couple weeks? Or, at least, we believe they're drones. Nobody has really gone up there to confirm,

Drone spotted through the treetops in New Jersey. (Scott Davis photo)

and no one has brought one down to take a look at these things. Instead, for some bizarre reason, we've just been letting them fly around up there, causing a ruckus in the news and most government officials to simply shrug their shoulders. Are they new government technology, drones from a foreign adversary, a hobbyist project, or are they UFOs and UAPs?

Let's start with what might probably be the easiest explanation. Most officials who have looked into the matter have stated these drones are not a hobbyist project. Given the scale of these objects, the numbers of them, and the sophistication of the technology they seem to display, if this were to be some sort of side project by a drone enthusiast, then this particular person (or group) would have to be wealthy or, at least, very well-funded. Sure, I could purchase a good-quality commercial drone for a few hundred dollars, but that's not what we're talking about here. These particular drones appear to be about six feet in diameter and contain a technology that eludes radar detection and is making it difficult for officials to track. The couple times police helicopters have gone up to take a look, the drones have turned off their lights and have seemingly disappeared into the night sky. However, to this point, these craft have only been witnessed over New Jersey which indicates a local point of origin. Could this be a billionaire's practical joke?

This morning, in response to claims by Rep. Jeff Van Drew, R-NJ, that an Iranian "mothership" was lurking in international waters in the Atlantic and launching the craft over America, the Pentagon stated these drones were not from a foreign adversary. Could the Pentagon's statement just be one to quell any fears in the citizens of New Jersey? Sure, of course, and if these drones originate from some foreign adversary, whether that was Iran, China, or some other opposing nation, wouldn't we have already scrambled the jets and shot them down out of the sky? New Jersey's governor, Phil Murray, has stated he has no problem with them being shot down, leaving no roadblocks in the way of such a course of action. The U.S. has launched jets into the skies before when we've had unidentified objects in the sky over our airspace (yes, that does, technically, make these drones UFOs), so why haven't we now?

That brings us to our next possibility. Are we not doing anything about these drones because, well, they're ours? We wouldn't scramble the jets and shoot them down out of the sky if they were our own technology. But the Pentagon has also stated these craft are not ours, and in congressional hearing, the FBI stated they simply have no idea what they are. However, if this was some sort of secret U.S. military project, would they really admit to that? Of course not – hence, the word "secret." This could be a secret project in a couple different ways. Yes, they could be testing the technology aboard these drones. How well can they avoid radar detection? How well can they avoid approaching aircraft like the police helicopters? It could also be a secret project to gauge the reaction by the public. Is there going to be a mass panic? This idea goes back to the Brookings Report in 1960 and the implications of humanity's response to the possibilities of extraterrestrial life. Are those days behind us now that we've had several decades to grow accustomed to the idea that there's other life out there in the universe and it may be visiting our planet? Perhaps ... although a few years ago we certainly didn't handle the toilet paper scare very well.

For the most part, the possibility that these drones might not have a human source hasn't been talked about in traditional media, but why not? At this point, they are Unidentified Flying Objects – objects flying in the sky that no one has been able to (or is willing to) identify. An interesting aspect of the "Iranian mothership" idea is that, reportedly, the U.S. Coast Guard has witnessed these craft approaching the land by sea. If that's true, and that's the origin for, at least, some of these, and it's not a foreign adversary's ship, then what's the source? If it's a secret government project, then sure, these could be coming off some sort of U.S. Navy vessel. However, could these also be coming from some underwater extraterrestrial or ultraterrestrial base? If that were the case, then this would also be a situation in which the U.S. government would not try attempting to shoot these things down. Risking provocation with a highly advanced civilization, or at least one in which we don't understand, probably wouldn't be a wise course of action.

It will be interesting to see how all of this unfolds, and it seems as if more information is coming out by the minute. Just as I was typing up this blog this morning more reports were coming out on the matter (although much of it was repetitious of details we'd already learned over the past couple weeks). What do *you* think these drones are? Hobbyists? The U.S. Government or military? A foreign adversary? Or could they even be the work of some other intelligent lifeforms residing on this planet ... or beyond?

Droning on in New Jersey

Drone Theories, Project Blue Beam, & Portals

December 16, 2024

The mystery of the New Jersey drones continues into its fourth week, but now citizens all across the country — and even the entire world — are beginning to report their own sightings of these mysterious objects. Are these just copycats of what's happening here in the United States, or is there really some strange phenomenon occurring that started here and has started to spread out around the globe? Why won't our governments give us any information about these things? And what are the latest theories as to what they are? Inquiring minds want to know.

My last blog article – and this one following – was supposed to be a piece on the audiobook I just released for *Portals to the Stars*, but here we are again trying to make sense of this bizarre drone activity. Frustratingly, the United States government has remained silent as to what is going on in our airspace. If they've been testing some sort of technology, you'd think they'd at least say, "We've been running some tests. No cause for alarm." They don't have to tell us what it is they're testing, but why leave us completely in the

Photo of a drone overhead in New Jersey from Scott Davis.

dark?

In a recent development, one amateur drone pilot tried chasing after one of these with his own, and while passing into restricted airspace in pursuit, his drone was immediately shutdown while the mystery drone kept flying. The intrigue deepens.

The video clips I've posted from my latest Mike's Morning Mug video discussing the drones have attracted a bevy of attention, and response comments have been plentiful. There have been a multitude of different ideas and theories that have been postulated within those comments, so I'm going to try to cover some of those in this space. I won't rehash the ideas in my previous article.

One of the more popular theories that keeps being tossed my way is that some sort of nuclear material has been smuggled into the United States and these drones are being used to try to find it. To me, this theory is just meant to scare people. If this idea is true, then why are the drones only being used at night? If there was something as serious as some sort of nuclear material or even a bomb out there as some have stated, then authorities would also be searching for that during the day. You would also have ground forces mobilized, bomb-sniffing dogs deployed, and much more to neutralize that kind of deadly threat. A covert nighttime operation makes no sense for that dangerous scenario.

Some people believe this is the Project Blue Beam conspiracy theory springing into action. What is Project Blue Beam? This was a theory popularized by Canadian journalist Serge Monast who stated there was a plot to establish a new world order by using NASA technology and a fabricated extraterrestrial attack to eradicate Abrahamic religions (Christianity, Judaism and Islam) and install a totalitarian government. However, there has been no sign whatsoever of aggressive behavior by these drones, so it's hard to see this as any sort of invasion. At the most, the drones are a bit of a nuisance, but aliens aren't attacking, and most major news outlets – the ones who actually enjoy riling up the masses for attention – are leaning toward human technology rather than extraterrestrial. Relax, please. This is another theory meant to drum up fear.

"It's demonic beings." Um, no.

"Pizza Hut delivery drones." That's a lot of pizza.

One idea that certainly has some legs is a false flag operation or a psyop by the government. Basically, this would be some sort of distraction to disguise some other operation that is actually taking place around us, diverting our attention from the real action. What that hidden operation could possibly be is anyone's guess – although, there have been plenty, and you've seen one of those above in Project Blue Beam. What could possibly be going on in New Jersey that you'd need to buzz the populous with drones for nearly a month straight?

In the Mike's Morning Mug video I posted the other day, I addressed photos that had emerged from a photographer trying to capture images of a drone that, basically, turned out to be a giant ball of light rather than a mechanical craft. This was sent my way by my friend and colleague, Ronny LeBlanc, and we'll be addressing it in further detail, along with Scott Davis, on *Connecting the Universe's Edge of the Rabbit Hole* on Wednesday night. I didn't have this in time for my last written blog, so I'll tackle it here, and since then there's been another clip that was posted by ABC7 News that also looked distinctly like a giant ball of light. Taken at different times of the evening, they look rather similar in shape.

The short of it is the possibility that the accompanying balls of light with these drones, if these are something from elsewhere – whether that's elsewhere in the cosmos or another dimension – could actually be the portals used by these machines to enter our world. What do I mean? Let me provide an excerpt from *Portals to the Stars* to try to explain:

> "Classically, we've come to view wormholes as some sort of tunnel through space, and while the traditional models of this do show two points in space connected via a tunnel, the entry point from either side likely would not be just a floating circular hole in the middle of space. That would look odd, indeed. In three-dimensional space, a circle becomes a sphere, so when we start looking for these in nature, we should probably be looking for something rather spherical in nature, a type of large orb, perhaps. The 2014 Christopher Nolan film *Interstellar* does a wonderful job of illustrating this, placing a star-filled sphere near the planet Saturn for the movie's spacefarers to pass through to another galaxy. This also begs us to question the existence of light orbs countless numbers of people have witnessed out in the wilderness and elsewhere. Believed by many to be spirits, fairies, or other beings (and some, I believe, certainly are), could some of these orbs actually be naturally occurring portals, manifesting as a three-dimensional sphere rather than a vertically standing tunnel, an energy field, or a type of magical hole on the ground? Might one kind of stargate actually be the ability for an intelligent life form to harness

One of the many glowing balls of light witnessed during the flap. What were these?

and control one of these orbs?"

This opens up a whole other realm of possibilities. If these are surveillance drones, are they ones from some other civilization in the universe or one that is living right here alongside us in another dimension accessible via these spherical portals or stargates? Might they even be time travelers, humans or some other intelligent civilization in the future, using this type of mode of transportation to get a glimpse of the planet's past? This is a rabbit hole we could venture down for a while, but I'm just going to leave you with that food for thought right now. The mystery continues ...

Plasmoids, Portals, or Extraterrestrials?

What's Going on With the Orbs in Our Skies?

January 6, 2025

Article Notes: While the new administration that came into office later in January stated the Drone Flap was simply testing (why didn't the Pentagon simply say that when they were asked back in November and December?) they never actually addressed the glowing balls of light and the drones which were seen moving in and out of those. They also never addressed the fact that this wasn't simply relegated to New Jersey and had been happening, not only all over the country, but across the entire world.

Following the mysterious drone escapades of November and December (they haven't stopped, the media just pulled back on coverage), there seems to have been an uptick of other phenomena appearing in our skies, primarily giant balls of light. Generally seen in conjunction with the drone sightings, these strange lighted objects have seemingly become more prevalent in recent weeks – or were they always there and just became noticed more because we were

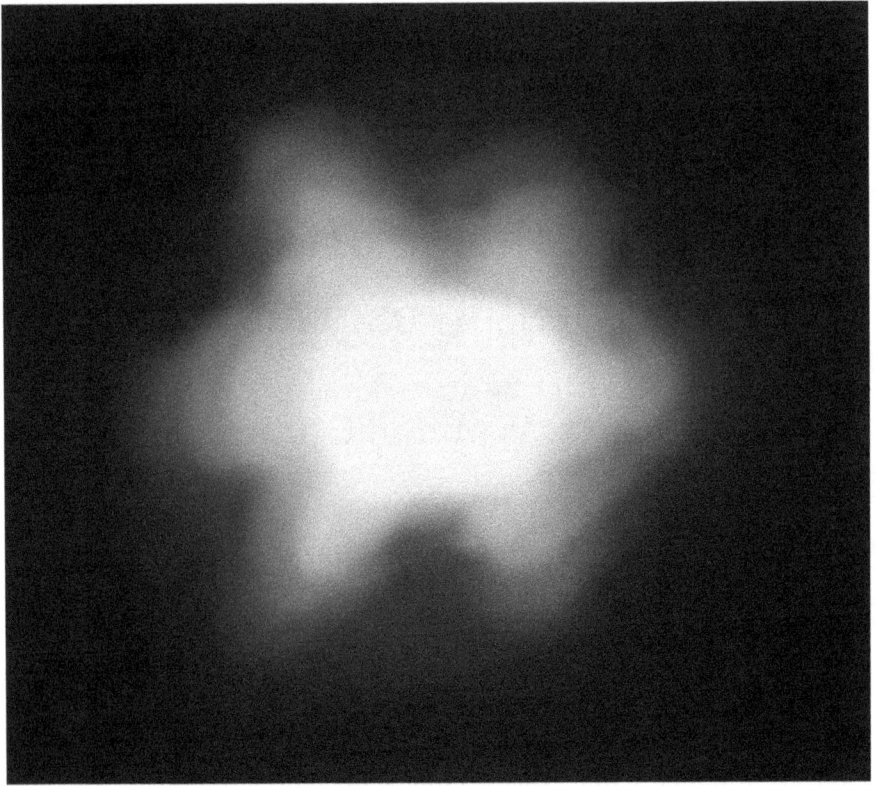

Brilliant ball of light captured in the sky by Katherine Swinn on December 20, 2024, near Edinburgh, Scotland. Many others also witnessed this.

now looking upward? Moreover, what exactly are these things? Some say they're plasmoids, some say they're portals, and some say they're extraterrestrials. Could they, in a way, be all three?

Just before Christmas, I received multiple messages from people near Edinburgh, Scotland, who witnessed a strange bit of light phenomenon in the sky, occurring in approximately the same area within about an hour of each other that evening. In one particular video clip sent to me by QHHT Practitioner Katherine Swinn, the light was shining brilliantly in almost a pulsating manor, and it was more oval in shape than the customary circular orb. From another angle further south and a little earlier in the evening, another witness, Christina, captured the phenomenon as more diamond in shape. Strange, indeed. After sharing their clips on social media, I had several more people reach out to me from Scotland reporting the same phenomenon on multiple occasions throughout the holiday season. Something significant was certainly happening!

As I shared this information and these clips, more people from across the world shared their sightings, and there was much discussion following as to what exactly these were. Let's tackle a few of these starting with *plasmoids*. What's a plasmoid? By definition, a plasmoid is "a coherent shape of plasma and magnetic fields that has a characteristic shape." Plasma is our fourth state of matter after solids, liquids, and gasses, and I cover it in *Portals to the Stars*. Plasma is an ionized gas in which the electrons are ripped away from the atoms creating a positive charge in a fluid-like state, and while it might not be as familiar to us as the other three states of matter we interact with all the time, we see plasma in the Sun and stars, auroras, cracks of lightning, and more, including those old plasma television sets. Ball lightning is a type of plasmoid, and some have speculated that these strange lights in the sky may be that, except ball lightning generally isn't as large as these reported sightings, don't usually last more than a minute, and in most cases are associated with thunderstorms or powerlines. But while ball lightning doesn't really fit the description, that still doesn't rule out plasmoids, and those plasmoids could be a type of portal.

Of course, it should go without saying that I do cover the idea of plasmoids, orbs, and giant balls of lights as possibly being portals in my latest book, *Portals to the Stars*, and I begin this discussion by breaking down X-points, or portals in space recognized by our scientific community. According to plasma physicist Jack Scudder of the University of Iowa, "We call them X-points or electron diffusion regions. They're places where the magnetic field of Earth connects to the magnetic field of the Sun, creating an uninterrupted path leading from our own planet to the Sun's atmosphere 93 million miles away."

Magnetospheric Multiscale Mission. (NASA illustration)

Since NASA started deepening their research into this phenomenon in 2015 by launching four satellites known as the Magnetospheric Multiscale Mission, they've renamed X-points to "magnetic reconnection" (my personal opinion is this is to further distance itself from the more metaphysical sounding "portals"). One of the more interesting findings from this still-ongoing mission was the observation of "magnetic reconnection in magnetic flux ropes — giant magnetic tubes, which can form in the wake of previous magnetic reconnection events, and in Kelvin-Helmholtz vortices, the same phenomenon that are created when wind blows over water to create waves on the surface." Yes, you read that correctly. When these magnetic fields in space reconnect at the X-point they have the capability of creating giant magnetic tubes to transfer this energy from the Sun to the Earth. It sounds eerily familiar to the imagery we've conjured in our minds as to what a portal or a wormhole in space actually looks like.

So, what does a giant magnetic tube have to do with giant balls of light in the sky? It has to do with what the ends of those tubes

Are the light anomalies sometimes seen near Sasquatch actually the portals they are using to enter our plane of existence?

would look like to the human eye. The end of a circular tube would look like, well, just like that – a circle. However, a circle is a two-dimensional object, and the skies of the Earth are in three-dimensional space. What's a circle in three dimensions? A sphere. Thus, the dazzling spherical light orbs we see in the skies or out in the wilderness could very well be the exit and entry points of portals leading to other dimensions, other places in the cosmos, or other points in time. In addition to *Portals to the Stars*, I cover this a bit more in my blog articles "Are Portals Hiding in the Wilderness?" and "Mysterious Lights in the Woods." Do beings like Sasquatch, the fairies of old, or extraterrestrials use these balls of lights as portals to enter into our world? Have the mysterious drones been using these?

That brings us to our next big question: are the light anomalies actually extraterrestrials? A plasma study in the early 2000s and published in 2007 in the *New Journal of Physics* stated, "These interacting complex structures exhibit thermodynamic and evolutionary features thought to be peculiar only to living matter such as bifurcations that serve as 'memory marks,' self-duplication, and more." That there are properties of plasma which are reminiscent of living matter certainly tells us there is more going on with this matter than we currently understand, which is pretty much the same thing we say when we talk about the other six dimensions above the fourth we live in. Some theorists have contested these balls of lights are, themselves, some sort of organism or have some sort of lifeform living inside them; they are the actual beings or visitors themselves. That could very well be.

According to our theoretical physicists, there are up to 11 hyperspatial dimensions, 0 – 10, but our fourth-dimensional consciousness living in a three-dimensional body doesn't have the physical geometry to properly see objects and beings from dimensions higher than our own. We may get a glimpse of them from time to time, but we will not be able to completely see these objects and beings in their full form because we don't have the physical capability to do so. (I don't have time to delve deep into the 2-D Flatland analogy here, but I do make a deeper reference to it in *Travels Through Time*.)

Personally, I believe we are witnessing a mix of things, and there is no one definitive answer for what these orbs and balls of light truly are. Context likely matters here. A giant ball of light hovering in the sky could be a portal while a light anomaly that zips across it could be a glimpse of some craft from another dimension. Likewise, a large glowing orb in the treetops of a forest could be the access point for a variety of different beings, while smaller points of light seen drifting about could be the beings themselves. Our continuing research over the coming years should, hopefully, provide a better understanding of what it is we're experiencing.

(Not So) Final Thoughts

How do you wrap up something that is ongoing and still in midstream? I would have loved to have included all the articles about the Giza Plateau scans and the news that's been coming out of the Egyptian Labyrinth, but to do so would have had added several hundred pages to this work. Originally, I was going to bookend the volume with my original "Our Place in the Universe" article from 2021 with an updated "Our Place in the Universe" article I wrote this past August. Doing so would have made this book a door stop. It actually works out pretty well, because now what I can do is simply publish one of these every year and make it almost like an annual yearbook of the year's news according to the Connected Universe. I don't know if anyone does that – publish their blog in book form yearly, but if that becomes the intention, then you can expect the second volume early in 2026, springtime at the latest.

I've already started contemplating what other older works I might include with that one like I started off with this one. There's some great material that became the "Haunted Road Media Learning

Shorts" that were a prelude to everything that came after it. But I'm thinking out loud here as I type. But it also got me thinking about all of those scripts I wrote for the hundred-plus episodes of *Friday Night Ghost Frights* – that's a lot of material just sitting out there collecting virtual dust on old hard drives.

I need more projects, right? I'm only deep into two other books with the next volume in the Connecting the Universe series and my fiction work. There are also upcoming film projects once I've finally finished off *The Shadow Dimension: Beyond the Shadows*, and Kate and I are neck deep in research, events, and our own books together as well. Keep on the lookout for all of these things coming out in 2026!

Like I said in the acknowledgments, I have to thank all of those "time travelers" who have been members of the Connected Universe Portal, those longtime supporters of the work and research I've been conducting. This work absolutely is not possible without all of you, and I sincerely, sincerely appreciate it all. I'll say it one more time: we are not alone. Speak your truth. Your drop in the ocean may be the one that changes the world – or even the universe.

Index

37th Parallel 133

Above Space Developments 23, 26
Abu Simbel 199, 264
Abydos 41, 94, 102 – 103, 197 – 198, 217, 231 – 232, 234 – 237, 239, 242 – 244, 284, 310
acoustics 217, 219, 222 – 224, 234
Agilkia Island 265
Akashic Records 373
Akhenaten 103
alabaster 255
Alaska Triangle, The 38, 53 – 60, 106 – 107, 123 – 124, 126 – 127, 134 – 135, 150, 173 – 178, 189, 297, 319, 334, 340, 343, 345 – 346, 371 – 372, 397
Alaska's Mysterious Triangle 53, 123, 134, 143 – 144, 150, 164, 174, 176 – 177, 295, 297, 299 – 300, 357, 359, 363, 390, 397, 441
Albuquerque, New Mexico 321
alchemy 71, 73, 75
Alexander the Great 246

Alexandria, Egypt 73 – 75, 193, 232 – 233, 258, 284
  Great Library of 74 – 75, 193, 215, 218, 356, 358
  Great Lighthouse of 193, 215, 218
  Mouseion 75 – 75
Algonquian 296
Aliens (see extraterrestrials)
Alien Highway 133
Alton, Illinois 142 – 143
Ancient Aliens 45, 126, 133
ANITA Project 66 – 67
Antarctica 65 – 67, 164 – 166, 285, 357 – 368, 438
Anthony, Mark 63
Anunnaki 154
Area 51 110
Aristotle 352
Ark of the Covenant 41, 263, 267 – 269
artificial intelligence 308, 374
As Above, So Below (see duality)
astral plane 51
Aswan 97, 194, 198 – 199, 217, 263 – 264, 266

Aswan dams 263 – 265
Athena 353
Atlantis 42, 60, 123, 163, 241, 257, 260, 278, 279, 286, 302, 318, 320, 327 – 330, 351 – 360, 367, 418
Australia 267
Avatar 27

Babylon 279
Back to the Future 31
Bacon, Sir Francis 88
Ballynacarigga Castle 82
Barker, Gray 48 – 49
barque hall 253, 309 – 310
Barsanti, Alessandro 308
Bean, Sean 420 – 421
Begich, Nick 107, 175
Bender, Albert K. 45, 48 – 50
Bent Pyramid (see pyramids)
Bermuda Triangle 53, 56, 105 – 106, 112 – 114, 127, 175, 300, 363
Big Bang 68 – 69, 370
Big Foot (see Sasquatch)
Bimini Road 114, 358
black hole 99, 167 – 169
Black Pyramid (see pyramids)
Blarney Castle 79 – 81
block universe 92
Boca Negra Canyon 321 – 326
Boggs, Hale 107, 175
Book of the Dead, Egyptian 164, 354 – 355
bootstrap paradox 30 – 31, 176

Boston Red Sox 187 – 189
boomerangs 267, 270
Braden Gregg 90
brain organoids 153
Bridgewater Triangle 107 – 109
Brookings Report 446
Burke, John 333 – 334
Byrd, Admiral Richard E. 360, 364 – 367

Caesar, Julius 73 – 74
Cahir Castle 79 – 80
Cahokia Mounds 141 – 142
Cairo, Egypt 38, 42 – 43, 97, 199 – 200, 207, 225, 272, 281, 403
Callahan, John 176
Calvert, Frank 417
Campfire Tales: Midwest 395
Cano, Brian 422
Cape Girardeau, Missouri 138 – 139
de Carvajal, Friar Gaspar 416
Catch-22 33 – 34
Center for Palaeogenetics 150
Chaco Canyon 324
Chandra X-Ray Telescope 370
Charles de Gaulle Airport 205
Charles Fort 81 – 82, 84
Charleville Castle 85 – 86, 147, 339 – 342
cheese paradox 160
Church, Jimmy 409
Circles of Silence 333, 378
Civilization Museum (Egypt) 280

Clearwater Lake, Missouri 140
Cleopatra VII 73
Cleveland Browns 119
Cleveland, Ohio 179, 183, 189, 315, 346 – 349, 419, 440
cloning 149 – 154, 246
Colossi of Memnon 254 – 255
Columbus, Christopher 112
consciousness 180, 240, 242, 306, 337
conspiracy
    Government 59
Coleman, Loren 107 – 108
Copts 246, 281
Cosmism 27
*Critia*s 328, 352, 354, 358
cuneiform 186

Dalén, Love 150
Dark Pyramid (see pyramids)
Dahshur 103, 192, 222 – 224, 233 – 234, 307
Davis, Scott 431, 443, 449
Deadly Heirs 126, 387, 392, 394
Democritus 75
Dendera 41 – 42, 123, 196 – 197, 203 – 204, 231, 239 – 242
Dendera lightbulb 196 – 197, 240
Dendera Zodiac 197
Derinkuyu 251, 440 – 442
Desmond Castle 85
Devil's Tuning Fork 36
dimensions 63, 89, 94, 123, 169 – 172, 228, 277, 299, 306, 311, 317, 326, 337, 368, 372, 377, 402, 450 – 451, 457 – 458
djed pillar 102, 203 – 204
Donner, George 109
dowsing rods 82, 333, 340 – 342
Dragon Project 333, 377 – 378
Dragon Triangle 111 – 112, 127, 363
Dreamtime (Aboriginal) 125 – 126
Drem, Scotland 215, 237 – 238
Drombeg Stone Circle 82, 85, 94, 147, 217 – 218, 335 – 338
drones 374, 435, 453, 457
    New Jersey 443 – 451
Dropkick Murphys 189
duality 69, 86, 285, 342
Dublin, Ireland 88
Dungeons and Dragons 389 – 390
Dunn, Christopher 97 – 98, 100

Eady, Dorothy 234 – 236, 244
Earth 25 – 26, 46, 49, 134, 168, 184, 354, 370
    Core 105, 134, 371
    energy (see energy, Earth)
    magnetism 135, 370 – 372, 440 – 442
Edfu 42, 257 – 260, 286 – 288, 304, 327 – 330, 354
Edwards, I.E.S 355
Egypt 27, 37 – 43, 69, 71 – 75, 78, 82, 97 – 103, 118, 122, 124, 173, 178, 191 – 200, 203 – 290, 301 – 305, 307 – 311, 327 – 330, 351 – 356,

358 – 359, 363, 383 – 384, 398, 401 – 404, 409 – 410, 418, 424, 442
Egyptian Labyrinth 402
Egypt's Area 51 (see Zawyet El Aryan)
Einstein, Albert 90, 92, 98 – 99, 307
electronic fog 114
Elephantine Island 41, 263, 267 – 270, 310 – 311
elongated skulls 280 – 281
Encounters with the Paranormal 394 – 395
energy
   Earth 92, 106, 123 – 124, 126, 134, 142, 156, 165, 220, 241, 265, 304, 314, 324, 333 – 334, 340, 363, 371, 375, 377 – 378, 397
   negative anomalies 135
   purple 233
   serpent symbolism 100
   serpentine 135, 310
   wireless 373 – 377
electromagnetism 55, 175
Eternal Knowledge 373, 403
Expedition Bigfoot 296
extraterrestrials 46, 48, 51, 57 – 58, 108, 133 – 144, 176, 318 – 319, 326, 369, 437 – 439, 446, 449, 457

fairies 78, 407 – 408, 457
Faiyum 401 – 402
Fermi Paradox 34 –35
Feynes Mansion 118

Flamm, Ludwig 99
Flight 19 113 – 114
Flower of Life 103, 232 – 233
Fort, Charles 363
Fort Knox, Kentucky 137 – 138
Fosset, Steven 111
Friday Night Ghost Frights 29

Gaia TV 38, 210, 301 – 302, 307, 313, 319, 401, 402
Galaxy 35
Gardiner, Sir Alan H. 356
Geb 203
general relativity 99, 307
geothermal heating 366
Gernon, Bruce 114, 175, 300
Ghosrian Case Files 395
ghosts 59, 82, 108 – 109, 111, 177, 364, 369, 388
Ghosts and Legends of Oklahoma 394
Ghosts of Maryland 393 – 394
giants 58
Giza Plateau 38, 39 – 40, 191 – 192, 209 – 212, 288 – 289, 356, 363, 459
Giza power plant 274 – 276
Giza pyramids (see pyramids)
Glanworth, Ireland 84 – 85
Goddard, Sir Robert Victor 238
Godman Field 137 – 138
Goldenrod Showboat 394, 407 – 408
Grandfather paradox 31 – 33, 160 – 161
Grange Stone Circle 85, 336

gravity ring 24
gravity wave 111
great cataclysm 354, 359, 418, 438, 440
Great Library of Alexandria (see Alexandria, Egypt)
Great Lighthouse of Alexandria (see Alexandria, Egypt)
Great Northern Eclipse 180 – 181, 183 – 185
Great Pyramid of Giza (see pyramids)
Great Sphinx 40, 212, 233, 290
Grusch, David 318
Gutro, Rob 147

HAARP 59, 175
Hanging Church 279, 281
Hapgood, Charles 358
harmonic resonance chambers 222 – 223, 233 –234
Harry Potter and the Sorcerer's Stone 34
Hathor 41, 239, 241 – 242, 265 – 266
Hatshepsut 280
Hatshepsut's Temple 94, 99 – 101, 194 – 196, 245, 252 – 254, 267, 309 – 310
Haunted Road Media 381, 394 – 396, 411, 427
Hawara 402
Heinlein, Robert A. 31, 71
Heliopolis 352, 355
Hell Fire Club 77 – 78
Heller, Joseph 33

hieroglyphs 102
Hinsdale House 405 – 408
Historic Anchorage Hotel 177
Hitler, Adolf 359 – 360
Hittites 440 – 441
Hockomock Swamp 108
Hollow Earth 366, 437
Homer 163, 226
Hondius, Henricus II 165
Hopkinsville, Kentucky 139 – 140
Horus 99, 195, 252, 260
Howe, Linda Moulton 178
Hudson, David 310
Huffman, Rev. William 138 – 139
Hum, The 440
Hume, Thomas 109
hydrometer 73
Hypatia 74 – 75

Ibrahim, Mohamed 37 – 38, 40, 42, 97 – 98, 102, 123, 191 – 192, 196 – 197, 203 – 205, 212, 217, 222, 227 – 228, 231, 236 – 237, 240, 244, 245, 259, 263, 269, 272, 280 – 281, 286, 288, 304, 310, 398, 412
Illiad 163, 226
Illinois River UFO sighting 144
illusion 90
Indiana Jones 210, 216, 398
interdimensional beings 47, 63, 431, 457 – 458
interdimensional hypothesis 317, 326
interdimensional travel 438 – 439

International Flying Saucer Bureau 48
Interstellar 36, 89, 94, 172, 450
Inventory Building 355 – 356
Ireland 77 – 88, 147, 335 – 342
Ireland Triangle 339 – 340
Isis 265 – 266

Japa Airlines Flight 1628 176
Jet Propulsion Laboratory 180
Jonny Quest 210
Jung, Carl 373
Junior's 422
Jurassic Park 149, 152

Kaio Maru No. 5 112 - 113
Karnak 103, 134, 225 – 230, 231, 247
Keel, John 317, 439
Khan, Kublai 111
Khnum, Temple of 268
Khufu 356
Kom Ombo 260, 266
kushtaka 177

Lake Michigan Triangle 109
Lake Vostok 360, 366
Leap Castle 86 – 87
LeBlanc, Ronny 296 – 297, 412, 431, 443, 449
LeMaitre, Michael 298
Lemuria 279
levitation of the temple 260
ley lines 55, 123 – 124
LiDAR 416

light anomalies 405 – 408, 450, 453 – 455
Long Room, The 88
Loomis, Chris 129
Looper 33
Lord of the Rings 313
Luxor 194, 225 – 226, 245 – 248, 258
Lynn, Heather Dr. 346, 412

Mackinac Island 92
magnetic anomalies 55, 298, 372, 397
magnetosphere 306, 370, 455 – 456
Magnetospheric Multiscale Mission 456
Mahooty, Clifford 318
Mallett, Ronald 167 – 169
mammisi 242
Ma'mun, Caliph al 273 – 274
Man and Time 89, 92 – 94
Mandela Effect 155 – 159
Mantell, Thomas F. 137 – 138
Mantell UFO Incident 137 – 138
Marconi, Guglielmo 376
Marquette, Jaques 142 – 143
Mars 25, 27 – 28
Marshall, Mary 63, 94 – 95
Masons 86, 340
Masters, Michael Paul 317
Maya (see illusion)
Mayan headdress 41, 267, 311
meditation 180, 223
Men in Black 48 – 49
Mesopotamia 186
Mineral Springs Hotel 142, 394

mirror universe (see parallel universe)
Missing 411 297
missing airplanes 55, 106, 109 – 111, 143, 174 – 176
missing people 109, 296
Mississippi River 142
Moore High Cross 78
monatomic white gold 228, 244, 310 – 311
Montezuma's Well 440
Montpelier Hill 78
Morgan, J.P. 376 – 377
Mount Denali 178
Mount Marathon race 298
Mount Sanitas 315
mountain wave (see gravity wave)
Mouseion (see Alexandria)
MUFON 129, 295
mummy 280 – 281
murder pudding 261, 272
Music Mound 315
Muskogee, Oklahoma 47
Mystery of the Sphinx 209 – 210, 398
Mythical Origin of the Egyptian Temple, The 329 – 330, 354

Nady, Ahmed 212, 254, 259 – 260, 267, 272, 286
Napta Playa 198, 266
NASA 35, 180, 295 – 296, 298, 306, 449, 456
National Leprechaun Museum 77
National Security Agency (NSA) 50

Nazis 359 – 360
Neith 353
Neoplatonism 73 – 74
Neuschwabenland 359
neutrino research 65 – 68, 165, 285, 367 – 368
Newgrange 267
New Jersey drones (see drones, New Jersey)
New York City 118
Nevada Triangle 110 – 111
Nile River 40, 198, 225, 255, 258, 263 – 264, 267, 270, 272, 311, 352 – 353, 402
Nolan, Christopher 36, 172, 450
Noory, George 302, 307, 319, 401, 402, 409
North Pole 363, 364
Nova Totius Terrarum Orbis Geographica ac Hydrographica Tabula 165
Novikov Self-Consistency Principle 160 – 161
Nubian Museum 42, 266
Nut 204, 250 – 251, 284 – 286

Odyssey 163, 226
Old Cork City Gaol 83 – 84
Om Ali 261
Omm Sety (see Eady, Dorothy)
Operation Highjump 360, 364
Optical illusions 35 – 36
Orbis Terrarum 165 – 166

Orbital Assembly Corportaion (see Above: Space Developments)
de Orellana, Francisco 416
Osirion 103, 198, 217, 232, 243 – 244
Osiris 102, 164, 198, 244, 355
ouroboros 71 – 75, 284 – 285

panpsychism 27
Papyrus of Ani 164
Paracus skulls 280
paradoxes 29 – 36, 155, 159 – 162, 176
parallel universe 65 – 70, 72, 249, 284 – 286
paranormal activity 58, 106, 108 – 109, 134, 177, 364, 371, 393, 396
Pari, Dustin 346
Paris, France 205 – 206
Parsons, Gov. Mike 140
Pasadena, California 118
past life regression 295
Paulides, David 297
Pavlopetri, Greece 351
Pelecanos, Theodoros 72, 75
pendulum 341 – 342
peripheral vision 61 – 64
petroglyphs 322 – 326
Philae 41, 198 – 199, 263 – 266
Phrygians 441
Piasa caves 142
Piedmont, Missouri 140 – 141
Piri Reis map 164 – 166, 357 – 358
Pittman, Shane 369
plasmoids 454 – 455, 458

Plato 27, 260, 327, 351 – 352, 356, 358
Pleiades 247
Plutarch 328, 352, 355
Polchinski, Joe 161 – 162
Polchinski's Paradox 162
pole shift 165, 441 – 442
Pompey's Pillar 217
portal 54 – 55, 105, 114, 142, 143, 180, 228, 280, 295 – 301, 304, 306, 308, 314, 322 – 326, 366, 372, 377, 397, 450 – 451, 456
portal stones 337
Portals to the Stars 173, 203 – 204, 293, 295, 301, 326, 327 – 328, 333, 361, 381, 383, 398 – 399, 401, 406, 408 – 413, 418, 423 – 431, 438, 447, 455, 457
Predestination 31 – 32, 71
Priestly, J.B. 89, 92 – 94
Primeval Ones 260, 328 – 329, 351, 355
Project Blue Beam 449
Ptolomy XIII 73 – 74
Punt Land 254, 267
purple energy (see energy, purple)
pyramids 156, 233, 401
    Bent Pyramid 38, 178, 192, 222 – 223, 233 – 234, 307
    Dark (Black) Pyramid 60
    on Elephantine Island 267, 270, 310
    Giza 38, 178, 191 – 192

Great Pyramid 39, 43, 192, 210, 212, 217 – 218, 233, 270, 271 – 278, 288 – 289, 378
   at Hatshepsut's Temple 100, 195, 253, 310
   Red Pyramid 192, 219, 222 – 223, 233 – 234, 307
   Step Pyramid 38, 82, 192, 221 – 222
   of Unas 221
   Unfinished 308

Qaitbay Citadel 218
QHHT 295, 301
Queensrÿche 396
Quitt, Jason 295

Ramsses II 281
Ramsses V/VI tomb 249, 284 – 286
rātā tree 313
Ray, Billy 139 – 140
Reeve, Christopher 92
regeneration chambers 220
resonance 156, 265, 336 – 337
reverse time 285
Reymond, E.A.E 327, 329 – 330, 354
Robins, Don 333, 378
Rock of Cashel 79
Rocky III 388
Room of Ships 234 – 237, 244, 284
Rollright stones 378
Roswell UFO Incident 138, 319
Rowling, J.K 34

saba 284, 287, 310
Said, Usama 38
Sais (see Temple of Sais)
Salk Institute for Biological Studies 152
Sanderson, Ivan T. 126, 165, 362 – 363
Sanford Research Facility (SURF) 65
Santorini 356
Saqqara 82, 102, 192, 219 – 221
Sasquatch 58, 108, 134, 296 – 297, 301 – 302, 369, 457
Schliemann, Heinrich 417
Schoch, Robert 209 – 210, 398
Schrader, Dave 416
Sea of the Devil (see Dragon Triangle)
Secret of My Success, The 34
Sedone 363
Sekhmet 227 – 228
Senruset III 402
Serapeum (Alexandria) 74 – 75
Serapeum (Saqqara) 192, 219 – 221, 233
Serapis 74
Shadow Dimension, The 45, 62 – 63, 94, 142, 145 – 146, 405 – 406, 425, 460
shadow people 45 – 51, 61 – 64, 396
   in the Alaska Triangle 56 – 57
   wearing hats 49 – 50
Shakespeare, William 88
Shatner, William 117 – 118, 156, 158 – 159
Shawshank Redemption, The 441

Shining Ones 329 – 330
Sintra Quinta da Regaleira 216
sheela na gig 82
shipwreck 56, 109, 163
simulated universe 91
Skinwalker Ranch 324, 372
Snag, Yukon Territory 106
Sneferu 222
Sobek 260 – 261
Socrates 29, 352
solar disc 252
solar eclipse 179 – 181. 183 – 187
solar wind 298, 306, 370
Sole Survivor 158 – 159
Solon 260, 328, 351 – 352, 354 – 356
Somalia 254
Somewhere in Time 92, 94, 170, 398
Sonchis 328, 352 – 353
South Pole 165, 358, 360, 363 – 365, 367
space-time continuum 92, 298
spaghettification 168
Spike Island 84
spirals 280, 323 – 326
Sputnik 27
St. Declan's Monastery 83
St. George's Church 281
Stacked Time Theory 89 – 95, 123, 172
Star door 243
star house 221, 285
star people 322 – 326
Stargate (film) 398

stargates 94, 97 – 103, 142, 173, 191, 194 – 196, 203 – 204, 220 – 221, 226 – 228, 236, 240, 242 – 244, 247, 252 – 254, 259 – 260, 267 – 268, 278, 286 – 288, 302 – 311, 314, 328, 349, 366, 383 – 384, 401 – 403, 410, 450 – 451
Step Pyramid (see pyramids)
stone circle 80, 82, 85, 94, 110, 156, 322, 324, 335 – 338, 377 – 378, 440
Stonehenge 94, 110
supernova 25 – 26
Sutton, Elmer 139 – 140
Stranger Things 389
Sverreborg, King Sverre 415
Swinn, Katherine 204, 215, 223, 228, 233, 237 – 238, 247 – 248, 268, 295, 301, 412, 454
symmetry
  CPT 68
  universal 69, 368
Synesius 73 – 75
System of the Dead 394, 424

Taddy Heather, 133, 369
Talbert, Meghan 405 – 408
telepathy (see thought transference)
Templar, Knights 216
Temple of Sais 328, 330, 352 – 353
Temple of Satet 311
Temple of the Seven Gates 228
Templemichael Castle 82 – 83

Tesla, Nikola 156, 373 – 378
Tex Murphy (series) 391
Thebes, Egypt (see Luxor)
Theophilus 74
Thorne, Kip 161
Thoth 356
thought transference 49
thunderbirds 143 – 144, 176
Thutmose III 228, 247, 268, 280
Tillery, Adam D. 398, 424
Timaeus 328, 352, 354
time
    reverse 67 – 70, 72
    travel (see time travel)
Time Channeler Chronicles 398, 423 – 424
Time Machine, The 167 – 170
time slips 237 – 238
time travel 31 – 33, 57, 89 – 95, 114, 167 – 172, 237 – 238, 368, 398, 402
time travelers 226, 242, 258
Titanic 84
Tolkien, J.R.R 313 – 314
Tomb of Ty 221 – 222
transitive property of equality 160
Travels Through Time 29, 65, 71, 89, 123, 125, 129, 156 – 159, 161, 164, 167 – 170, 173, 195, 215, 237 – 238, 254, 278, 285, 298, 302, 309, 354, 360, 369, 373, 384, 388, 398, 409, 411, 458
Trinity College 88

Troy 163, 416 – 417
Tullamore, Ireland 87
telluric currents (see energy, Earth)
Tutankhamun 71 – 72, 103, 199
Tsiolkovsky, Konstantin 26 – 27

UAPs (see UFOs)
UFO Superhighway (see 37th Parallel)
UFOs 48 – 49, 57 – 58, 106, 110, 128, 131, 133 – 144, 155, 165, 176, 318 – 319, 360, 364 – 365, 371 – 372, 402, 408, 431, 437, 440, 444 – 446
Uintah Basin 372
ultraterrestrials 439, 446
Unas, Pyramid of (see pyramids)
Unbelievable, The 419 – 422
Undecidable Monument 36
underground civilizations 251, 365, 435, 437 – 442
Underground Neutrino Experiment (DUNE) 65
Unfinished Obelisk 198, 263 – 264, 266 – 267
UnXplained, The 117 – 118, 361
USS Cyclops 112 – 113

Vallée, Jacques 317
Valley of the Kings 196, 245, 249 – 252, 284 – 286, 442
Valley Temple 232 – 233
Verde Valley 440
Vikings 84
Vile Vortices 124, 126, 165, 362 – 363

vortex 54 – 55, 124, 134
Voyager Station 24

Waine, Amy 412
Walk in the Shadows, A 45, 56, 61, 64, 90, 383, 396
Wardenclyffe Tower 375 – 377
Waset (see Luxor)
Weir, Darcy 45
Wells, H.G. 167 – 169
West, John Anthony 209 – 210, 398
Westcar Papyrus 356
white hole 99
"WiFi" glyph 260
winemaking 147 – 148
wireless energy (see energy, wireless)
woolly mammoth 149 – 153
World War II 359
wormhole 298 – 299, 302, 306, 372, 450

X-Points 298 – 299, 306, 455 – 456

Zawyet El Aryan 103, 307 – 308, 370
Zep Tepi 260, 329
Zeus 328
Zukowski, Chuck 133

About the Author

Researcher Mike Ricksecker is the author of the award-winning *Travels Through Time*, Amazon best-sellers *Portals to the Stars*, *A Walk In The Shadows* and *Alaska's Mysterious Triangle*, as well as several historic paranormal books. He has appeared on multiple television shows and programs, including History Channel's *Ancient Aliens* and *The UnXplained*, Travel Channel's *The Alaska Triangle*, Discovery+'s *Fright Club*, Animal Planet's *The Haunted*, multiple series on Gaia TV, and more. Mike is the producer and director of the docu-series, *The Shadow Dimension*, available on several streaming platforms, and produces additional full-length content on ancient wisdom, lost civilizations, UFOs, and the supernatural on his extensive YouTube channel.

For more than eight years he has hosted *The Edge of the Rabbit Hole* livestream show and he also hosts the *Connecting the Universe* interactive class on his online learning platform, the Connected Universe Portal. He operates his own book publishing and video production company, Haunted Road Media, representing a number of authors, and winning the award for Excellent Media In The Paranormal Field at the 2019 Shockfest Film Festival.

Mike also hosts the annual Stargates of Ancient Egypt Tour, an exploration of Egypt's pyramids and temples for lost advanced technologies, the secrets of esoteric alchemy, and ancient stargates.

A native of Cleveland, Ohio, Mike is a U.S. Air Force veteran with a background in Intelligence and a degree in computer simulation programming. He's been researching unexplained phenomena across the world for over 30 years.

Join us at the Connected Universe Portal:
www.connecteduniverseportal.com

Watch Mike on Gaia TV at:
https://www.gaia.com/portal/mike

Tune into the *Connecting the Universe* podcast on your favorite podcast platform, including Apple Podcasts, iHeart Radio, Spotify, and more!

What has been lost can be found, and what has been found can be lost.

www.ingramcontent.com/pod-product-compliance
Lightning Source LLC
Chambersburg PA
CBHW070606030426
42337CB00020B/3700